Fuzzy Database Modeling with XML

ADVANCES IN DATABASE SYSTEMS

Series Editor

Ahmed K. Elmagarmid

Purdue University
West Lafayette, IN 47907

Other books in the Series:

Fuzzy Database Modeling with XML

by

Zongmin Ma
Université de Sherbrooke
Canada

 Springer

Zongmin Ma
Département de Mathématiques et Informatique
Université de Sherbrooke
Canada

Library of Congress Cataloging-in-Publication Data

A C.I.P. Catalogue record for this book is available
from the Library of Congress.

Fuzzy Database Modeling with XML
by
Zongmin Ma, *Université de Sherbrooke, Canada*

Advances in Database Systems Volume 29

ISBN 978-1-4419-3708-7   e-ISBN 978-0-387-24249-1

Printed on acid-free paper.

Printed in the United States of America.

9 8 7 6 5 4 3 2 1

springeronline.com

To

my parents

and to

my wife Li, my daughter Ruizhe, and my son Jiaji

This book is dedicated to my younger brother *Zonghua*.

TABLE OF CONTENTS

LIST OF FIGURES

LIST OF TABLES

FOREWORD
Advances in Fuzzy Databases

Databases have evolved from early models such as hierarchical and network approaches, through the seminal relational model as defined by Codd [1], to current object-oriented and object-relational models that can represent more complex data such as multi-media data. As these developments occurred, realization of the desirability of capturing the incompleteness and imprecision manifest in the real world became apparent. In the relational model the use of null values was an attempt to resolve aspects of this problem. The single null value proved to be insufficiently powerful for this and was overloaded semantically with numerous interpretations. Other approaches such as range values of data [2], incompleteness models [3], and probabilistic models [4] have also been considered.

Fuzzy database approaches were first created in the late 1970s by several research groups [5, 6, 7]. Over the past thirty years a significant body of research in the area of fuzzy databases / fuzzy information systems has been developed. All database models including network, relational, entity-relationship and object-oriented databases have been the target of extensions utilizing fuzzy sets. Recent interests have been seen in the application of fuzzy database approaches to problems in areas such as geographic information systems (GIS) and the semantic web. Although there have been edited collections of fuzzy database papers, it has been nearly 10 years since a comprehensive monograph has appeared in this area [8] and so this volume by Dr. Zongmin Ma satisfies the obvious need for an updating. The book is quite self-contained as it surveys the necessary database and fuzzy set background to appreciate the concepts involved in fuzzy database approaches. It provides a complete coverage of fuzzy database models from relational to nested relational and object-oriented models. The currency of the volume is shown by chapters covering fuzzy set approaches to UML and XML and their relationships to other models. This book should provide a standard reference for this area for a significant number of years and should of broad interest to researchers and developers interested in the applications of fuzzy sets in the database area.

[1] E. Codd. "A Relational Model for Large Shared Data Banks," *Communications of the ACM*, 13, 377-387, 1970.

[2] J. Grant, "Incomplete Information in a Relational Database", *Fundamenta Informaticae*, 3, 363-378, 1980.

[3] W. Lipski, "On Semantic Issues Connected with Incomplete Information Databases," *ACM Trans. Database Syst.*, 4, 262-296, 1979

[4] E. Wong, "A Statistical Approach to Incomplete Information in Database Systems", *ACM Trans. on Database Systems*, 7, 479-488, 1982

[5] C. Giardina, "Fuzzy Databases and Fuzzy Relational Associative Processors", *Technical Report*, Stevens Institute of Technology, Hoboken NJ, 1979.

[6] B. Buckles and F. Petry, "A Fuzzy Model for Relational Databases", *Int. Jour. Fuzzy Sets and Systems*, 7, 213-226, 1982.

[7] M. Umano, "FREEDOM-0: A Fuzzy Database System", *Fuzzy Information and Decision Processes*, (eds. M. Gupta and E. Sanchez), North-Holland, Amsterdam, 339-347, 1982.

[8] F. Petry, Fuzzy Databases: Principles and Applications, Kluwer Press, 1996.

Frederick E. Petry
Center for Intelligent and Knowledge Based Systems
Tulane University, New Orleans LA USA

PREFACE

A major goal for database research has been the incorporation of additional semantics into the data model. Classical data models often suffer from their incapability of representing and manipulating imprecise and uncertain information that may occur in many real world applications. Since the early 1980's, Zadeh's fuzzy logic has been used to extend various data models. The purpose of introducing fuzzy logic in database modeling is to enhance the classical models such that uncertain and imprecise information can be represented and manipulated. This resulted in numerous contributions, mainly with respect to the popular relational model or to some related form of it. It should be noticed that, however, rapid advances in computing power have brought opportunities for databases in emerging applications in CAD/CAM, multimedia, geographic information systems, and etc. These applications characteristically require the modeling and manipulation of complex objects and semantic relationships. The advances of object-oriented databases are acknowledged outside the research and academic worlds. It proved that the object-oriented paradigm lends itself extremely well to the requirements. Since classical relational database model and its extension of fuzziness do not satisfy the need of modeling complex objects with imprecision and uncertainty, currently many researches have been concentrated on fuzzy conceptual data models and fuzzy object-oriented database models in order to deal with complex objects and uncertain data together. The research on fuzzy conceptual models and fuzzy object-oriented databases is receiving increasing attention in addition to fuzzy relational database model. In addition, with rapid advances in network and Internet techniques, the databases have been applied under the environment of distributed information systems. So it is essential to integrate multiple fuzzy database systems. And the fact that the databases are commonly employed to store and manipulate XML data puts a requirement on how to model fuzzy information with XML and how to map fuzzy XML model to the fuzzy databases. There have been few efforts at investigating these issues.

The material in this book is the outgrowth of research the author has conducted in recent years. The topics include conceptual data modeling, logical database modeling, and conceptual design of fuzzy logical databases. Concerning the fuzzy conceptual data modeling, in addition to the ER/EER data models, the UML model and the XML model are extended for fuzzy data modeling. Concerning the fuzzy logical database modeling, in addition to data models and constraints, the query and operations in the fuzzy databases and multiple fuzzy relational database integration are investigated. Concerning conceptual design of fuzzy logical databases, in addition to the mapping from the fuzzy EER model to the fuzzy nested relational databases, the mapping from the fuzzy UML model to the fuzzy object-oriented databases is developed. In particular, the mapping from the fuzzy UML model to the fuzzy XML model and the mapping from the fuzzy XML model to the fuzzy relational database model are introduced in this book.

This proposed book aims to provide a single record of current research and practical applications in the fuzzy databases. The objective of the proposed book is to provide state of the art information to the database researcher and while at the same time serving the information technology professional faced with a non-traditional application that defeats conventional approaches. Researchers, graduate students, and information technology professionals interested in databases and soft computing will find this book a starting point and a reference for their study, research and development.

ACKNOWLEDGEMENTS

My first debt of gratitude is to all of the researchers in the area of fuzzy databases. Based on both their publications and the many discussions with some of them, their influence on this book is profound. I have attempted to be comprehensive in describing their efforts and hope I have not unintentionally omitted anyone.

Much of the material presented in this book is a continuation of the initial research work that I did during my Ph.D. studies at City University of Hong Kong. I am grateful for the financial support from City University of Hong Kong through a research studentship. Additionally, the assistances and facilities of University of Saskatchewan and University of Sherbrooke, Canada, and Oakland University and Wayne State University, USA, are deemed important, and are highly appreciated.

I would like to express my sincere gratitude and appreciation to the anonymous referees for their reviews of the outlines of this book.

Special thanks go to the publishing team at Kluwer Academic Publishers. In particular to Susan Lagerstrom-Fife and to her assistant Sharon Palleschi for their advice and help to propose, prepare and publish this book. This book will not be completed without the support from them.

Finally I wish to thank my family for their patience, understanding, encouragement, and support when I needed to devote many time in development of this book. This book will not be completed without their love.

Zongmin Ma
Northeastern University, China

PART I

BACKGROUND INFORMATION

1. **Conceptual Data Modeling**

2. **Logical Database Models**

3. **Fuzzy Sets and Possibility Distributions**

Chapter 1

CONCEPTUAL DATA MODELING

Database systems are the key to implementing information modeling. Information modeling in databases can be carried out at two different levels: *conceptual data modeling* and *logical database modeling*. Correspondingly, we have *conceptual data models* and *logical database models* for information modeling. Generally the conceptual data models are used for information modeling at a high level of abstraction and at the level of data manipulation, i.e., a low level of abstraction, the logical database model is used for information modeling. Database modeling generally starts from the conceptual data models and then the developed conceptual data models are mapped into the logical database models.

The logical database models will be discussed in Chapter 2. In this chapter, we focus on the conceptual data models. We will briefly introduce the entity-relationship (ER) model, the enhanced (extended) entity-relationship (EER) model, and the class model of the Unified Modeling Language (UML). In addition, with the popularity of Web-based applications, the requirement has been put on the exchange and share of data over the Web. The XML (eXtensiable Markup Language) provides a Web-friendly and well-understood syntax for the exchange of data and impacts on data definition and share on Web (Seligman and Rosenthal, 2001). So this chapter will briefly present the XML.

1.1   Entity-Relationship (ER) and Enhanced ER (EER) Models

The entity-relationship (ER) model was incepted by P. P. Chen (Chen, 1976) and has played a crucial role in database design and information systems analysis. In spite of its wide applications, the ER model suffers from its incapability of modeling complex objects and semantic relationships. So a number of new concepts have been introduced into the ER model by various researchers (Dos Santos, Neuhold and Furtado, 1979; Elmasri, Weeldreyer and Hevner, 1985; Gegolla and Hohenstein, 1991; Scheuermann, Schiffner and Weber, 1979) to enrich its usefulness and expressiveness, forming the notion of the enhanced entity-relationship (EER) model.

1.1.1   ER Model

The ER data model proposed by Chen (1976) can represent the real world semantics by using the notions of *entities, relationships*, and *attributes*. ER data schema described by the ER data model is generally represented by the *ER diagram*.

Entity

Entity is a concrete thing or an abstract notion that can be distinguishable and can be understood. A set of entities having the same characteristics is called an *entity set*. A named entity set can be viewed as the description of an *entity type*, while each entity in an entity set is an instance of that entity type. For example, "Car" is an entity set. The descriptions of the features of a car belong to the entity type, while an actual model car, for example, "Honda Civic DX", is an instance of the car entity. Sometimes entity type is called entity for short.

Attribute and key

The characteristics of an entity are called *attributes* of the entity. Each attribute has a range of values, called a *value set*. Value sets are essentially the same as attribute domains in relational databases.

Attributes in entities, however, can be not only simple attributes having one value set but also complex attributes having several value sets, called a *composite attribute*. For example, attributes "name" and "post address" of a person are a simple attribute and a complex attribute, respectively. In addition, an attribute can be *single-valued* or *multivalued*. For example, the attributes "Age" and "Email address" for a person are single-valued and multivalued attributes, respectively.

Like relational databases, a minimal set of attributes of an entity that can uniquely identify the entity is called a *key* of the entity. An entity may have more than one keys and one of them is designated as the *primary key*.

Relationship

Let e_1, e_2, ..., e_n be entities. A relationship among them is represented as r (e_1, e_2, ..., e_n). The relationship is 2-ary if n = 2 and is multiple-ary if n > 2. The set that consists of the same type of relationship is called *relationship set*. A relationship set can be viewed as a relationship among entity sets. R (E_1, E_2, ..., E_n) denotes the relationship set defined on entity sets E_1, E_2, ..., E_n. Relationship set is the type description of the entity relationship and a relationship among concrete entities is an instance of the corresponding relationship set. The same entity set can appear in a relationship set several times. A named relationship set can be viewed as the description of a *relationship type*. Sometimes relationship type is called relationship for short.

In the ER data model, a 2-ary relationship can be one-to-one, one-to-many, or many-to-many relationships. This classification can be applied to n-ary relationships as well. The constraint of a relationship among entities is called *cardinality ratio constraint*. In the ER data model there is an important semantic constraint called *participation constraint*, which stipulates the way that entities participate in the relationship. The concept *participation degree* is used to express the minimum number and maximum number of an entity participating in a relationship, expressed as (min, max) formally, where max ≥ min ≥ 0 and max ≥ 1. When min = 0, the way an entity participates in a relationship is called *partial participation*, and is called *total participation* otherwise. The cardinality ratio constraint and participation constraint are, sometimes, referred to as the structure constraint.

Note that relationships in the ER data model also have attributes, called the *relationship attributes*.

There is a special relationship in the real world, which represents the ownership among entities and is called the *identifying relationship*. Such a relationship has two characteristics:

(a) The entity owned by another entity depends on an owning entity, and does not exist separately, which must totally participate in relationship.

(b) The entity owned by another entity may not be the entity key of itself.

Because the entity owned by another entity has such characteristics, it is called the *weak entity*. A weak entity can be regarded as an entity as well as a complex attribute of its owning entity.

ER diagram

In the ER diagram, entities, attributes and relationships should be represented, where a rectangle denotes an entity set, a rectangle with double lines denotes a weak entity set, and a diamond denotes a relationship.

Rectangles and rhombus are linked by arcs and the cardinality ratios of relationships are given. If an arc is a single line, it represents that the entity is a partial participation. If an arc is a double line, it represents that the entity is a total participation. Participation degrees may be given if necessary.

In the ER diagram, a circle represents an attribute and it is linked to the corresponding entity set with an edge. If an attribute is an entity key or a part of the entity key, it is pointed out that in the ER diagram by underlining the attribute name or adding a short vertical line on the edge. If an attribute is complex, a tree structure will be formulated in the ER diagram.

Figure 1-1 shows ER diagram notations.

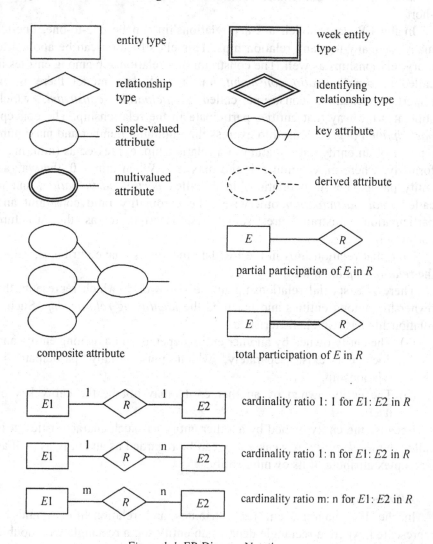

Figure 1-1. ER Diagram Notations

1.1.2   EER Model

The ER model based on *entities, relationships* and *attributes* is called the basic ER model. In order to model the complex semantics and relationships in the applications such as CAD/CAM, CASE, GIS, and so on, some new concepts have been introduced in the ER model and the enhanced (extended) entity-relationship (EER) data model is formed. In the EER model, the following notions are introduced.

Specialization and generalization

Generalization can summarize several entity types with some common features to an entity type and define a superclass. Specialization can divide an entity type into several entity types according to a particular feature and define several subclasses. For example, entity type "Automobile" is specialized into several subclasses such as "Car" and "Truck" while entity types "Faculty", "Technician", and "Research Associate" are generalized into a superclass "Staff".

Symbolically, a superclass E and several subclasses S_1, S_2, ..., S_n satisfy the relationship $S_1 \cup S_2 \cup ... \cup S_n \subseteq E$. Let $F = \cup_i S_i$ ($1 \leq i \leq n$). Then if $F = E$, F is a total specialization of E, or it is a partial one. In addition, F is a disjoint if $S_i \cap S_j = \Phi$ ($i \neq j$), or it is overlapping with $G = \cup_i S_i$ ($1 \leq i \leq n$). It should be noted that a subclass may not only inherit all attributes and relationships of its superclasses, but also have itself attributes and relationships.

In order to represent specialization and generalization in the ER diagram, the ER diagram should be extended and some new symbols are introduced into the EER diagram as shown in Figure 1-2.

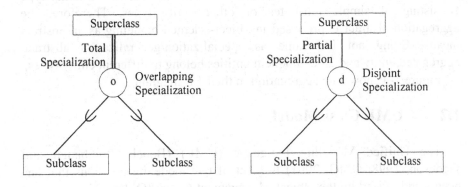

Figure 1-2. EER Diagram of the Specialization

Category

A category is a subclass of the union of the superclasses with different entity types. For example, entity type "Account" may be entity types "Personal" or "Business". Symbolically, a category E and the supclasses S_1, S_2, ..., S_n satisfy the relationship $E \subseteq S_1 \cup S_2 \cup ... \cup S_n$. The difference between the category and the subclass with more than one superclass should be noticed. Let E be a subclass and S_1, S_2, ..., S_n be its superclasses. One has then $E \subseteq S_1 \cap S_2 \cap ... \cap S_n$.

Figure 1-3 shows the category in the EER diagram.

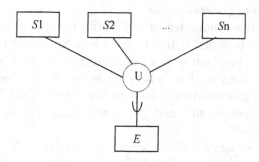

Figure 1-3. EER Diagram of the Category

Aggregation

A number of entity types, say S_1, S_2, ..., S_n, are aggregated to form an entity type, say E. In other words, E consists of S_1, S_2, ..., and S_n. For example, an entity type "Automobile" is aggregated from some entity types such as "Engine", "Gearbox", and "Interior", where "Interior" consists of "Seat" and "Dashboard". Here, S_i (i = 1, 2, ..., n) can be viewed as a kind of composite attribute, but it is not a simple attribute, which is an entity type consisting of simple attributes or other entity types. Therefore, the aggregation abstract is proposed in object-oriented modeling as an abstract means. Being not the same as specialization/generalization abstract, aggregated entity and all component entities belong to different entity types.

Figure 1-4 shows the aggregation in the EER diagram.

1.2   UML Class Model

The Unified Modeling Language (UML) (Booch, Rumbaugh and Jacobson, 1998; OMG, 2001) is a set of OO modeling notations that has been standardized by the Object Management Group (OMG). The power of the UML can be applied for many areas of software engineering and knowledge engineering (Mili *et al.*, 2001). The complete development of relational and object relational databases from business requirements can be described by the UML. The database itself traditionally has been described by notations called entity relationship (ER) diagrams, using graphic representation that is similar but not identical to that of the UML. Using the UML for database design has many advantages over the traditional ER notations (Naiburg, 2000). The UML is based largely upon the ER notations, and includes the ability to capture all information that is captured in a traditional data model. The additional compartment in the UML for methods or operations allows you to capture items like triggers, indexes, and the various types of constraints directly as part of the diagram. By modeling this, rather than using tagged values to store the information, it is now visible on the modeling surface, making it more easily communicated to everyone involved. So more and more, the UML is being applied to data modeling (Ambler, 2000a; Ambler, 2000b; Blaha and Premerlani, 1999; Naiburg, 2000). More recently, the UML has been used to model XML conceptually (Conrad, Scheffiner and Freytag, 2000).

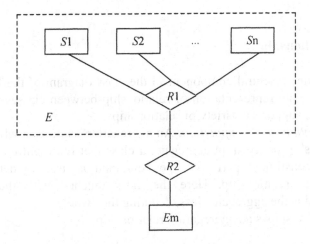

Figure 1-4. EER Diagram of the Aggregation

From the database modeling point of view, the most relevant model is the class model. The building blocks in this class model are those of classes and relationships. We briefly review these building blocks in the following.

1.2.1   Class

Being the descriptor for a set of objects with similar structure, behavior, and relationships, a class represents a concept within the system being modeled. Classes have data structure and behavior and relationships to other elements.

A class is drawn as a solid-outline rectangle with three compartments separated by horizontal lines. The top name compartment holds the class name and other general properties of the class (including stereotype); the middle list compartment holds a list of attributes; the bottom list compartment holds a list of operations. Either or both of the attribute and operation compartments may be suppressed. A separator line is not drawn for a missing compartment. If a compartment is suppressed, no inference can be drawn about the presence or absence of elements in it. Figure 1-5 shows a class.

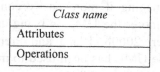

Figure 1-5. The Class Icon of the UML

1.2.2   Relationships

Another main structural component in the class diagram of the UML is relationships for the representation of relationship between classes or class instances. UML supports a variety of relationships.

(a) *Aggregation and composition.* An aggregation captures a whole-part relationship between an aggregate, a class that represent the whole, and a constituent part. An open diamond is used to denote an aggregate relationship. Here the class touched with the white diamond is the aggregate class, denoting the "whole".
Figure 1-6 shows an aggregation relationship.

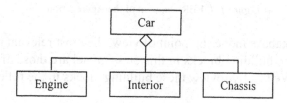

Figure 1-6. An Aggregation Relationship in the UML

Aggregation is a special case of composition where constituent parts directly dependent on the whole part and they cannot exist independently. Composition mainly applies to attribute composition. A composition relationship is represented by a black diamond.

(b) *Generalization.* Generalization is used to define a relationship between classes to build taxonomy of classes: one class is a more general description of a set of other classes. The generalization relationship is depicted by a triangular arrowhead. This arrowhead points to the superclass. One or more lines proceed from the superclass of the arrowhead connecting it to the subclasses. Figure 1-7 shows a generalization relationship.

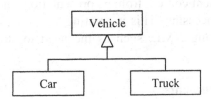

Figure 1-7. A Generalization Relation in the UML

(c) *Association.* Associations are relationships that describe connections among class instances. An association is a more general relationship than aggregation or generalization. A role may be assigned to each class taking part in an association, making the association a directed link. An association relationship is expressed by a line with an arrowhead drawn between the participating classes. Figure 1-8 shows an association relationship.

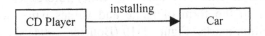

Figure 1-8. An Association Relation in UML

(d) *Dependency.* A dependency indicates a semantic relationship between two classes. It relates the classes themselves and does not require a set of instances for its meaning. It indicates a situation in which a change to the target class may require a change to the source class in the dependency. A dependency is shown as a dashed arrow between two classes. The class at the tail of the arrow depends on the class at the arrowhead. Figure 1-9 shows a dependency relationship.

Figure 1-9. A Dependency Relationship in the UML

1.3 XML

The eXtensible Markup Language (XML) (Bray, Paoli and Sperberg-McQueen, 1998), a data formatting recommendation proposed by the W3C as a simplified form of the Standard Generalized Markup Language (SGML), is becoming the de facto standard for data description and exchange between various systems and databases over the Internet. As a new markup language, XML supports user-defined tags, encourages the separation of document content from its presentation, and is able to automate web information processing. This is creating a new set of data management requirements involving XML, such as the need to store and query XML documents.

1.3.1 XML Documents

An XML document has a logical and a physical structure (Bray, Paoli and Sperberg-McQueen, 1998). The physical structure is consists of entities that are ordered hierarchically. The logical structure is explicitly described by markups that comprise declarations, elements, comments, character references, and processing instructions.

XML documents that conform to the rules of XML mark-up are called "well-formed"; for example, each document must have a single top-level (root) element, and all tags must be correctly nested. A number of additional instructions arc permitted, such as comments, processing instructions, unparsed character data and entity references. Tags can also contain attributes in the form of name and values pairs, with the values enclosed in quotation marks. Figure 1-10 (Bourret, 2004) shows an example XML document.

```
<SalesOrder SONumber="12345">
  <Customer CustNumber="543">
    <CustName>ABC Industries</CustName>
    <Street>123 Main St.</Street>
    <City>Chicago</City>
    <State>IL</State>
    <PostCode>60609</PostCode>
  </Customer>
  <OrderDate>981215</OrderDate>
  <Item ItemNumber="1">
    <Part PartNumber="123">
      <Description>
        <p><b>Turkey wrench:</b><br/>
        Stainless steel, one-piece construction, lifetime guarantee.</p>
      </Description>
      <Price>9.95</Price>
    </Part>
```

```
        <Quantity>10</Quantity>
      </Item>
      <Item ItemNumber="2">
        <Part PartNumber="456">
          <Description>
            <p><b>Stuffing separator:<b><br/>
            Aluminum, one-year guarantee.</p>
          </Description>
          <Price>13.27</Price>
        </Part>
        <Quantity>5</Quantity>
      </Item>
    </SalesOrder>
```

Figure 1-10. Sales Order XML Document

Essentially, XML documents can be associated with and validated against a schema specification in terms of a *document type definition (DTD)* (Bray, Paoli and Sperberg-McQueen, 1998) or by using the more powerful *XML* Schema language (Thompson *et al.*, 2001; Biron and Malhotra, 2001). In the following, we only focus on the DTD. Then XML document structure consists of an optional document type declaration containing the DTD and a document instance. The purpose of a DTD is to provide a grammar for a class of documents. DTDs consist of markup declarations.

1.3.2   XML DTD Constructs

According to the XML specification, DTDs consist of markup declarations namely element declarations, attribute-list declarations, entity declarations, notation declarations, processing instructions, and comments (Bray, Paoli and Sperberg-McQueen, 1998). As for these declarations, they are the elementary building blocks on which a DTD can be designed.

Element Type and Attribute-list Declarations
Element type and attribute-list declarations make up the core of DTDs and declare the valid structures of a document instance, namely, the nested element tags with their additional attributes. An elements type declaration associates the element content. XML provides a variety of facilities for the construction of the element content, namely, *sequence* of elements, *choice* of elements, *cardinality* constructors (?, *, +), the types of EMPTY, ANY, #PCDATA, and *mixed* content. *Sequence* requires elements to have a fixed order, whereas *choice* expresses element alternatives. An EMPTY element has no content, whereas ANY indicates that the element can contain data of type #PCDATA or any other element defined in the DTD. Mixed is useful

when elements are supposed to obtain character data (#PCDATA), optionally interspersed with child elements.

The name of attribute list must match the name of the corresponding element. The list of attribute declaration consists of the attribute names, their types and default declarations.

Entity Declarations

Entity declarations serve the reuse of DTD fragments and text as well as the integration of unparsed data. An entity declaration binds an entity to an identifier. Being external entities, unparsed entities always have notation references.

Notation Declarations

Notation Declarations provide a name for the format of an unparsed entity. They might be used as reference in entity declarations, and in attribute-list declaration as well as in attribute specification.

Processing Instructions

Processing instructions play an important role while checking integrity constraints of valid document instances. They have to be checked while parsing a document instance. The XML parse validates the document instance first and consumes the processing instructions known to XML. Then an application can handle more specific processing instructions.

A simple DTD of the XML document in Figure 1-10 is given in Figure 1-11 as follows.

```
<!ELEMENT SaleOrder (Customer*, OrderDate, Item*)>
    <!ATTLIST SaleOrder SONumber IDREF #REQUIRED>
<!ELEMENT Customer (CustName?, Street?, City?, State?, PostCode?)>
    <!ATTLIST Customer CustNumber IDREF #REQUIRED>
<!ELEMENT CustName (#PCDATA)>
<!ELEMENT Street (#PCDATA)>
<!ELEMENT City (#PCDATA)>
<!ELEMENT State (#PCDATA)>
<!ELEMENT PostCode (#PCDATA)>
<!ELEMENT OrderDate (#PCDATA)>
<!ELEMENT Item (Part*, Quantity)>
    <!ATTLIST Item ItemNumber IDREF #REQUIRED>
<!ELEMENT Part (Description?, Price?)>
    <!ATTLIST Part PartNumber IDREF #REQUIRED>
<!ELEMENT Description (#PCDATA)>
<!ELEMENT Price (#PCDATA)>
<!ELEMENT Quantity (#PCDATA)>
```

Figure 1-11. The DTD of the XML Document in Figure 1-10

It should be noticed that, however, XML lacks sufficient power in modeling real-world data and their complex inter-relationships in semantics. Hence, it is necessary to use other methods to describe data paradigms and develop a true conceptual data model, and then transform this model into an XML encoded format, which can be treated as a logical model. Figure 1-12 depicts such a procedure to integrate conceptual data models and XML, making it easier to create, manage and retrieve XML documents.

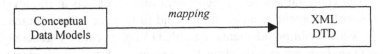

Figure 1-12. Transformation from Conceptual Data Models to XML DTD

Conceptual data modeling of XML schema (here XML schema refers to XML DTD or XML Schema, while XML Schema refers to the XML schema language proposed by W3C (Thompson *et al.*, 2001; Biron and Malhotra, 2001)) has been studied in the recent past. In (Conrad, Scheffiner and Freytag, 2000), UML was used for designing XML DTD. The idea is to use essential parts of static UML to model XML DTD. The mapping between the static part of UML (i.e., class diagrams) and XML DTDs was developed. To take advantage of all facets that DTD concepts offer, the authors further extended the UML language in an UML-compliant way. Focusing on conceptual modeling at XML Schema level instead of XML DTD level, Xiao *et al.* (2001) introduced a solution for modeling XML and the transformation from object-oriented (OO) conceptual models to XML Schema, where the OO features are more general and are not limited to UML. Also in (Mani, Lee and Muntz, 2001), a set of features found in various XML schema languages (e.g., XML DTD and XML Schema) was formalized into XGrammar and the conversion between an XGrammar and EER model was presented. The EER was also used in (Elmasri *et al.*, 2002) to generate customized hierarchical views and then further create XML schemas from the hierarchical views. In (Psaila, 2000), the ER model was extended to ERX so that one can represent a style sheet and a collection of documents conforming to one DTD in ERX model. But order was represented in ERX model by an additional order attribute.

XML DTDs can also be converted to conceptual models. In (dos Santos Mello and Heuser, 2001), a semi-automatic process for converting an XML DTD to a schema in a canonical conceptual model based on ORM/NIAM and extended ER models was described. A set of conversion rules, which was the core of this process, was hereby developed.

1.3.3   XML Databases

It is crucial for Web-based applications to model, storage, manipulate, and manage XML data documents. XML documents can be classified into *data-centric documents* and *document-centric documents* (Bourret, 2004).

Data-Centric Documents

Data-centric documents are characterized by fairly regular structure, fine-grained data (i.e., the smallest independent unit of data is at the level of a PCDATA-only element or an attribute), and little or no mixed content. The order in which sibling elements and PCDATA occurs is generally not significant, except when validating the document. Data-centric documents are documents that use XML as a data transport. They are designed for machine consumption and the fact that XML is used at all is usually superfluous. That is, it is not important to the application or the database that the data is, for some length of time, stored in an XML document.

As a general rule, the data in data-centric documents is stored in a traditional database, such as a relational (Kappel *et al.*, 2000; Lee and Chu, 2000), object-oriented (Chung *et al.*, 2001), object-relational (Surjanto, Ritter and Loeser, 2000), or hierarchical database. The data can also be transferred from a database to a XML document (Vittori, Dorneles and Heuser, 2001; Shanmugasundaram *et al.*, 2001; Carey *et al.*, 2000).

For the transfers between XML documents and databases, the mapping relationships between their architectures as well as their data should be created (Lee and Chu, 2000; Surjanto, Ritter and Loeser, 2000). Note that it is possible to discard some information such as the document and its physical structure when transferring data between them. It must be pointed out, however, that the data in data-centric documents such as semistructured data can also be stored in a native XML database, in which a document-centric document is usually stored.

The sales order XML document shown in Figure 1-10 is data-centric.

Document-Centric Documents

Document-centric documents are characterized by less regular or irregular structure, larger grained data (that is, the smallest independent unit of data might be at the level of an element with mixed content or the entire document itself), and lots of mixed content. The order in which sibling elements and PCDATA occurs is almost always significant. Document-centric documents are usually documents that are designed for human consumption. As a general rule, the documents in document-centric documents are stored in a native XML database or a content management system (an application designed to manage documents and built on top of a native XML database). Native XML databases are databases designed especially for storing XML documents. The only difference of native XML databases from other databases is that their internal model is based on XML and not something else, such as the relational model.

In practice, however, the distinction between data-centric and document-centric documents is not always clear. So the above-mentioned rules are not of a certainty. Data, especially semistructured data, can be stored in native XML databases and documents can be stored in traditional databases when few XML-specific features are needed. Furthermore, the boundaries between traditional databases and native XML databases are beginning to blur, as traditional databases add native XML capabilities and native XML databases support the storage of document fragments in external databases.

The following product description given in Figure 1-13 is document-centric (Bourret, 2004).

```
<Product>

<Intro>
The <ProductName>Turkey Wrench</ProductName> from <Developer>Full
Fabrication Labs, Inc.</Developer> is <Summary>like a monkey wrench,
but not as big.</Summary>
</Intro>

<Description>

<Para>The turkey wrench, which comes in <i>both right- and left-
handed versions (skyhook optional)</i>, is made of the <b>finest
stainless steel</b>. The Readi-grip rubberized handle quickly adapts
to your hands, even in the greasiest situations. Adjustment is
possible through a variety of custom dials.</Para>

<Para>You can:</Para>

<List>
<Item><Link URL="Order.html">Order your own turkey wrench</Link></Item>
<Item><Link URL="Wrenches.htm">Read more about wrenches</Link></Item>
<Item><Link URL="Catalog.zip">Download the catalog</Link></Item>
</List>

<Para>The turkey wrench costs <b>just $19.99</b> and, if you
order now, comes with a <b>hand-crafted shrimp hammer</b> as a
bonus gift.</Para>

</Description>

</Product>
```

Figure 1-13. The Document-Centric XML Document of Product Description

References

Ambler, S. W., 2000a, The design of a robust persistence layer for relational databases, http://www.ambysoft.com/persistenceLayer.pdf.

Ambler, S. W., 2000b, Mapping objects to relational databases, http://www.AmbySoft.com/mappingObjects.pdf.

Biron, P. V. and Malhotra, A. (Eds), 2001, XML Schema Part 2: Datatypes, *W3C Recommendation*, http://www.w3.org/TR/xmlschema-2/.

Blaha, M. and Premerlani, W., 1999, Using UML to design database applications, http://www.therationaledge.com/rosearchitect/mag/archives/9904/f8.html.

Booch, G., Rumbaugh, J. and Jacobson, I., 1998, *The Unified Modeling Language User Guide*, Addison-Welsley Longman, Inc.

Bourret, R., 2004, XML and databases, http://www.rpbourret.com/xml/XMLAndDatabases.htm.

Bray, T., Paoli, J. and Sperberg-McQueen, C. M. (Eds), 1998, Extensible Markup Language (XML) 1.0, *W3C Recommendation*, http://www.w3.org/TR/1998/REC-xml-19980210.

Carey, M. J., Kiernan, J., Shanmugasundaram, J., Shekita, E. J. and Subramanian, S. N., 2000, XPERANTO: Middleware for publishing object-relational data as XML documents, *Proceedings of 26th International Conference on Very Large Data Bases*, 646-648.

Chen, P. P., 1976, The entity-relationship model: Toward a unified view of data, *ACM Transactions on Database Systems*, 1 (1): 9-36.

Chung, T. S., Park, S., Han, S. Y. and Kim, H. J., 2001, Extracting object-oriented database schemas from XML DTDs using inheritance, *Lecture Notes in Computer Science 2115*, 49-59.

Conrad, R., Scheffiner, D. and Freytag, J. C., 2000, XML conceptual modeling using UML, *Lecture Notes in Computer Science 1920*, 558-571.

dos Santos Mello, R. and Heuser, C. A., 2001, A rule-based conversion of a DTD to a conceptual schema, *Lecture Notes in Computer Science 2224*, 133-148.

dos Santos, C., Neuhold, E. and Furtado, A., 1979, A data type approach to the entity-relationship model, *Proceedings of the 1st International Conference on the Entity-Relationship Approach to Systems Analysis and Design*, 103-119.

Elmasri, R., Weeldreyer, J. and Hevner, A., 1985, The category concept: an extension to the entity-relationship model, *International Journal on Data and Knowledge Engineering*, 1 (1): 75-116.

Elmasri, R., Wu, Y. C., Hojabri, B., Li, C. and Fu, J., 2002, Conceptual modeling for customized XML schemas, *Lecture Notes in Computer Science 2503*, 429-443.

Gegolla, M. and Hohenstein, U., 1991, Towards a semantic view of an extended entity-relationship model, *ACM Transactions on Database Systems*, 16 (3): 369-416.

Kappel, G., Kapsammer, E., Rausch-Schott, S. and Retschitzegger, W., 2000, X-Ray: Towards integrating XML and relational database systems, *Lecture Notes in Computer Science 1920*, 339-353.

Lee, D. W. and Chu, W. W., 2000, Constraints-preserving transformation from XML document type definition to relational schema, *Lecture Notes in Computer Science 1920*, 323-338.

Lee, M. L., Lee, S. Y., Ling, T. W., Dobbie, G. and Kalinichenko, L. A., 2001, Designing semistructured databases: a conceptual approach, *Lecture Notes in Computer Science 2113*, 12–21.

Mani, M., Lee, D. W. and Muntz, R. R., 2001, Semantic data modeling using XML schemas, *Lecture Notes in Computer Science 2224*, 149–163.

Mili, F., Shen, W., Martinez, I., Noel, Ph., Ram, M. and Zouras, E., 2001, Knowledge modeling for design decisions, *Artificial Intelligence in Engineering*, 15: 153-164.

Naiburg, E., 2000, Database modeling and design using rational rose 2000, http://www.therationaledge.com/rosearchitect/mag/current/spring00/f5.html.

OMG, 2001, Unified Modeling Language (UML), version 1.4, http://www.omg.org/technology/documents/formal/uml.htm.

Psaila, G., 2000, ERX: A data model for collections of XML Documents, *Proceedings of the 2000 ACM Symposium on Applied Computing*, 2: 898-903.

Scheuermann, P., Schiffner, G. and Weber, H., 1979, Abstraction capabilities and invariant properties modeling within to the entity-relationship approach, *Proceedings of the 1st International Conference on the Entity-Relationship Approach to Systems Analysis and Design*, 121-140.

Seligman, L. and Rosenthal, A., 2001, XML's impact on databases and data sharing, *IEEE Computer*, June, 59-67.

Shanmugasundaram, J., Shekita, E. J., Barr, R., Carey, M. J., Lindsay, B. G., Pirahesh, H. and Reinwald, B., 2001, Efficiently publishing relational data as XML Documents, *VLDB Journal*, 10 (2-3): 133-154.

Surjanto, B., Ritter, N. and Loeser, H., 2000, XML content management based on object-relational database technology, *Proceedings of the First International Conference on Web Information Systems Engineering*, 1, 70-79.

Thompson, H. S., Beech, D., Maloney, M. and Mendelsohn, N. (Eds), 2001, XML Schema Part 1: Structures, *W3C Recommendation*, http://www.w3.org/TR/xmlschema-1/.

Vittori, C. M., Dorneles, C. F. and Heuser, C. A., 2001, Creating XML documents from relational data sources, *Lecture Notes in Computer Science 2115*, 60-70.

Xiao, R. G., Dillon, T. S., Chang, E. and Feng, L., 2001, Modeling and transformation of object-oriented conceptual models into XML schema, *Lecture Notes in Computer Science 2113*, 795-804.

Chapter 2

LOGICAL DATABASE MODELS

The evolution of database systems was initially driven by the requirements of traditional data processing. Hierarchical and network data models were adopted by database management systems (DBMS) as database models in the 1960s and 1970s. The hierarchical and network data models have the drawbacks that the data models couple with the need for a formally based database model, which clearly separate the physical and logical model. Relational database model, put forward by E. F. Codd in 1970s (Codd, 1970), has a simple structure and a solid mathematical foundation. It rapidly replaced the hierarchical and network database models and became the dominant database model for commercial database systems.

With the breadth and depth of database uses in many emerging areas as diverse as biology and genetics, artificial intelligence, computer aided design, and geographical information systems, it was realized that the relational database model as defined by Codd, had semantic and structured drawbacks when it came to modeling of such specialized applications. The next evolution of database models took the form of rich data models such as the object-oriented data model (Abiteboul, Hull and Vianu, 1995; Elmasri and Navathe, 1994; Kim and Lochovsky, 1989) and the semantic data models (Abiteboul and Hull, 1987; Elmasri and Navathe, 1994; Hammer and McLeod, 1981).

Relational database model and object-oriented database model are typical the representatives of the logical database models. Based on these two basic database models, there exists a kind of hybrid database model called object-relational database model. In addition, new developments in artificial intelligence and procedure control have resulted in the appearances of deductive databases, active databases, temporal databases, and spatial databases. These databases generally adopt either one of the above-mentioned two basic database models or a hybrid database model.

2.1 The Relational Database Model

Relational database model introduced first by Codd (1970) is the most successful one and relational databases have been extensively applied in most information systems in spite of the increasing populations of object-oriented databases. A relational database is a collection of relations.

2.1.1   Attributes and Domains

The representations for some features are usually extracted from real-world things. The features of a thing are called *attributes*. For each attribute, there exists a range that the attribute takes values, called *domain* of the attribute. A domain is a finite set of values and every value is an atomic data, the minimum data unit with meanings.

2.1.2   Relations and Tuples

Let A_1, A_2, ..., A_n be attribute names and the corresponding attribute domains be D_1, D_2, ..., D_n (or Dom (A_i), $1 \le i \le n$), respectively. Then relational schema R is represented as

$$R = (D_1/A_1, D_2/A_2, ..., D_n/A_n)$$

or

$$R = (A_1, A_2, ..., A_n),$$

where n is the number of attributes and is called the degree of relation.

The instances of R, expressed as r or r (R), are a set of n-tuples and can be represented as $r = \{t_1, t_2, ..., t_m\}$. A tuple t can be expressed as $t = <v_1, v_2, ..., v_n>$, where $v_i \in D_i$ ($1 \le i \le n$), i.e., $t \in D_1 \times D_2 \times ... \times D_n$. The quantity r is therefore a subset of Cartesian product of attribute domains, i.e., $r \subseteq D_1 \times D_2 \times ... \times D_n$. Viewed from the content of a relation, a relation is a simple table, where tuples are its rows and attributes are its columns. Note that there is no complex data in relational table. The value of a tuple t on attribute set S is generally written $t [S]$, where $S \subseteq R$.

2.1.3   Keys

If an attribute value or the values of an attribute group in a relation can solely identify a tuple from other tuples, the attribute or attribute group is called a *super key* of the relation. If any proper subsets of a super key are not a super key, such super key is called a *candidate key* or shortly *key*.

For a relation, there may be several candidate keys. One chooses one candidate as the *primary key*, and other candidates are called *alternate key*. It is clear that the values of primary key of all tuples in a relation are different and are not null. The attributes included in a candidate key are called *prime attributes* and not included in any candidate key called *non-prime attributes*. If an attribute or an attribute group is not a key of relation *r* but it is a key of relation s, such attribute (group) is called *foreign key* of relation *r*.

2.1.4   Constraints

There are various constraints in the relational databases. We identify these constraints as follows.

(a) *Domain integrity constraints*. The basic contents of domain integrity constraints are that attribute values should be the values in the domains. In addition, domain integrity constraints are also prescribed if an attribute value could be null.

(b) *Entity integrity constraints*. Every relation should have a primary key and the value of the primary key in each tuple should be sole and cannot be null.

(c) *Referential integrity constraints*. Let a relation *r* have a foreign key *FK* and the foreign key value of a tuple *t* in *r* be *t* [*FK*]. Let *FK* quote the primary key *PK* of relation *r'* and *t'* be a tuple in *r'*. Referential integrity constraint demands that *t* [*FK*] comply with the following constraint: *t* [*FK*]= *t'* [*PK*]/null.

(d) *General integrity constraints*. In addition to the above-mentioned three kinds of integrity constraints that are most fundamental in relational database model, there are other integrity constraints related to data contents directly, called *general integrity constraints*. Because numbers of them are very large, only a few of them are considered in current relational DBMSs. Among these constraints, *functional dependencies (FD)* and *multivalued dependencies (MVD)* are more important in relational database design theory and widely investigated.

The functional dependencies (*FD*) in relational databases represent the dependency relationships among attribute values in relation. In the relational databases, functional dependencies can be defined as follows.

Definition: For a relation r (R), in which R denotes the schema, its attribute set is denoted by U, and X, $Y \subseteq U$, we say r satisfies the functional dependency *FD*: $X \rightarrow Y$, if

$$(\forall t \in r)\,(\forall s \in r)\,(t\,[X] = s\,[X] \Rightarrow t\,[Y] = s\,[Y]).$$

Based on the concept of functional dependency, the partial/full functional dependencies and the transitive functional dependency can be defined as follows.

Definition: For a relation r (R), in which R denotes the schema, its attribute set is denoted by U, and X, $Y \subseteq U$, we say Y is fully functionally dependent on X, denoted by $X \rightarrow_f Y$, if and only if $X \rightarrow Y$ and there does not exit $X' \subset X$ $(X' \neq \Phi)$ such that $X' \rightarrow Y$. If such X' exits, then Y is partially functionally dependent on X, denoted by $X \rightarrow_p Y$.

The notion of keys can consequently be defined in terms of *FD*s.

Definition: For a relation r (R), in which R denotes the schema, its attribute set is denoted by U, and $K \subseteq U$, we say K is a candidate key of R if and only if $K \rightarrow_f U$.

Multivalued dependencies (*MVD*) originated by Fagin (1977) are another important data dependencies that are imposed on the tuples of relational databases, relating an attribute value or a set of attribute values to a set of attribute values, independent of the other attributes in the relation. In classical relational databases, multivalued dependencies can be defined as follows.

Definition: For a relation r (R), in which R denotes the schema, its attribute set is denoted by U, X, $Y \subseteq U$, and $Z = U - XY$, we say r satisfies the multivalued dependency *MVD*: $X \rightarrow\rightarrow Y$, if

$$(\forall\, t \in r)\,(\forall\, s \in r)\,(t\,[X] = s\,[X] \Rightarrow (\exists\, u \in r)\,(u\,[X] = t\,[X] \wedge u\,[Y] = t\,[Y] \wedge u\,[Z] = s\,[Z])).$$

In the relational databases, the functional and multivalued dependencies satisfy the inference rules, namely, the *axiom systems* (Armstrong, 1974; Beeri, Fagin and Howard, 1977). For the functional dependency, for example, the *Armstrong axioms* (1974) can be used to derive all possible FDs implied by a given set of dependencies. Let r (R) be a relation on schema R, its attribute set be denoted by U, and X, Y, $Z \subseteq U$. Then the following is a set of Armstrong axioms.

(a) *Inclusion rule*: if $X \supseteq Y$, then $X \rightarrow Y$.
(b) *Transitivity rule*: if $X \rightarrow Y$ and $Y \rightarrow Z$, then $X \rightarrow Z$.
(c) *Augmentation rule*: If $X \rightarrow Y$, then $X \cup Z \rightarrow Y \cup Z$.

2.1.5   The Relational Algebra

Relational database model provides some operations, called the *relational algebra operations*. These operations can be subdivided into two classes:

(a) the operations for relations only (*select, project, join,* and *division*) and

(b) the set operations (*union, difference, intersection,* and *Cartesian product*).

In addition, some new operations such as *outerjoin, outerunion* and *aggregate* operations are developed for database integration or statistics and decision support. By using these operations, one can query or update relations.

Union ($\cup$)

Union is a binary set operation on two relations that are union-compatible. That means they have the same number of attributes with the same domains pairwisely. Formally let r and s be two union-compatible relations on the scheme R (A1, A2, ..., An). Then

$$r \cup s = \{t \mid t \in r \vee t \in s\}$$

It is clear that the result of $r \cup s$ is a relation on the schema R that includes all tuples which are either in r or in s or in both r and s. Of course, duplicate tuples, if any, must be eliminated.

Difference ($-$)

Difference is a binary set operation on two relations that are union-compatible. Formally let r and s be two union-compatible relations on the scheme R (A1, A2, ..., An). Then

$$r - s = \{t \mid t \in r \wedge t \notin s\}$$

It can be seen that the result of $r - s$ is a relation on the schema R that includes the tuples which are only in r but not in s.

Cartesian product ($\times$)

Cartesian product is a binary set operation on two relations. Formally let r and s be two fuzzy relations on schema R and S, respectively. Then

$$r \times s = \{t (R \cup S) \mid t [R] \in r \wedge t [S] \in s\}$$

That is, the result of $r \times s$ is a relation on the schema $R \cup S$, in which a tuple is a combination of a tuple from r and a tuple from s. So $|r \times s| = |r| \times |s|$. Here $|r|$ denotes the number of tuples in r.

Projection (Π)

Projection is a unary operation on a relation. Formally let r be relation on the scheme R (A1, A2, ..., An). Then the projection of r over attribute subset S ($S \subset R$) is defined as follows.

$$\Pi_S (r) = \{t (S) \mid (\forall x) (x \in r (S) \wedge t = x [S])\}$$

In other words, the result of $\Pi_S (r)$ is a relation on the schema S that only includes the columns of relational table r which are given in S. It should noticed that, if the attributes in S are all non-key attributes of r (R), duplicate tuples may appear in $\Pi_S (r)$ and must be eliminated.

Selection (σ)

Selection is a unary operation on a relation. Formally let r be relation on the scheme R (A1, A2, ..., An). Then the selection of r based on a selection condition P specified by a Boolean expression in forms of a single or composite predicate is defined as follows.

$$\sigma_P (r) = \{t \mid t \in r \wedge P (t)\}$$

Clearly, the result of $\sigma_P (r)$ is a relation on the schema R that only includes the tuples in r which satisfy the given selection condition P.

The five relational operations given above are called the primitive operations in the relational databases. In addition, there are three additional relational operations, namely, intersection, join (and natural join), and division. But the three operations can be defined by the primitive operations.

Intersection (∩)

Intersection is a binary set operation on two relations that are union-compatible. Formally let r and s be two union-compatible relations on the scheme R (A1, A2, ..., An). Then

$$r \cap s = \{t \mid t \in r \wedge t \in s\} \text{ or } r \cap s = r - (r - s)$$

The result of $r \cap s$ is a relation on the schema R that includes the tuples which are both in r and in s.

Join (⋈)

Join is a binary set operation on two relations. Formally let r (R) and s (S) be any two relations. Let P be a conditional predicate in the form of $A \theta B$, where $\theta \in \{>, <, \geq, \leq, =, \neq\}$, where $A \in R$, and $B \in S$. Then

$$r \bowtie_P s = \{t (R \cup S) \mid t [R] \in r \wedge t [S] \in s \wedge P (t [R], t [S])\} \text{ or}$$

$$r \bowtie_P s = \sigma_P (r \times s)$$

The result of $r \bowtie_P s$ is a relation on the schema $R \cup S$, in which a tuple is a combination of a related tuple from r and a related tuple from s. Not being the same as the Cartesian product operation, the two combined tuples respectively from r and s must satisfy the given condition.

When attributes A and B are identical and "θ" takes =, the join operation becomes the natural join operation, denoted $r \bowtie s$. Let $Q = R \cap S$. Then

$$r \bowtie s = \{t (R \cup (S - Q)) \mid (\exists x) (\exists y) (x \in r (R) \wedge y \in s (S) \wedge x [Q] = y$$
$$[Q] \wedge t [R] = x [R] \wedge t [S - Q] = y [S - Q] \}$$

Division (÷)
Division, referred to quotient operation sometimes, is used to find out the sub-relation $r \div s$ of a relation r, containing sub-tuples of r which have for complements in r all the tuples of a relation s. Then the division operation is defined by

$$r \div s = \{t \mid (\forall u) (u \in s \wedge (t, u) \in r)\},$$

where u is a tuple of s and t is a sub-tuple of r such that (t, u) is a tuple of r.

Alternatively, let $r (R)$ and $s (S)$ be two relations, where $S \subset R$. Let $Q = R - S$. Then the division of r and s can be defined as follows.

$$r \div s = \Pi_Q (r) - \Pi_Q (r (Q) \times s - r)$$

2.1.6   Relational Database Design

Overall Design of Databases
The objective of database design is to capture the essential aspects of some real-world enterprise for which one wishes to construct a database (Petry, 1996). Figure 2-1 shows a simplified description of the database design process (Elmasri and Navathe, 1994). Then four major steps are applied for the database design process, which are the *requirements collection & analysis, conceptual data modeling, logical database model,* and *physical database model,* respectively.

In the first step, the database designers collect and analyze the data requirements from prospective database users. As a result of this step, a concisely written set of users' requirements is formed.

In the second step, the conceptual data models (e.g., ER/EER and UML) are used to create a conceptual schema for the database. Here, the conceptual schema is a concise descriptions of the data requirements of the users and includes detailed descriptions of the data types, relationships, constraints, and etc. But there are no any implementation details in the conceptual schema. So it should be easy to share the conceptual schema with non-technical users. It is worth mentioning that a complex database is generally designed cooperatively by a design group and each member of the group may have different background. So using multiple conceptual data models to create the conceptual schema can facilitate the database designers with different background to design their conceptual data schemas easily by using one of the conceptual data models they are familiar with. But finally all these conceptual schemas designed by different members should be converted into a union conceptual schema. There are already some efforts for converting different conceptual schemas (Cherfi, Akoka and Comyn-Wattiau, 2002).

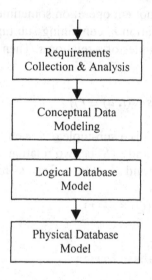

Figure 2-1. Database Design Process

In the third step, the logical database model is designed through mapping the conceptual schema represented by the conceptual data model. The result of this step is perhaps a relational or object-oriented database model. In (Teorey, Yang and Fry, 1986), for example, relational databases were logically designed using the ER model.

Finally, in the fourth step, the physical database model is design. Of course, this step is mostly already formulated with a commercial DBMS.

Relational Database Design Theory

In the context of relational databases, the relational database model should be designed in terms of a set of *good* schemas such that update anomalies and data redundancy are minimized. Here update anomalies mean that the undesired consequences occur when updating the data in the relational databases (e.g., inserting, deleting or modifying the tuples). The reason is that there exist certain undesired dependency relationships between the attributes of a relation.

The relational database design theory has been developed for minimizing update anomalies and data redundancy, which core is the normalization theory. The process of normalization is the process of relation schema decomposition so that certain undesired dependency relationships are removed to lead to certain *normal forms* (NFs).

Let r (R) be a relation on schema R, U be the attribute set of R, and X, K, $A \subseteq U$. Here K is the candidate key of R. Then we have the following major NFs in the relational databases.

(a) *The first normal form* (1NF): R is in 1NF, denoted by $R \in$ 1NF, if and only if every attribute value in r (R) is atomic.

(b) *The second normal form* (2NF): R is in 2NF, denoted by $R \in$ 2NF, if and only if $R \in$ 1NF and for any non-prime attribute A, $K \rightarrow_f A$.

(c) *The third normal form* (3NF): R is in 3NF, denoted by $R \in$ 3NF, if and only if $R \in$ 1NF and for any $X \rightarrow A$ $(A \not\subseteq X)$, either X is a superkey of R or A is a set of prime attributes.

(d) *The Boyce-Codd normal form* (BCNF): R is in BCNF, denoted by $R \in$ BCNF, if and only if $R \in$ 1NF and for any $X \rightarrow A$ $(A \not\subseteq X)$, either X is a superkey of R.

A lower NF can be normalized into a higher NF through relation schema decomposition (via projection). Figure 2-2 shows the details (Chen 1999).

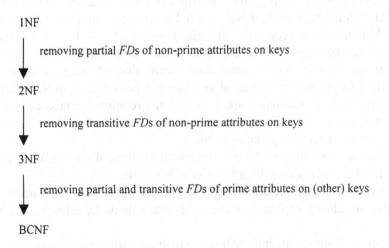

Figure 2-2. Normal Forms Based on Functional Dependencies

It should be noticed that the schema decomposition should satisfy the following properties:

    (a) *lossless-join*. It means that the relation reconstructed from the resultant relations of the decomposition will be the same as the original relation with respect to information contents.

    (b) *dependency-preservation*. It means that the functional dependencies in the original relation are preserved by the resultant relations of the decomposition.

The four NFs discussed above are based on the functional dependency. In addition, there are other kinds of normal forms such as the *fourth normal form* (4NF) and the *fifth normal form* (5NF), which are related with multivalued dependency and join dependency, respectively.

2.2   The Nested Relational Database Model

The normalization, being one kind of constraints, is proposed in traditional relational databases. Among various normalized forms, first normal form (1NF) is the most fundamental one, which assumes that each attribute value in a relational instance must be atomic. As we know, the real-world applications are complex, and data types and their relationships are rich as well as complicated. The 1NF assumption limits the expressive power of traditional relational database model. Therefore, some attempts to relax 1NF limitation are made and one kind of data model, called non-first normal (or nested) relational database model have been introduced,

The first attempt to relax first-normal formal limitation is made by Makinouchi (1977), where, attribute values in the relation may be atomic or set-valued. Such relation is thereby called non-first normal form (NF^2) one. After Makinouchi's proposal, NF^2 database model is further extended (Ozsoyoglu, Ozsoyoglu and Matos, 1987; Schek and Scholl, 1986). The NF^2 database model in common sense now means that attribute values in the relational instances are either atomic or set-valued and even relations themselves. So NF^2 databases are called nested relational databases also. In this paper, we do not differentiate these two notions. A formal definition of NF^2 relational schema is given as follows.

Definition. An attribute Aj is a structured attribute if its schema appears on the left-hand side of a rule; otherwise it is simple.

Definition. An NF^2 relational schema may contain any combination of simple or structured attributes on the right-hand side of the rules. Formally,

Schema:: Simple_attribute | Simple_attribute, Structured_attributes

Structured_attributes:: Simple_attribute | Simple_attribute, Structured_attributes

A schema is called flat if and only if all of its attributes are simple. It is clear that a classical schema, namely, a flat relational schema, is a special case of a nested relational schema. Two nested schemas are called union-compatible, meaning the ordered attributes have the same nesting structure, if and only if the corresponding simple attributes and structured attributes are union-compatible.

Let a relation r have schema $R = (A1, A2, ..., An)$ and let D1, D2, ..., Dn be corresponding domains from which values for attributes (A1, A2, ..., An) are selected. A tuple of an NF^2 relation is an element in r and denoted as <a1, a2, ..., an> consisting of n components. Each component a_j ($1 \leq j \leq n$) may be an atomic or null value or another tuple. If Aj is a structureed attribute, then the value aj need not be a single value, but an element of the subset of the Cartesian product of associated domains Dj1, Dj2, ..., Djm.

Based on the NF^2 database model, the ordinary relational algebra has been extended. In addition, two new restructuring operators, called the *Nest* and *Unnest* (Ozsoyoglu, Ozsoyoglu and Matos, 1987; Roth, Korth and Batory, 1987) (as well as *Pack* and *Unpack* (Ozsoyoglu, Ozsoyoglu and Matos, 1987)), have been introduced. The Nest operator can gain the nested relation including complex-valued attributes. The Unnest operator is used to flatten the nested relation. That is, it takes a relation nested on a set of attributes and desegregates it, creating a "flatter" structure. The formal definitions and the properties of these operators as well as the ordinary relational algebra for the NF^2 data model have been given (Colby, 1990; Venkatramen and Sen, 1993).

2.3　The Object-Oriented Database Model

Although there has been great success in using the relational databases for transaction processing, the relational databases have some limitations in some non-transaction applications such as computer-aided design and manufacturing (CAD/CAM), knowledge-based systems, multimedia, and GIS. Such limitations include the following.

(a) The data type is very restricted.
(b) The data structure based on the record notion may not match the real-world entity.
(c) Data semantics is not rich, and the relationships between two entities cannot be represented in a natural way.

Therefore, some non-traditional data models were developed in succession to enlarge the application area of databases since the end of the 1970s. Since these non-traditional data models appeared after the relational data model, they are called post-relational database models. Object-oriented database model is one of the post-relational database models.

Object-oriented (OO) data model is developed by adopting some concepts of semantic data models and knowledge expressing models, some ideas of object-oriented program language and abstract data type in data structure/programming.

2.3.1   Objects and Identifiers

All real-world entities can be simulated as *objects*, which have no unified and standard definition. Viewing from the structure, an object consists of *attributes, methods* and *constraints*. The attributes of an object can be simple data and other objects. The procedure that some objects constitute a new object is called *aggregation*. A method in an object contains two parts: signature of the method that illustrates the name of the method, parameter type, and result type; implementation of the method.

In general, attributes, methods and constraints in an object are encapsulated as one unit. The state of an object is changed only by passing message between objects. *Encapsulation* is one of the major features in OO data models.

In OO data models, each object has a sole and constant identifier, which is called *object identifier* (OID). For two objects with same attributes, methods and constraints, they are different objects if they have a different OID. The OID of an object is generated by system and cannot be changed by the user.

The OID generated by system can be divided into two kinds, i.e., *logical object identifier* and *physical object identifier*. Logical object identifier is mapped into physical one when an object is used because only physical object identifier concerns the storage address of the object.

2.3.2   Classes and Instances

In OO data models, objects with the same attributes, methods and constraints can be incorporated into a *class*, where objects are called *instances*. In a class, attributes, methods and constraints should be declared. Note that the attributes in a class can be classified into two kinds: instance variables and class variables. Instance variables are the attributes for which values are different in different objects of the class, while class variables are the attributes for which values are the same in different objects of the class.

In fact, classes can also be regarded as objects. Then, classes can be incorporated into another new class, called *meta class*. The instances of a meta class are classes. Therefore, objects are distinguished into *instance objects* and *class objects*.

2.3.3 Class Hierarchical Structure and Inheritance

A subset of a class, say A, can be defined as a class, say B. Class B is called a *subclass* and class A is called *superclass*. A subclass can further be divided into new subclasses. A *class hierarchical structure* is hereby formed, where it is permitted that a subclass has several direct or indirect superclasses. The relationship between superclass and subclass is called *IS-A relationship*, which represents a *specialization* from top to bottom and a *generalization* from bottom to top. Because one subclass can have several direct superclasses, a class hierarchical structure is not a tree but a class *lattice*.

Because a subclass is a subset of its superclass, the subclass inherits the attributes and methods in its all superclasses. Besides inheritance, a subclass can define new attributes and methods or can modify the attributes and methods in the superclasses. If a subclass has several direct superclasses, the subclass inherits the attributes and methods from these direct superclasses. This is called *multiple inheritance*.

When inheriting, the naming conflict may occur, which should be resolved.

(a) Conflict among superclasses. If several direct superclasses of a subclass have the same name of attributes or methods, the conflict among superclasses appear. The solution is to declare the superclass order inherited, or to be illustrated by user.

(b) Conflict between a superclass and a subclass. When there are conflicts between a subclass and a superclass, the definition of attributes and methods in subclass would override the same definition in the superclass.

Note that a naming method may have a different meaning in different classes. The feature that a name has a multiple meaning is called *polymorphism*. The method with polymorphism is called *overloading*. Because the method in an object is polymorphism, the procedure corresponding to the method name cannot be determined while compiling program and do while running program. The later combination of the method name and implementing procedure of a method is called *late binding*.

References

Abiteboul, S. and Hull, R., 1987, IFO: A formal semantic database model, *ACM Transactions on Database Systems*, 12 (4): 525-565.

Abiteboul, S., Hull, R. and Vianu, V., 1995, *Foundations of Databases*, Addison Wesley.

Armstrong, W. W., 1974, Dependency structures of data base relationships, *Proceedings of the IFIP Congress*, 580- 583.

Beeri, C., Fagin, R. and Howard, J. H., 1977, A complete axiomatization for functional and multivalued dependencies in database relations, *ACM SIGMOD Conference*, 47-61.

Chen, G. Q., 1999, *Fuzzy Logic in Data Modeling; Semantics, Constraints, and Database Design*, Kluwer Academic Publisher.

Cherfi, S. S., Akoka, J. and Comyn-Wattiau, I., 2002, Conceptual modeling quality: from EER to UML schemas evaluation, *Lecture Notes in Computer Science*, 2503: 414-428.

Codd, E.F., 1970, A relational model of data for large shared data banks, *Communications of the ACM*, 13 (6): 377-387.

Colby, L. S., 1990, A recursive algebra for nested relations, *Information Systems*, 15 (5): 567–662.

Elmasri, R. and Navathe, S. B., 1994, *Fundamentals of Database Systems*, Second Edition, Benjamin/Cummings.

Fagin, R., 1977, Multivalued dependencies and a new normal form for relational databases, *ACM Transactions on Database Systems*, 2 (3): 262-278.

Hammer, M. and McLeod, D., 1981, Database description with SDM: a semantic database model, *ACM Transactions on Database Systems*, 6 (3): 351-386.

Kim, W. and Lochovsky, F. H., 1989, *Object-Oriented Concepts, Databases and Applications*, Addison Wesley.

Makinouchi, A., 1977, A consideration on normal form of not-necessarily normalized relations in the relational data model, *Proceedings of Third International Conference on Very Large Databases*, Tokyo, Japan, October, 447–453.

Ozsoyoglu, G., Ozsoyoglu, Z. M. and Matos, V., 1987, Extending relational algebra and relational calculus with set-valued attributes and aggregate functions, *ACM Transactions on Database Systems*, 12 (4): 566-592.

Petry, F. E., 1996, *Fuzzy Databases: Principles and Applications*, Kluwer Academic Publisher.

Roth, M. A., Korth, H. F. and Batory, D. S., 1987, SQL/NF: A query language for non-1NF relational databases, *Information Systems*, 12: 99-114.

Schek, H. J. and Scholl, M. H., 1986, The relational model with relational-valued attributes, *Information Systems*, 11 (2): 137–147.

Teorey, T. J., Yang, D. Q. and Fry, J. P., 1986, A logical design methodology for relational databases using the extended entity-relationship model, *ACM Computing Surveys*, 18 (2): 197-222.

Venkatramen, S. S. and Sen, A., 1993, Formalization of an IS-A based extended nested relation data model, *Information Systems*, 20 (1): 53–57.

Chapter 3

FUZZY SETS AND POSSIBILITY DISTRIBUTIONS

Fuzzy set theory (Zadeh, 1965), which is interchangeably referred as fuzzy logic, is a generalization of the set theory and provides a means for the representation of imprecision and vagueness. In real-world applications, information is often imperfect. So fuzzy set theory has been applied in a number of real applications crossing over a broad realm of domains and disciplines (Cox, 1995; Munakata and Jani, 1994) since its formal start in 1965. Typically, for example, fuzzy set theory has extensively been applied in the navigation of mobile robots under unknown environments (Lee and Wu, 2003).

One of the major areas of research in database has been the continuous effort to enrich existing database models with a more extensive collection of semantic concepts. One of the semantic needs not adequately addressed by traditional models is that of imprecision and uncertainty. Traditional models assume the database model to be a correct reflection of the world being captured and assume that the data stored is known, accurate, and complete. It is rarely the case in real life that all or most of these assumptions are met. Different data models have been proposed to handle different categories of data quality (or lack thereof) with fuzzy set theory.

3.1 Imperfect Information in Database Modeling

There have been some attempts at classifying various possible kinds of imperfect information. Inconsistency, imprecision, vagueness, uncertainty, and ambiguity are five basic kinds of imperfect information in database systems (Bosc and Prade, 1993; Motor, 1990; Motor and Smets, 1997).

Inconsistency is a kind of semantic conflict when one aspect of the real world is irreconcilably represented more than once in a database or several different databases. For example, one has "*married*" value and "*single*" value for Tom's marital status. Information inconsistency usually comes from information integration.

Intuitively, imprecision and vagueness are relevant to the content of an attribute value, and it means that a choice must be made from a given range (interval or set) of values but it is not known exactly which one to choose per se. For example, "*between 20 and 30 years old*" and "*young*" for the attribute *Age* are imprecise and vague values, respectively. In general, vague information is represented by linguistic terms.

Uncertainty is related to the degree of truth of its attribute value, and it means that one can apportion some, but not all, of our belief to a given value or a group of values. For example, the sentence that "*I am 95 percent sure that Tom is married*" represents information uncertainty. Notice that the random uncertainty is described using probability theory.

The ambiguity means that some elements of the model lack complete semantics, leading to several possible interpretations. For example, it may not be clear if one person's salaries stated are per week or month.

Generally, several different kinds of imperfect information can co-exist with respect to the same piece of information. For example, that it is almost sure that John is very young involves information uncertainty and vagueness simultaneously.

3.1.1   Null Values and Partial Values

Imprecise values generally denote a set of values in the form of [ai1, ai2, ..., aim] or [ai1, ai2] for the discrete and continuous universe of discourse, respectively, meaning that exactly one of the values is the true value for the single-valued attribute, or at least one of the values is the true value for the multivalued attribute. So imprecise information here have two interpretations: disjunctive information and conjunctive information.

One kind of imprecise information that has been studied extensively is the well-known null values (Codd, 1986 & 1987; Motor, 1990; Parsons, 1996; Zaniola, 1986), which were originally called incomplete information. The possible interpretations of null values include

    (a) "*existing but unknown*" (denoted by *unk* or φ in this thesis),

    (b) "*nonexisting*" or "*inapplicable*" (denoted by *inap* or ⊥), and

    (c) "*no information*" (denoted by *nin*).

A null value on a multivalued object, however, means an "open null value" (denoted by *onul*) (Gottlob and Zicari, 1988), i.e., the value may not exist, has exactly one unknown value, or has several unknown values.

Null values with the semantics of "existent but unknown" can be considered as the special type of partial values that the true value can be any one value in the corresponding domain, i.e., an applicable null value corresponds to the whole domain. The notion of a partial value is illustrated as follows (DeMichiel, 1989; Grant, 1979).

Definition. A partial value on a universe of discourse U corresponds to a finite set of possible values in which exactly one of the values in the set is the true value, denoted by $\{a_1, a_2, ..., a_m\}$ for discrete U or $[a_1, a_n]$ for continua U, in which $\{a_1, a_2, ..., a_m\} \subseteq U$ or $[a_1, a_n] \subseteq U$. Let η be a partial value, then *sub* (η) and *sup* (η) are used to represent the minimum and maximum in the set.

Note that crisp data can also be viewed as special cases of partial values. A crisp data on discrete universe of discourse can be represented in the form of $\{p\}$, and a crisp data on continua universe of discourse can be represented in the form of $[p, p]$. Moreover, a partial value without containing any element is called an *empty partial value*, denoted by $\perp$. In fact, the symbol $\perp$ means an inapplicable missing data (Codd, 1986 & 1987). Null values, partial values, and crisp values are thus represented with a uniform format.

3.1.2   Probabilistic Values

Information with a stochastic nature is very common in real-world applications. In order to represent such random uncertainty, probabilistic values are used (Barbara, Garcia-Molina and Porter, 1992; Cavallo and Pittarelli, 1987; Dey and Sarkar, 1996; Eiter *et al.*, 2001; Lakshmanan *et al.*, 1997; Pittarelli, 1994; Zimanyi, 1997). For a discrete universe of discourse U, a probabilistic value in U is described by a probability distribution ψ_P. Here, A probabilistic measure Prob (u) for each $u \in U$ is needed, which denotes the probability that ψ_P takes u, where $0 \leq$ Prob (u) ≤ 1. Formally, the probability distribution ψ_P is represented as follows.

$$\psi_P = \{\text{Prob } (u_1)/u_1, \text{Prob } (u_2)/u_2, ..., \text{Prob } (u_n)/u_n\}$$

It should be noted that, for a probability distribution ψ_P, the following must hold.

$$\sum_{i=1}^{n} \text{Prob } (u_i) \leq 1$$

This is not the same as a fuzzy value to be presented in Section 3.2.

3.1.3   Fuzzy Sets in Database Modeling

A large number of data models have been proposed to handle uncertainty and vagueness. Most of these models are based on the same paradigms. Vagueness and uncertainty are generally modeled with fuzzy sets and possibility theory (Zadeh, 1965 & 1978). Many of the existing approaches dealing with imprecision and uncertainty are based on the theory of fuzzy sets. Fuzzy information has been extensively investigated in the context of the relational model (Petry, 1996; Chen, 1999). Recent efforts have extended these results to object-oriented databases by introducing the related notions of classes, generalization/specialization, and inheritance (de Caluwe, 1998; Ma, 2005). In addition, fuzzy data modeling has been investigated in the context of the conceptual data models such as ER (Zvieli and Chen, 1986), EER (Chen and Kerre, 1998) and IFO (Vila *et al.*, 1996; Yazici, Buckles and Petry, 1999; Yazici and Merdan, 1996). More recently, XML data management is increasingly receiving attention due to the extensive use of Internet. Fuzzy information modeling in XML is hereby one of the foundations of implementing Web-based intelligent information processing (Lee and Fanjiang, 2003).

In the following sections, the basic concepts of fuzzy set theory are briefly introduced, which are of interest or relevance to the discussions of successive chapters.

3.2   Representations of Fuzzy Sets and Possibility Distributions

In 1965, Lofti Zadeh published his innovating paper "Fuzzy Set" in the journal of *Information and Control* (Zadeh, 1965). Since then fuzzy set has been infiltrating into almost all branches of pure and applied mathematics that are set-theory-based. This has resulted in a vast number of real applications crossing over a broad realm of domains and disciplines.

Fuzzy data is originally described as fuzzy set by Zadeh (1965). Let U be an universe of discourse. A fuzzy value on U is characterized by a fuzzy set F in U. A membership function

$$\mu_F: U \to [0,1]$$

is defined for the fuzzy set F, where $\mu_F(u)$, for each $u \in U$, denotes the degree of membership of u in the fuzzy set F. Thus the fuzzy set F is described as follows.

$$F = \{\mu_F(u_1)/u_1, \mu_F(u_2)/u_2, ..., \mu_F(u_n)/u_n\}, \text{ or}$$

$$F = \int_{u \in U} \mu_F(u)/u$$

When $\mu_F(u)$ is viewed to be a measure of the possibility that a variable X has the value u in this approach, where X takes values in U, a fuzzy value is described by a possibility distribution π_X (Zadeh, 1978).

$$\pi_X = \{\pi_X(u_1)/u_1, \pi_X(u_2)/u_2, ..., \pi_X(u_n)/u_n\}$$

Here, $\pi_X(u_i)$, $u_i \in U$, denotes the possibility that u_i is true. Let π_X and F be the possibility distribution representation and the fuzzy set representation for a fuzzy value, respectively. It is apparent that $\pi_X = F$ is true (Raju and Majumdar, 1988).

3.3   Support, Kernel, and α-Cut of a Fuzzy Set

Let U be a universe of discourse and F a fuzzy set in U with the membership function $\mu_F: U \rightarrow [0,1]$. We have then the following notions related to fuzzy sets.

Support. The set of the elements that have non-zero degrees of membership in F is called the support of F, denoted by

supp $(F) = \{u|\ u \in U$ and $\mu_F(u) > 0\}$.

Kernel. The set of the elements that completely belong to F is called the kernel of F, denoted by

ker $(F) = \{u|\ u \in U$ and $\mu_F(u) = 1\}$.

α-Cut. The set of the elements which degrees of membership in F are greater than (greater than or equal to) α, where $0 \leq \alpha < 1$ $(0 < \alpha \leq 1)$, is called the strong (weak) α-cut of F, respectively denoted by

$$F_{\alpha+} = \{u|\ u \in U \text{ and } \mu_F(u) > \alpha\}$$

and

$$F_\alpha = \{u|\ u \in U \text{ and } \mu_F(u) \geq \alpha\}.$$

The relationships among the support, kernel, and α-cut of a fuzzy set can be illustrated in Figure 3-1.

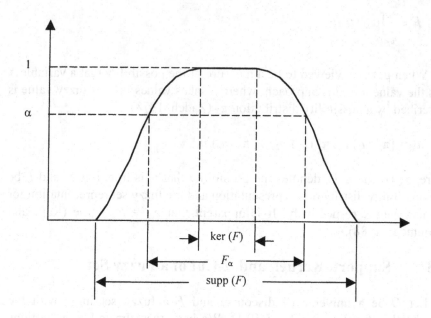

Figure 3-1. Support, Kernel, and α-Cut of Fuzzy Sets

Consider the example of a preliminary product design. The value of the performance parameter *capacity* is "about 2.5e+03", which is represented by the following fuzzy set

F = {1.0/2.5e+03, 0.96/5.0e+03, 0.88/7.5e+03, 0.75/1.0e+04,

0.57/1.25e+04, 0.32/1.5e+04, 0.08/1.75e+04}.

Then, we have

supp (F) = {2.5e+03, 5.0e+03, 7.5e+03, 1.0e+04, 1.25e+04, 1.5e+04, 1.75e+04},

ker (F) = {2.5e+03},

$F_{0.88+}$ = {2.5e+03, 5.0e+03}, and

$F_{0.88}$ = {2.5e+03, 5.0e+03, 7.5e+03}.

3.4   Zadeh's Extension Principle

The extension principle introduced by Zadeh (1975) has been regarded as one of the most basic ideas of fuzzy set theory. By providing a general method, the extension principle has been extensively employed to extend nonfuzzy mathematical concepts. The idea is to induce a fuzzy set from a number of given fuzzy sets through a mapping.

Zadeh's extension principle can also be referred to maximum-minimum principle sometimes. Let X1, X2, ..., Xn and Y be ordinary sets, f be a mapping from $X1 \times X2 \times \ldots \times Xn$ to Y such that $y = f(x1, x2, \ldots, xn)$, P (Xi) and P (Y) be the power sets of Xi and Y ($0 \le i \le n$), respectively. Here, P (Xi) = $\{C|C \subseteq Xi\}$ and P (Y) = $\{D|D \subseteq Y\}$. Then f induces a mapping from $P(X1) \times P(X2) \times \ldots \times P(Xn)$ to P (Y) with

$$f(C1, C2, \ldots, Cn) = \{f(x1, x2, \ldots, xn)|xi \in Ci, 0 \le i \le n\},$$

where $Ci \subseteq Xi, 0 \le i \le n$. Now, let F (Xi) be the class of all fuzzy sets on Xi, i.e., F (Xi) = $\{\}$, $0 \le i \le n$ and F (Y) be the class of all fuzzy sets on Y, i.e., F (Y) = $\{\}$, then f induces a mapping from $F(X1) \times F(X2) \times \ldots \times F(Xn)$ to F (Y) such that for all $Ai \in F(Xi)$, f (A1, A2, ..., An) is a fuzzy set on Y with

$$f(A1, A2, \ldots, An)(y) =$$

$$\begin{cases} \sup\limits_{\substack{f(x1,x2,\ldots,xn)=y \\ xi \in Xi\,(i=1,2,\ldots,n)}} (\min(\mu_{A1}(x1), \mu_{A2}(x2), \ldots, \mu_{An}(xn)), f^{-1}(y)) \ne \Phi \\ 0, f^{-1}(y) = \Phi \end{cases}$$

3.5   Operations on Fuzzy Sets

In order to manipulate fuzzy sets (as well as possibility distributions), several operations, including set operations, arithmetic operations, relational operations, and logical operations, should be defined.

3.5.1   Set Operations of Fuzzy Sets

Let A and B be fuzzy sets on the same universe of discourse U with the membership functions μ_A and μ_B, respectively. Then we have

Union. The union of fuzzy sets A and B, denoted $A \cup B$, is a fuzzy set on U with the membership function $\mu_{A \cup B} \colon U \to [0,1]$, where

$$\forall u \in U, \mu_{A \cup B}(u) = \max(\mu_A(u), \mu_B(u)).$$

Intersection. The intersection of fuzzy sets A and B, denoted $A \cap B$, is a fuzzy set on U with the membership function $\mu_{A \cap B} \colon U \to [0,1]$, where

$$\forall u \in U, \mu_{A \cap B}(u) = \min(\mu_A(u), \mu_B(u)).$$

Complementation. The complementation of fuzzy set $\bar{A}$, denoted by $\bar{A}$, is a fuzzy set on U with the membership function $\mu_{\bar{A}} \colon U \to [0,1]$, where

$\forall u \in U, \mu_{\bar{A}}(u) = 1 - \mu_A(u).$

Difference. Based on the above-defined operations, we can obtain the difference of fuzzy sets B and A.

$B - A = B \cap \bar{A}$

Being the same as the classical set theory, the operations on fuzzy sets satisfy the following properties. Let A, B, and C be fuzzy sets on U:
   (a) Commutativity laws: $A \cup B = B \cup A, A \cap B = B \cap A,$
   (b) Associativity laws: $(A \cup B) \cup C = A \cup (B \cup C), (A \cap B) \cap C = A \cap (B \cap C),$
   (c) Distribution laws: $A \cup (B \cap C) = (A \cup B) \cap (A \cup C), A \cap (B \cup C) = (A \cap B) \cup (A \cap C),$
   (d) Absorption laws: $A \cup (A \cap B) = A, A \cap (A \cup B) = A,$
   (e) Idempotency laws: $\underline{A \cup A = A, A \cap A = A,}$ and
   (f) de Morgan laws: $\overline{A \cup B} = \bar{A} \cap \bar{B}, \overline{A \cap B} = \bar{A} \cup \bar{B}.$

3.5.2   Arithmetic Operations of Fuzzy Sets

Utilizing Zadeh's extension principle, which can also be referred to maximum-minimum principle sometimes, arithmetic operations can be defined. Let A and B be fuzzy sets on the same universe of discourse U with the membership functions μ_A and μ_B, respectively, and "θ" be an infix operator. $A\ \theta\ B$ is a fuzzy set on U with the membership function $\mu_{A\,\theta\,B}: U \to [0,1]$, where

$$\forall z \in U, \mu_{A\theta B}(z) = \max_{z = x \theta y} (\min(\mu_A(x), \mu_B(y))).$$

3.5.3   Relational Operations of Fuzzy Sets

Fuzzy relational operations are various kinds of comparison operations on fuzzy sets, namely, *equal* (=), *not equal* (≠), *greater than* (>), *greater than or equal* (≥), *less than* (<), and *less than or equal* (≤). The definitions of these fuzzy relational operations are essentially related to the closeness measures between fuzzy sets and the given thresholds. Semantic equivalence degree (*SE*) for fuzzy sets, which will be depicted in Chapter 7, can be used for this purpose.

Let A and B be fuzzy sets on the same universe of discourse U with the membership functions μ_A and μ_B, respectively, and β be a given threshold value. Then we have

(a) $A \approx_\beta B$ if $SE(A, B) \geq \beta$,

(b) $A \not\approx_\beta B$ if $SE(A, B) < \beta$,

(c) $A \succ_\beta B$ if $SE(A, B) < \beta$ and max (supp (A)) > max (supp (B)),

(d) $A \prec_\beta B$ if $SE(A, B) < \beta$ and max (supp (A)) < max (supp (B)),

(e) $A \succeq_\beta B$ if $A \succ_\beta B$ or $A \approx_\beta B$, and

(f) $A \preceq_\beta B$ if $A \prec_\beta B$ or $A \approx_\beta B$.

Now let us have a close look at the fuzzy sets being operators. Three kinds of fuzzy sets can be identified: simple (atomic) fuzzy set, modified (composite) fuzzy set, and compound fuzzy set.

Simple (atomic) fuzzy set. A simple fuzzy set such as *young* or *tall* is defined by a fuzzy number with membership function.

Modified (composite) fuzzy set. A modified fuzzy set such as *very young* or *more or less tall* is described by a fuzzy number with membership function. Note that its membership function is not defined but computed through the membership function of the corresponding simple fuzzy set. In order to compute the membership function of modified fuzzy set, some semantic rules should be used. Let F is a simple fuzzy set represented by a fuzzy number in the universe of discourse U and its membership function is $\mu_F: U \rightarrow [0,1]$, then we have the following rules.

Concentration rule: $\mu_{\text{very } F}(u) = (\mu_F(u))^2$

More generally, $\mu_{\text{very very ... very } F}(u) = (\mu_F(u))^{2 \times \text{(times of very)}}$

Dilation rule: $\mu_{\text{more or less } F}(u) = (\mu_F(u))^{1/2}$

Compound fuzzy set. A compound fuzzy set such as *young $\cap$ very tall* is represented by simple fuzzy sets or modified fuzzy sets connected by union ($\cup$), intersection ($\cap$) or complementation connectors.

Generally speaking, the results of fuzzy relational operations are fuzzy Boolean. They can be combined with logical operators such as *not* ($\neg$), *and* ($\wedge$), and *or* ($\vee$) to form complicated logical expression. Such expression can be used to represent logical conditions for information retrieval and so on. In the above definitions of the fuzzy relational operations, classical two-valued logic (2VL), namely, true (T) and false (F), is used because of the use of threshold values.

In the relational operations of fuzzy sets, there may be some fuzzy relations such as *(not) close to/around*, *(not) at lease*, and *(not) at most* etc. with crisp values in addition to the traditional operators such as >, <, =, $\neq$, $\geq$, and $\leq$. Now consider fuzzy relations as operators and crisp values as operands. For $A \tilde{\theta} Y$, where A is an attribute, $\tilde{\theta}$ is a fuzzy relation, and Y is a crisp value, $\tilde{\theta} Y$ is a fuzzy number.

Firstly let's focus on fuzzy relation "*close to (around)*". According to (Chen and Jong, 1997), the membership function of the fuzzy number "*close to Y (around Y)*" on the universe of discourse can be defined by

$$\mu_{close\ to\ Y}(u) = \frac{1}{1 + (\frac{u - Y}{\beta})^2}$$

The membership function of the fuzzy number "*close to Y*" is shown in Figure 3-2.

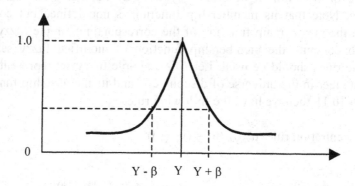

Figure 3-2. Membership Function of the Fuzzy Number "*close to Y*"

It should be noted that the fuzzy number above is a simple fuzzy term. Based on it, we have the following modified fuzzy terms: "*very close to Y*", "*very very ... very close to Y*", and "*more or less close to Y*", which membership functions can be defined as

$$\mu_{very\ close\ to\ Y}(u) = (\mu_{close\ to\ Y}(u))^2,$$

$$\mu_{very\ very\ ...\ very\ close\ to\ Y}(u) = (\mu_{close\ to\ Y}(u))^{2\ \times\ (times\ of\ very)}, \text{ and}$$

$$\mu_{more\ or\ less\ close\ to\ Y}(u) = (\mu_{close\ to\ Y}(u))^{1/2}.$$

In addition, based on fuzzy number "*close to Y*", a compound fuzzy term "*not close to Y*" can be defined. Its membership function is as follows.

$$\mu_{\text{not close to } Y}(u) = (1 - \mu_{\text{close to } Y}(u))$$

Secondly let's focus on fuzzy relation *"at least"* (Bosc and Pivert, 1995 & 1997). The membership function of the fuzzy number *"at least Y"* on the universe of discourse can be defined by

$$\mu_{\text{at least } Y}(u) = \begin{cases} 0, u \leq \omega \\ \dfrac{u-\omega}{Y-\omega}, \omega < u < Y. \\ 1, u \geq Y \end{cases}$$

The membership function of the fuzzy number *"at least Y"* is shown in Figure 3-3.

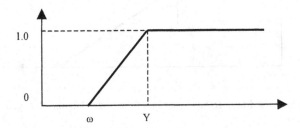

Figure 3-3. Membership Function of the Fuzzy Number *"at least Y"*

Based on fuzzy number *"at least Y"*, a compound fuzzy term *"not at least Y"* can be defined. Its membership function is as follows.

$$\mu_{\text{not at least } Y}(u) = (1 - \mu_{\text{at least } Y}(u))$$

Finally let's focus on fuzzy relation *"at most"*. The membership function of the fuzzy number *"at most Y"* on the universe of discourse can be defined by

$$\mu_{\text{at most } Y}(u) = \begin{cases} 1, u \leq Y \\ \dfrac{\delta - u}{\delta - Y}, Y < u < \delta. \\ 0, u \geq \delta \end{cases}$$

The membership function of the fuzzy number *"at most Y"* is shown in Figure 3-4.

Based on fuzzy number "*at most Y*", a compound fuzzy term "*not at most Y*" can be defined. Its membership function is as follows.

$\mu_{\text{not at most Y}}(u) = (1 - \mu_{\text{at most Y}}(u))$

The fuzzy relations "close to", "not close to", "at least", "at most", "not at least", and "not at most" can be viewed as "fuzzy equal to", "fuzzy not equal to", "fuzzy greater than and equal to", "fuzzy less than and equal to", "fuzzy greater than", and "fuzzy less than", respectively. Using these fuzzy relations and crisp values, the fuzzy query condition with fuzzy operators, which has the form A $\tilde{\theta}$ Y, is formed.

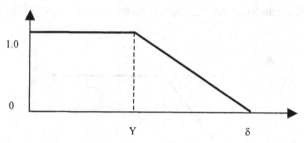

Figure 3-4. Membership Function of the Fuzzy Number "*at most Y*"

3.5.4   Logical Operations of Fuzzy Sets

Fuzzy logical operations dependent on the representation of fuzzy Boolean values as well as fuzzy logic. Three logical operations *fuzzy not* ($\tilde{\neg}$), *fuzzy and* ($\tilde{\wedge}$), and *fuzzy or* ($\tilde{\vee}$), which operands are fuzzy Boolean value(s) represented by fuzzy sets, are defined in this section.

Fuzzy and. The result of *fuzzy and* is a fuzzy Boolean value. *Fuzzy and* can be defined with "intersection" kinds of operations such as "min" operation. Let A: $\mu_A(u)$ and B: $\mu_B(u)$ be two fuzzy Boolean values represented by fuzzy sets on the same universe of discourse U. Then

$A \tilde{\wedge} B$: min ($\mu_A(u)$, $\mu_B(u)$), $u \in U$.

Fuzzy or. The result of *fuzzy or* is a fuzzy Boolean value. *Fuzzy or* can be defined with "union" kinds of operations such as "max" operation. Let A: $\mu_A(u)$ and B: $\mu_B(u)$ be two fuzzy Boolean values represented by fuzzy sets on the same universe of discourse U. One has

$A \tilde{\vee} B$: max ($\mu_A(u)$, $\mu_B(u)$), $u \in U$.

Fuzzy not. The result of *fuzzy not* is a fuzzy Boolean value. *Fuzzy not* can be defined with "complementation" kinds of operations such as "subtraction" operation. Let A: $\mu_A (u)$ be a fuzzy Boolean values represented by fuzzy sets on the universe of discourse U. One has

$$\eqsim A: (1 - \mu_A (u)), u \in U.$$

References

Barbara, D., Garcia-Molina, H. and Porter, D., 1992, The management of probabilistic data, *IEEE Transactions on Knowledge and Data Engineering*, 4 (5): 487-502.

Bosc, P. and Pivert, O., 1995, SQLf: a relational database language for fuzzy querying, *IEEE Transactions on Fuzzy Systems*, 3 (1): 1–17.

Bosc, P. and Pivert, O., 1997, Extending SQL retrieval features for the handing of flexible queries, *Fuzzy Information Engineering: A Guided Tour of Applications*, D. Dubois, H. Prade, and R. R. Yager eds., Wiley Computer Publishing, 233–251.

Bosc, P. and Prade, H., 1993, An introduction to fuzzy set and possibility theory based approaches to the treatment of uncertainty and imprecision in database management systems", *Proceedings of the Second Workshop on Uncertainty Management in Information Systems: From Needs to Solutions*.

Cavallo, R. and Pittarelli, M., 1987, The theory of probabilistic databases, *Proceedings of the 13th VLDB Conference*, 71-81.

Chen, G. Q. and Kerre, E. E., 1998, Extending ER/EER concepts towards fuzzy conceptual data modeling, *Proceedings of the 1998 IEEE International Conference on Fuzzy Systems*, 2: 1320-1325.

Chen, G. Q., 1999, *Fuzzy Logic in Data Modeling; Semantics, Constraints, and Database Design*, Kluwer Academic Publisher.

Chen, S. M. and Jong, W. T., 1997, Fuzzy query translation for relational database systems, *IEEE Transactions on Systems, Man and Cybernetics–Part B: Cybernetics*, 27 (4): 714–721.

Codd, E. F., 1986, Missing information (applicable and inapplicable) in relational databases, *SIGMOD Record*, 15: 53-78.

Codd, E. F., 1987, More commentary on missing information in relational databases (applicable and inapplicable information), *SIGMOD Record*, 16 (1): 42-50.

Cox, E., 1995, *Fuzzy Logic for Business and Industry*, Massachusetts: Charles River Media, Inc.

de Caluwe, R., 1998, *Fuzzy and Uncertain Object-Oriented Databases: Concepts and Models*, World Scientific Pub Co.

Dey, D. and Sarkar, S. A., 1996, Probabilistic relational model and algebra, *ACM Transactions on Database Systems*, 21 (3): 339-369.

Eiter, T., Lu, J. J., Lukasiewicz, T. and Subrahmanian, V. S., 2001, Probabilistic object bases, *ACM Transactions on Databases Systems*, 26 (3): 264-312.

Gottlob, G. and Zicari, R., 1988, Closed world databases opened through null values, *Proceedings of the 1988 International Conference on Very Large Data Bases*, 50-61.

Grant, J., 1979, Partial values in a tabular database model, *Information Processing Letters*, 9 (2): 97-99.

Lakshmanan, L. V. S., Leone, N., Ross, R. and Subrahmanian, V. S., 1997, ProbView: A flexible probabilistic database system, *ACM Transactions on Database Systems*, 22 (3): 419-469.

Lee, J. and Fanjiang, Y. Y., 2003, Modeling imprecise requirements with XML, *Information and Software Technology*, 45 (7): 445-460.

Lee, T. L. and Wu, C. J., 2003, Fuzzy motion planning of mobile robots in unknown environments, *Journal of Intelligent and Robotic Systems*, 37 (2): 177–191

Ma, Z. M., 2005, *Advances in Fuzzy Object-Oriented Databases: Modeling and Applications*, Idea Group Publishing.

Motor, A. and Smets, P., 1997, *Uncertainty Management in Information Systems: From Needs to Solutions*, Kluwer Academic Publishers.

Motor, A., 1990, Accommodation imprecision in database systems: issues and solutions, *ACM SIGMOD Record*, 19 (4): 69-74.

Munakata, T. and Jani, Y., 1994, Fuzzy systems: an overview, *Communications of The ACM*, 37 (3): 69-76.

Parsons, S., 1996, Current approaches to handling imperfect information in data and knowledge bases, *IEEE Transactions on Knowledge Data Engineering*, 8: 353–372.

Petry, F. E., 1996, *Fuzzy Databases: Principles and Applications*, Kluwer Academic Publisher.

Pittarelli, M., 1994, An algebra for probabilistic databases, *IEEE Transactions on Knowledge and Data Engineering*, 6 (2): 293-303.

Raju, K. V. S. V. N. and Majumdar, A. K., 1988, Fuzzy functional dependencies and lossless join decomposition of fuzzy relational database system, *ACM Transactions on Database Systems*, 13(2): 129-166.

Vila, M. A., Cubero, J. C., Medina, J. M. and Pons, O., 1996, A conceptual approach for deal with imprecision and uncertainty in object-based data models, *International Journal of Intelligent Systems*, 11: 791-806.

Yazici, A. and Merdan, O., 1996, Extending IFO data model for uncertain information, *Proceedings of Information Processing and Management of Uncertainty in Knowledge-Based Systems*, 3: 1283-1288.

Yazici, A., Buckles, B. P. and Petry, F. E., 1999, Handling complex and uncertain information in the ExIFO and NF^2 data models, *IEEE Transactions on Fuzzy Systems*, 7 (6): 659–676.

Zadeh, L. A., 1965, Fuzzy sets, *Information and Control*, 8 (3): 338-353.

Zadeh, L. A., 1975, The concept of a linguistic variable and its application to approximate reasoning, *Information Sciences*, 8: 119-249 & 301-357; 9: 43-80.

Zadeh, L. A., 1978, Fuzzy sets as a basis for a theory of possibility", *Fuzzy Sets and Systems*, 1 (1): 3-28.

Zaniolo, C., 1984, Database systems with null values, *Journal of Computer and System Sciences*, 28 (2): 142- 166.

Zimanyi, E., 1997, Query evaluation in probabilistic relational databases, *Theoretical Computer Science*, 171: 179-219.

Zvieli, A. and Chen, P. P., 1986, Entity-relationship modeling and fuzzy databases, *Proceedings of the 1986 IEEE International Conference on Data Engineering*, 320-327.

PART II

FUZZY CONCEPTUAL DATA MODELING

Chapter 4

THE FUZZY ER AND FUZZY EER MODELS

4.1   Introduction

Conceptual data modeling involves conceptual (semantic) data models. The conceptual data models, as described in Chapter 1, provide the designers with powerful mechanisms in generating the most complete specification from the real world. The conceptual data models, e.g., ER/EER and UML, represent both complex structures of entities and complex relationships among entities as well as their attributes. Hence, the conceptual data models play an important role in conceptual data modeling and database conceptual design.

A major goal for database research has been the incorporation of additional semantics into the data model. Classical data models often suffer from their incapability to represent and manipulate imprecise and uncertain information that may occur in many non-traditional applications in the real world (e.g., decision-making and expert systems). In order to deal with complex objects and imprecise and uncertain information in conceptual data modeling, one needs fuzzy extension to conceptual data models, which allow imprecise and uncertain information to be represented and manipulated at a conceptual level.

Fuzzy databases have been extensively studied in last two decades in the context of the relational database model (see Chapter 7). Current efforts have been concentrated on fuzzy object-oriented databases (see Chapter 9). However, less research has been done in modeling imprecision and uncertainty in conceptual data model. In (Zvieli and Chen, 1986), fuzzy set theory was applied to some of the basic ER concepts. Fuzzy entity sets, fuzzy relationship sets and fuzzy attribute sets were introduced in addition to fuzziness in entity and relationship occurrences and in attribute values. Consequently, fuzzy extension to the ER algebra (Chen, 1976) has been sketched. Other efforts to extend the ER model can be found in (Ruspini, 1986; Vandenberghe, 1991). The fuzzy extensions of several major EER concepts were introduced in (Chen and Kerre, 1998), including superclass/subclass, generalization/specialization, category, and the subclass with multiple superclasses. In this chapter, a full fuzzy extension to ER and EER models and the graphical representations will be presented.

4.2   The Fuzzy ER Model

The extension to the ER data model to incorporate fuzziness was proposed by Zvieli and Chen (1986), where fuzzy entities, attributes and relationships are represented in the graphical model. Consequently, fuzzy extension to Chen' ER algebra has been sketched.

4.2.1   Three Levels of Fuzziness in Entities, Relationships and Attributes

The classical ER model, as shown in Chapter 1, describes the real-world semantics in the terms of entities, relationships, and attributes. Here the attributes refer to the entity attributes and the relationship attributes. An ER model generally contains a set of entity types and a set of relationship types among these entity types, and each entity or relationship type may contain a set of attributes on one hand. It should be noticed that these sets of entity types, relationship types, and attributes are crisp. On the other hand, each entity type, relationship, or attribute may have a number of values.

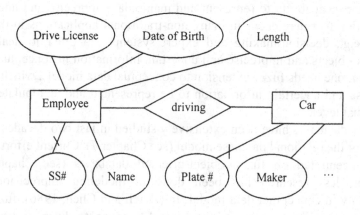

Figure 4-1. A Simple ER DataModel

Example. Let us consider a simple ER model in Figure 4-1, which contains two entity types and a relationship type, namely, entity types "Employee" and "Car", and relationship type "driving". Assume entity type "Employee" contains attributes "SS#", "Drive License", "Name", "Date of Birth", and "Length". Also assume that "John Smith" is a value of "Employee", which has attribute values <375275613, M000988014861, John Smith, 9/18/1963, 174>.

Viewed hierarchically from the discussion above, it is not difficult to find that the ER data model is described in three levels. The first level is model level, referring to the entity type, relationship type and attribute. In the example mentioned above, the first level refers to

- entity types: "Employee" and "Car", "driving",
- relationship type: "driving", and
- attributes: "SS#", "Drive License", "Name", "Date of Birth", and "Length" for "Employee".

The second level is type/instance level, referring to the instances of an entity type or a relationship type. In the example mentioned above, the second level refers to

- entity type/instance: "John Smith" for "Employee".

The third level is attribute value level, referring to the attribute values of an entity or relationship instance. In the example mentioned above, the third level refers to

- attribute values: "375275613", "M000988014861", "John Smith", "9/18/1963", "174" for "John Smith".

The fuzzy extension to the ER data model is hereby carried out in the three levels. At the first level, entity types, relationship types and attributes may all be fuzzy sets. That means we only have the partial knowledge that they possibly belong to the corresponding types, i.e., the ER model. In the above-mentioned example, for example, relationship type "driving" may indefinitely belong to the ER model. Since the entity types, relationship types and attributes may be fuzzy sets in the fuzzy ER model, membership functions of the fuzzy entity type set, fuzzy relationship type set, and fuzzy attribute set must be introduced, respectively.

Formally, let E, R, and A be the fuzzy entity type set, fuzzy relationship type set, and fuzzy attribute set of the fuzzy ER model, respectively, and μ_E, μ_R, and μ_A be their membership functions. Then

- for an entity type, say Ei, we have $\mu_E(Ei)/Ei$, where $\mu_E(Ei)$ is the degree of Ei belonging to E and $0 \leq \mu_E(Ei) \leq 1$,
- for a relationship type, say Ri, we have $\mu_R(Ri)/Ri$, where $\mu_R(Ri)$ is the degree of Ri belonging to R and $0 \leq \mu_R(Ri) \leq 1$, and

- for an attribute of entity type or relationship type, say Ai, we have μ_A $(Ai)/Ai$, where μ_A (Ai) is the degree of Ai belonging to A and $0 \le \mu_A$ $(Ai) \le 1$.

So in a fuzzy ER model, for example, its entity types may look like {0.9/Employee, 1.0/Car} and its relationship type may look like {0.7/driving}. Note that in the classical ER model, the values of μ_E, μ_R and μ_A should always be 0 or 1. We omit the entity types, relationship types, and attributes which membership degrees are 0.

At the second level, for each entity type and relationship type, the sets of their instances can be fuzzy sets. That is, they reflect possible partial belonging of the corresponding values to their types.

Formally, let e and r be the fuzzy instance sets of an entity type, say Ei, and a relationship type, say Ri, respectively, and μ_e and μ_r be their membership functions. Then

- for an entity instance of fuzzy instance set e to the (fuzzy) entity type, say ei, we have μ_e $(ei)/ei$, where μ_e (ei) is the degree of ei belonging to e and $0 \le \mu_e$ $(ei) \le 1$, and
- for a relationship instance of fuzzy instance set r to the (fuzzy) relationship type, say ri, we have μ_r $(ri)/ri$, where μ_r (ri) is the degree of ri belonging to r and $0 \le \mu_r$ $(ri) \le 1$.

Also μ_e $(ei)/ei$ can be represented by μ_{Ei} $(ei)/ei$ and μ_r $(ri)/ri$ by μ_{Ri} $(ri)/ri$, where μ_{Ei} (ei) is the degree of ei being the entity instance of Ei and μ_{Ri} (ri) is the degree of ri being the relationship instance of Ri.

In a fuzzy ER model, for example, its entity instances to an entity type may look like {1.0/<375275613, M000988014861, John Smith, 9/18/1963, 174>, 0.8/<914825583, M000909116501, Chris Chen, 10/1/1984, 170>}. Note that in the classical ER model, the values of μ_e and μ_r should always be 0 or 1. We omit the entity instances and relationship instances which membership degrees are 0 in all entity types and relationship types.

At the third level, for each attribute, any of its values can be a fuzzy set. Suppose we have attribute "Length" and its two values may be "tall" and "short".

The three levels of fuzziness in the fuzzy ER data model were presented in (Zvieli and Chen, 1986). Also the fuzzy ER diagram was introduced to represent the fuzziness. In order to represent the fuzziness at the first level in the fuzzy ER diagram graphically, each of the entity types, relationship types and attributes is connected with a membership degree to replace the originals, and they are enclosed in the rectangle, diamond-shaped box, and oval, respectively.

Let Ei, Ri, and Ai be a fuzzy type, fuzzy relationship type, and attribute, respectively. Then Figure 4-2 shows fuzzy ER diagram notations with the first level of fuzziness.

Fuzziness at the second and third levels is represented with symbol "*f*" labeled in the fuzzy ER diagram in (Zvieli and Chen, 1986).

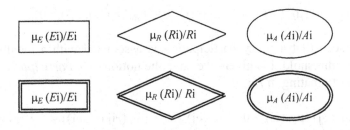

Figure 4-2. The Fuzzy ER Diagram Notations with the First Level of Fuzziness

4.2.2 Relationships and Constraints

The participation constraints and the cardinality constraints are two important semantic constraints in the ER model. Both of them related to the number of entity instances of each participating entity type. In the classical ER model, it is not difficult to get the number of entity instances of each participating entity type because it is known for sure if an entity instance belongs to the entity type. For the fuzzy ER model, however, there exits the fuzziness at the second (type/instance) level. An entity instance may be associated with a degree that the entity instance belongs to the entity type. The participation constraints and the cardinality constraints should be extended in a fuzzy context. Without loss of generality, only binary relationships are considered in the following discussions.

Formally, let Rij be a relationship type of entity types Ei and Ej, denoted Rij (Ei, Ej). Then Ei is called totally participating in Rij, if

$$(\forall \ ei) \ (\exists \ ej) \ (\mu_{Ei} \ (ei) > 0 \wedge \mu_{Ej} \ (ej) > 0 \wedge \mu_{Rij} \ (rij \ (ei, ej)) = 1).$$

Here ei (ej) is the instance of Ei (Ej), which degree belonging to Ei (Ej) is greater than 0. And rij (ei, ej) is a relationship instance of entity instances ei and ej. The totally participation means that every ei of Ei participates in at least one relationship instance of Rij with a membership degree 1. Besides, Ei is called partially participating in Rij, if

$$(\exists \ ei) \ (\exists \ ej) \ (\mu_{Ei} \ (ei) > 0 \wedge \mu_{Ej} \ (ej) > 0 \wedge \mu_{Rij} \ (rij \ (ei, ej)) = 0).$$

The totally participation requires that for any ***. It is clear that such a requirement is too strict. Generally the totally participation can be extended into the notion of *fuzzy participation*. For any ei of Ei, there exists an ej of Ej, such that μ_{Rij} (rij (ei, ej)) > 0. We call Ei fuzzily participates in Rij, if

$$(\forall\ ei)\ (\exists\ ej)\ (\mu_{Ei}\ (ei) > 0 \wedge \mu_{Ej}\ (ej) > 0 \wedge \mu_{Rij}\ (rij\ (ei, ej)) > 0).$$

It can be seen that a fuzzy participation is associated with a membership degree. If a threshold λ is given, we have the notion of *λ-participation*. Ei is called *λ-participating* in Rij, if

$$(\forall\ ei)\ (\exists\ ej)\ (\mu_{Ei}\ (ei) > 0 \wedge \mu_{Ej}\ (ej) > 0 \wedge \mu_{Rij}\ (rij\ (ei, ej)) \geq \lambda \wedge \lambda \in [0, 1]).$$

That is, Ei λ-participates in Rij if every ei of Ei participates in at least one relationship instance of Rij with a membership degree being greater than the given threshold λ.

In the fuzzy ER diagrams, total participation, partial participation, fuzzy participation and λ-participation are displayed as in Figure 4-3.

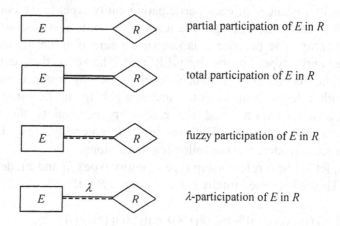

Figure 4-3. The Fuzzy ER Diagram of the Participation Constraints

Another constraint of concern for relationships is the cardinality constrain, referring to the correspondence between the numbers of the related entity types. Let Rij be the relationship type between entity types Ei and Ej. In the classical ER model, three kinds of cardinality can be identified: *one-to-one correspondence* (1: 1), *one-to-many correspondence* (1: n), and *many-to-many correspondence* (m: n). Here

- 1: 1 means that for each instance ei of Ei, there is at most one instance of Ej corresponding to ei, and vice versa,

- 1: n means that for each instance *ei* of *Ei*, there may exist more than one instance of *Ej* corresponding to *ei*, and for each instance *ej* of *Ej*, there is at most one instance of *Ei* corresponding to *ej*, and
- 1: n means that for each instance *ei* of *Ei*, there may exist more than one instance of *Ej* corresponding to *ei*, and vice versa.

It is clear that the number of the "many" side is a precise integer number in the classical ER model. In the fuzzy ER model, however, there may exist the fuzziness at the second level and sometimes the more information on the partial knowledge about the correspondence between related entity types have to be modeled. An example is that in a university, a student is allowed to select "about 10" courses or less in an academic year (Chen, 1999) and we have a fuzzy many-to-many correspondence for entity types "Student" and "Course" with relationship type "Select".

First of all, in the fuzzy ER model, we have *fuzzy one-to-many correspondence*, denoted 1: Ñ, for entity types *Ei* and *Ej* with relationship type *Rij*, where Ñ is a fuzzy set representing "how many" in the "many" side. That means that for each instance *ei* of *Ei*, there may exist as many as Ñ instance of *Ej* corresponding to *ei*, and for each instance *ej* of *Ej*, there is at most one instance of *Ei* corresponding to *ej*. Furthermore we can differentiate two kinds of *fuzzy many-to-many correspondence*, denoted m: Ñ and Õ: Ñ, respectively, for entity types *Ei* and *Ej* with relationship type *Rij*, where Õ and Ñ are fuzzy sets. For the former, m: Ñ means that for each instance *ej* of *Ej*, there may exist more than one instance of *Ei* corresponding to *ej*, and for each instance *ei* of *Ei*, there may exist as many as Ñ instance of *Ej* corresponding to *ei*. For the later, Õ: Ñ means that for each instance *ei* of *Ei*, there may exist as many as Ñ instance of *Ej* corresponding to *ei*, and for each instance *ej* of *Ej*, there may exist as many as Õ instance of *Ei* corresponding to *ej*.

In general, in the fuzzy ER model, there are 1: Ñ, m: Ñ, and Õ: Ñ in addition 1: 1, 1: n, and m: n. Figure 4-4 depicts diagrammatic representations of the fuzzy cardinality constrain.

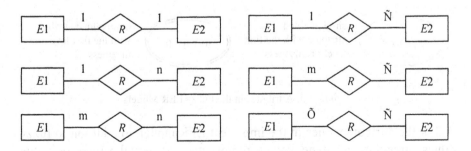

Figure 4-4. Fuzzy Cardinality Ratios

4.3   The Fuzzy EER Model

In order to model information fuzziness in the EER data model, some notions and notations are introduced in this section based on the issues of Zvieli and Chen (1986) and Chen and Kerre (1998).

4.3.1   Fuzzy Attribute

In an imperfect EER model, first attributes may have fuzziness at the first level in the fuzzy ER model, referring to fuzzy attribute sets. In addition, attribute values may be fuzzy ones based on possibility distribution, which are the same as the fuzziness at the third level in the fuzzy ER model. Moreover, there are two kinds of interpretation of a fuzzy attribute value because of single-valued and multivalued attributes, which are a fuzzy disjunctive attribute value and a fuzzy conjunctive attribute value. In connection to these two kinds of fuzzy attribute values, the fuzzy attributes can be classified into the fuzzy disjunctive one and the fuzzy conjunctive one. Also a composite attribute may be fuzzy too, either disjunctive or conjunctive, if one of its components is fuzzy.

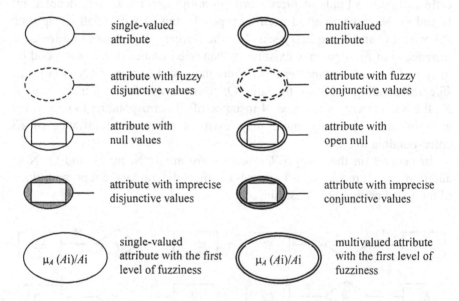

Figure 4-5. Attributes in the Fuzzy EER Model

For the attribute values in the imperfect EER model, in addition to fuzzy values, imprecise attribute values represented by partial values or value intervals (Grant, 1979; DeMichiel, 1989; Lipski, 1979) and missing attribute values should also be identified. Since attributes are either single-valued or multivalued, two kinds of imprecise attributes can be found, namely, disjunctive one and conjunctive one. Missing information, sometimes referred to *null* (Codd, 1986 & 1987), is considered as a special case of imprecise information. A null on a single-valued attribute means *no information, unknown information,* or *placeholder.* A null on a multivalued attribute, however, means an *open null* (Gottlob and Zicari, 1988). That is, the attribute value may not exist, has exactly an unknown value, or has several unknown values. A composite attribute consists of any kind of the attribute types above.

Graphical representations of the imperfect attributes mentioned above are shown in Figure 4-5.

4.3.2 Fuzzy Entity and Relationship

Being the same as the fuzzy ER model, there exist two levels of fuzziness in entity and relationship types of the fuzzy EER model, which are the first level fuzziness and the second level of fuzziness.

To graphically represent the entity type with the first level of fuzziness, one can place membership degrees inside the diagrams of entity and relationship types in the fuzzy EER data model. For example, let Ei be an entity type and μ (Ei) be its degree of membership in the model, then "μ $(Ei)/Ei$" is enclosed in the rectangle. If μ $(Ei) = 1$, "$1/Ei$" is usually denoted by "Ei" simply. In a similar way, the relationship type with the first level of fuzziness can be represented.

The graphical representations of the entity and relationship types with the first level of fuzziness are shown in Figure 4-6.

Figure 4-6. Entity and Relationship Types with the First Level of Fuzziness in Fuzzy EER Model

The graphical representations of the entity and relationship types with the second level of fuzziness are shown in Figure 4-7.

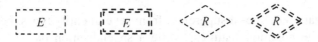

Figure 4-7. Entity and Relationship Types with the Second Level of Fuzziness in Fuzzy EER Model

It should be noted that in the fuzzy EER model, an entity type with the first and second level of fuzziness can be an weak one, a relationship type with the first and second level of fuzziness can be an ownership one, and an attribute of entity type or relationship type can be simple one, multivalued, composite, fuzzy (disjunctive or conjunctive), imprecise (disjunctive or conjunctive), or missing (null or open null).

4.3.3   Fuzzy Generalization/Specialization

Generalization and specialization describe subclass-superclass relationship between entity types. Under traditional environment, an entity type, say Sj, is called a subclass of another entity type, say Ei, and meanwhile Ei is called a superclass of Sj, if and only for any entity instance of Sj, it must be the entity instance of Ei. Formally,

$$(\forall\ e)\,(e \in Sj \Rightarrow e \in Ei)$$

In the fuzzy EER model, however, there exist three levels of fuzziness. Among these three levels of fuzziness, the second level of fuzziness is the fuzziness in entity type/instance. An entity instance may have a membership degree with respect to an entity type. The subclass-superclass relationship between such entity types must be redefined.

Now consider two entity types Ei and Sj on U such that they are all fuzzy sets with membership functions μ_{Ei} and μ_{Sj}, respectively. Then Sj is a fuzzy subclass of Ei and Ei is a fuzzy superclass of Sj if and only if the following is true.

$$(\forall\ e)\,(e \in U \wedge \mu_{Sj}\,(e) \leq \mu_{Ei}\,(e))$$

Suppose that superclass Ei has multiple subclasses $S1$, $S2$, ..., Sn and their membership functions are μ_{Ei}, μ_{S1}, μ_{S2}, ..., and μ_{Sn}, respectively, then

$$(\forall\ e)\,(e \in U \wedge \max\,(\mu_{S1}\,(e),\, \mu_{S2}\,(e),\, ...,\, \mu_{Sn}\,(e)) \leq \mu_{Ei}\,(e))$$

That is, the degree that an entity instance belongs to any of subclasses is not greater than the degree that the entity instance belongs to superclass of the subclasses.

A generalization defines a superclass from several entity types, generally being with some common features, while a specialization defines several subclasses from an entity type according to a certain feature. Considering a fuzzy superclass Ei and its fuzzy subclasses S_1, S_2, ..., S_n with membership functions μ_{Ei}, μ_{S1}, μ_{S2}, ..., and μ_{Sn}, respectively, The following relationship is true.

$$(\forall\ e)\ (\forall\ S)\ (e \in U \wedge S \in \{S_1, S_2, ..., S_n\} \wedge \mu_S\ (e) \leq \mu_{Ei}\ (e))$$

This means that for each subclass, the degree that an entity instance belongs to it must be less than or equal to the degree that the entity instance belongs to superclass of the subclasses.

Furthermore we have the fuzzy total specialization, fuzzy partial specialization, fuzzy disjoint specialization, and fuzzy overlapping specialization as follows.

- $S_1, S_2, ..., S_n$ are a fuzzy total specialization of Ei if

$$(\forall\ e)\ (\exists\ S)\ (e \in Ei \wedge S \in \{S_1, S_2, ..., S_n\} \wedge 0 < \mu_S\ (e) \leq \mu_{Ei}\ (e))$$

That is, for any of entity instances belonging to supclass with a non-zero degree, it must belong to one of its subclasses with a non-zero degree as well. In addition, the later non-zero degree is not greater than the former non-zero degree.

- $S_1, S_2, ..., S_n$ are a fuzzy partial specialization of Ei if

$$(\exists\ e)\ (\forall S)\ (e \in Ei \wedge S \in \{S_1, S_2, ..., S_n\} \wedge \mu_{Ei}\ (e) > 0 \wedge \mu_S\ (e) = 0)$$

In other words, there exists entity instance that belongs to supclass with a non-zero degree but belongs to any of subclasses with a zero degree.

- $S_1, S_2, ..., S_n$ are disjoint if

$$(\nexists e)\ (\forall S)\ (\forall S')\ (e \in U \wedge S \in \{S_1, S_2, ..., S_n\} \wedge S' \in \{S_1, S_2, ..., S_n\} \wedge$$
$$\min\ (\mu_S\ (e), \mu_{S'}\ (e)) > 0)$$

This means that there exists no entity instance that belongs to more than one subclass each with a non-zero degree.

- $S_1, S_2, ..., S_n$ are overlapping if

$$(\exists e)\ (\forall\ S)\ (\forall\ S')\ (e \in U \wedge S \in \{S_1, S_2, ..., S_n\} \wedge S' \in \{S_1, S_2, ..., S_n\} \wedge$$
$$\min\ (\mu_S\ (e), \mu_{S'}\ (e)) > 0)$$

That is, there exists entity instance that belongs to more than one subclass each with a non-zero degree.

Generalization is the inverse process of specialization. Therefore, there are fuzzy total generalization, fuzzy disjoint generalization, and fuzzy overlapping generalization according to the discussion above. It should be noticed that there is no fuzzy partial generalization, which is consistent with the situation in the classical EER model.

4.3.4   Fuzzy Category

Let S_1, S_2, ..., S_n and Ei be fuzzy entity sets with membership functions $\mu_{S1}, \mu_{S2, ...}, \mu_{Sn}$, and μ_{Ei}, respectively. Then Ei is a fuzzy category of S_1, S_2, ..., S_n if

$$(\forall\, e)\,(\exists\, S)\,(e \in Ei \wedge S \in \{S_1, S_2, ..., S_n\} \wedge \mu_S\,(e) \geq \mu_{Ei}\,(e) > 0)$$

That is, for any of entity instances belonging to category with a non-zero degree, it must belong to one of its superclasses with a non-zero degree as well. In addition, the former non-zero degree is not greater than the later non-zero degree.

Note that the fuzzy category is different from the fuzzy subclass with more than one fuzzy superclass. Let Ei be a fuzzy subclass and S_1, S_2, ..., S_n be its fuzzy superclasses and their membership functions are μ_{Ei}, μ_{S1}, $\mu_{S2, ...}$, and μ_{Sn}, respectively. Then

$$(\forall\, e)\,(\forall\, S)\,(e \in Ei \wedge S \in \{S_1, S_2, ..., S_n\} \wedge \mu_S\,(e) \geq \mu_{Ei}\,(e) > 0)$$

4.3.5   Fuzzy Aggregation

In addition to specialization/generalization, aggregation is an abstraction method for entity types and has been studied in object-oriented databases and the EER model. However, little attention has been paid to aggregation in fuzzy object-oriented databases and fuzzy EER data model.

Let Ei be a fuzzy aggregation of fuzzy entity sets S_1, S_2, ..., and S_n and their membership functions are μ_{Ei}, μ_{S1}, $\mu_{S2, ...}$, and μ_{Sn}, respectively. Then

$$(\forall\, e)\,(\exists\, e_1)\,(\exists\, e_2) ... (\exists\, e_n)\,(e \in Ei \wedge e_1 \in S_1 \wedge e_2 \in S_2 \wedge ... \wedge e_n \in S_n$$
$$\wedge \mu_{Ei}\,(e) = \mu_{S1}\,(e_1) \times \mu_{S2}\,(e_2) \times ... \times \mu_{Sn}\,(e_n) \neq 0).$$

In other words, for any of entity instances belonging to aggregation with a non-zero degree, it can be broken down into some parts and as an entity instance, each part must belong to one of its part entity types with a non-zero degree. In addition, the product of all of the later non-zero degrees forms the former non-zero degree.

The diagrammatic notations in Figure 4-8 are used to represent fuzzy specialization, category and aggregation in the fuzzy EER model, respectively.

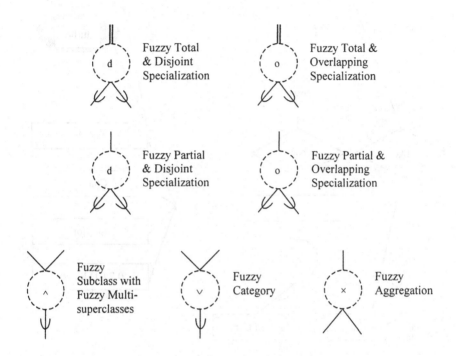

Figure 4-8. Fuzzy EER Diagram Notations of Specialization, Category, and Aggregation

Utilizing some notations introduced in this section, a simple fuzzy *EER* data model is given in Figure 4-9, where entity type *Car* is a superclass, and *New Car* and *Old Car* are its two fuzzy subclasses; i.e., they may have fuzzy instances. Fuzzy entity type *Young Employee* with fuzzy instances and entity type *Company* compose a category and entity type *Buyer* is formed. Entity types *Young Employee* and *Company* have a fuzzy relationship *like*; in particular, the fuzziness in this case is at the level of instance/schema. Entity type *Car* is aggregated by four entity types: *Engine, Chassis, Interior*, and *Radio*. Among these four entity types, *CD Player* is a fuzzy entity type with membership degree 0.7, which is the fuzziness at the level of schema. Entity type *Engine* has three attributes. The attribute *Id* is a key with perfect values whereas *size* and *turbo* are disjunctive fuzzy attribute and disjunctive imprecise attribute, respectively.

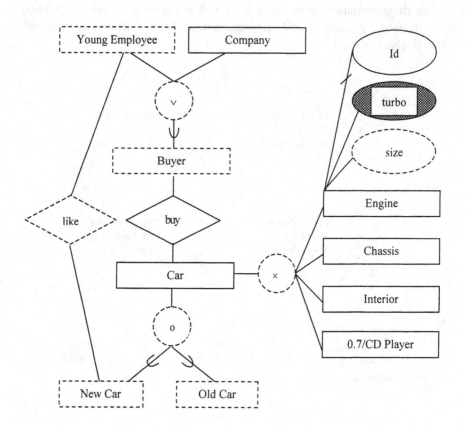

Figure 4-9. A Simple Fuzzy EER Data Model

4.4   Summary

This chapter presents fuzzy extended ER and EER data models to handle imperfect objects in the real world at a conceptual level. Three levels of fuzziness are identified in entity and relationship types, attributes, entity and relationship instances, and attribute values. In particular, based on the second level of fuzziness, i.e., the fuzziness in entity and relationship types/instances, some major notions in the EER data model are extended, including generalization/specialization, categorization, and aggregation. But the first level of fuzziness, i.e., the fuzziness in entity and relationship types is not considered when these notions are extended. The corresponding graphical representations of the fuzzy ER and EER data models are also developed in this chapter.

References

Chen, G. Q. and Kerre, E. E., 1998, Extending ER/EER concepts towards fuzzy conceptual data modeling, *Proceedings of the 1998 IEEE International Conference on Fuzzy Systems*, 2: 1320-1325.

Chen, G. Q., 1999, *Fuzzy Logic in Data Modeling; Semantics, Constraints, and Database Design*, Kluwer Academic Publisher.

Chen, P. P., 1976, The entity-relationship model: toward a unified view of data, *ACM Transactions on Database Systems*, 1 (1): 9-36.

Codd, E. F., 1986, Missing information (applicable and inapplicable) in relational databases, *SIGMOD Record*, 15 (4): 53-78.

Codd, E. F., 1987, More commentary on missing information in relational databases (applicable and inapplicable information), *SIGMOD Record*, 16 (1): 42-50.

DeMichiel, L. G., 1989, Resolving database incompatibility: an approach to performing relational operations over mismatched domains, *IEEE Transactions on Knowledge and Data Engineering*, 1 (4): 485-493.

Gottlob, G. and Zicari, R., 1988, Closed world databases opened through null values, *Proceedings of the 1988 International Conference on Very Large Data Bases*, 50-61.

Grant, J., 1979, Partial values in a tabular database model, *Information Processing Letters*, 9 (2): 97-99.

Lipski, W., 1979, On semantic issues connected with incomplete information databases, *ACM Transactions on Database Systems*, 4 (3): 262-296.

Ruspini, E. 1986, Imprecision and uncertainty in the entity-relationship model, *Fuzzy Logic in Knowledge Engineering*, Verlag TUV Rheinland.

Vandenberghe, R. M., 1991, An extended entity-relationship model for fuzzy databases based on fuzzy truth values, *Proceedings of the 1991 International Fuzzy Systems Association World Congress*, 280-283.

Zvieli, A. and Chen, P. P., 1986, Entity-relationship modeling and fuzzy databases, *Proceedings of the 1986 IEEE International Conference on Data Engineering*, 320-327.

Chapter 5

THE FUZZY UML DATA MODEL

5.1   Introduction

UML provides a collection of models to capture the many aspects of a software system (Booch, Rumbaugh and Jacobson, 1998; OMG, 2001). Notice that while the UML reflects some of the best OO modeling experiences available, it suffers from some lacks of necessary semantics. One of the lacks can be generalized as the need to handle imprecise and uncertain information although imprecise and uncertain information exist in knowledge engineering and database systems and have extensively being studied (Parsons, 1996).

In the context of the fuzzy conceptual data models, the ER model has been extended in (Zvieli and Chen, 1986) using fuzzy set theory. In addition, in (Chen and Kerre, 1998), fuzzy logic was applied to some of the basic EER concepts around the notions of subclass and superclass. However, the issues on fuzzy UML data model have received little attention in the literature.

In this chapter, different levels of fuzziness will be introduced into the class in the UML and the corresponding graphical representations are given. The class diagrams of the UML can hereby model fuzzy information.

5.2   The Fuzzy UML Class Model

This section extends the UML class diagrams to model fuzzy data. Since the constructs of the UML contain class and relationships, the extension to these constructs should be conducted based on fuzzy sets.

5.2.1   Fuzzy Class

The objects having the same properties are gathered into classes that are organized into hierarchies. Theoretically, a class can be considered from two different viewpoints:

(a) an extensional class, where the class is defined by the list of its object instances, and

(b) an intensional class, where the class is defined by a set of attributes and their admissible values.

A class is fuzzy because of the following several reasons.

(a) Some objects are fuzzy ones, which have similar properties. A class defined by these objects may be fuzzy. Then the objects belong to the class with membership degree of [0, 1].

(b) When a class is intensionally defined, the domain of an attribute may be fuzzy and a fuzzy class is formed.

(c) The subclass produced by a fuzzy class by means of specialization and the superclass produced by some classes (in which there is at least one class who is fuzzy) by means of generalization are also fuzzy.

Following on the footsteps of (Zvieli and Chen, 1986), we define three levels of fuzziness. In the context of classes, the three levels of fuzziness are defined as follows:

(a) Fuzziness in the extent to which the class belongs to the data model as well as fuzziness on the content (in terms of attributes) of the class.

(b) Fuzziness related to whether some instances are instances of a class. Even though the structure of an entity is crisp, it is possible that an instance of the class belongs to the class with degree of membership.

(c) The third level of fuzziness is on attribute values of the instances of the class. An attribute in a class defines a value domain. When this domain is a fuzzy subset or a set of fuzzy subset, the fuzziness of an attribute value appears.

In order to model the first level of fuzziness, i.e., an attribute or a class with degree of membership, the attribute or class name should be followed by a pair of words WITH *mem* DEGREE, where $0 \leq mem \leq 1$ and it is used to indicate the degree that the attribute belongs to the class or the class belongs to the data model (Marín, Vila and Pons, 2000). For example, "*Employee WITH 0.6 DEGREE*" and "Office Number *WITH 0.8DEGREE*" are class and attribute with the first level of fuzziness, respectively. Generally, an attribute or a class will not be declared when its degree is 0. In addition, "WITH 1.0 DEGREE" can be omitted when the degree of an attribute or a class is 1. It should be noted that attribute values might be fuzzy. In order to model the third level of fuzziness, a keyword FUZZY is introduced and is placed in the front of the attribute. The second level of fuzziness, we must indicate the degree of membership that an instance of the class belongs to the class. For this purpose, an additional attribute is introduced into the class to represent instance membership degree to the class, which attribute domain is [0, 1]. We denote such special attribute with μ. In order to differentiate the class with the second level of fuzziness, we use a dashed-outline rectangle to denote such class.

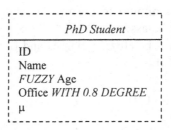

Figure 5-1. A Fuzzy Class in the Fuzzy UML

Figure 5-1 shows a fuzzy class *PhD Student*. Here, attribute *Age* may take fuzzy values, namely, its domain is fuzzy. Ph. D. students may or may not have their offices. It is not known for sure if class *PhD Student* has attribute *Office*. But we know Ph.D. students may have their offices with high possibility, say 0.8. So attribute *Office* uncertainly belongs to the class *PhD Students*. This class has the fuzziness at the first level and we use "with 0.8 membership degree" to describe the fuzziness in the class definition. In addition, we may not determine if an object is the instance of the class because the class is fuzzy. So an additional attribute μ is introduced into the class for this purpose.

5.2.2 Fuzzy Generalization

The concept of subclassing is one of the basic building blocks of the object model. A new class, called subclass, is produced from another class, called superclass by means of inheriting some attributes and methods of the superclass, overriding some attributes and methods of the superclass, and defining some new attributes and methods. Since a subclass is the specialization of the superclass, any one object belonging to the subclass must belong to the superclass. This characteristic can be used to determine if two classes have subclass/superclass relationship.

However, classes may be fuzzy. A class produced from a fuzzy class must be fuzzy. If the former is still called subclass and the later superclass, the subclass/superclass relationship is fuzzy. In other words, a class is a subclass of another class with membership degree of [0, 1] at this moment. Correspondingly, we have the following method for determining subclass/superclass relationship.

  (a) for any (fuzzy) object, if the membership degree that it belongs to the subclass is less than or equal to the membership degree that it belongs to the superclass, and

  (b) the membership degree that it belongs to the subclass is great than or equal to the given threshold.

The subclass is then a subclass of the superclass with the membership degree, which is the minimum in the membership degrees to which these objects belong to the subclass.

Formally, let A and B be (fuzzy) classes and β be a given threshold. We say B is a subclass of A if

$$(\forall e)\,(\beta \leq \mu_B\,(e) \leq \mu_A\,(e)).$$

The membership degree that B is a subclass of A should be $\min_{\mu_B\,(e)\,\geq\,\beta}\,(\mu_B\,(e))$. Here, e is object instance of A and B in the universe of discourse, and $\mu_A\,(e)$ and $\mu_B\,(e)$ are membership degrees of e to A and B, respectively.

It should be noted that, however, in the above-mentioned fuzzy generalization relationship, we assume that classes A and B can only have the second level of fuzziness. It is possible that classes A or B are the classes with membership degree, namely, with the first level of fuzziness. Assume that we have two classes A and B as follows.

  A WITH *degree_A* DEGREE
  B WITH *degree_B* DEGREE
Then B is a subclass of A if

$$(\forall e)\,(\beta \leq \mu_B\,(e) \leq \mu_A\,(e)) \wedge ((\beta \leq degree\_B \leq degree\_A).$$

That means that B is a subclass of A only if, in addition to the condition that the membership degrees of all objects to A and B must be greater than or equal to the given threshold and the membership degree of any object to A must be greater than or equal to the membership degree of this object to B, the membership degrees of A and B must be greater than or equal to the given threshold and the membership degree of A must be greater than or equal to the membership degree of B.

Considering a fuzzy superclass A and its fuzzy subclasses $B1$, $B2$, ..., Bn with instance membership degrees μ_A, μ_{B1}, $\mu_{B2, ...}$, and μ_{Bn}, respectively, which may have the degrees of membership *degree_A*, *degree_B1*, *degree_B2*, ..., and *degree_Bn*, respectively. Then the following relationship is true.

$(\forall e)$ (max (μ_{B1} (e), μ_{B2} (e), ..., μ_{Bn} (e))) $\leq \mu_A$ (e)) $\wedge$ (max (*degree_B*1, *degree_B*2, ..., *degree_B*n) $\leq$ *degree_A*)

It can be seen that we can assess fuzzy subclass/superclass relationships by utilizing the inclusion degree of objects to the class. Clearly such assessment is based on the extensional viewpoint of class. When classes are defined with the intensional viewpoint, there is no any object available. Therefore, the method given above cannot be used. At this point, we can use the inclusion degree (see Section 7.3) of a class with respect to another class to determine the relationships between fuzzy subclass and superclass.

Formally, let A and B be (fuzzy) classes and the degree that B is the subclass of A be denoted by μ (A, B). For a given threshold β, we say B is a subclass of A if

$$\mu (A, B) \geq \beta.$$

The membership degree that B is a subclass of A is clearly μ (A, B).

Now let us consider the situation that classes A or B are the classes with membership degree, namely, with the first level of fuzziness. Assume that we have two classes A and B as follows.

A WITH *degree_A* DEGREE
B WITH *degree_B* DEGREE
Then B is a subclass of A if

$$(\mu (A, B) \geq \beta) \wedge ((\beta \leq degree\_B \leq degree\_A).$$

That means that B is a subclass of A only if, in addition to the condition that the inclusion degree of A with respect to B must be greater than or equal to the given threshold, the membership degrees of A and B must be greater than or equal to the given threshold and the membership degree of A must be great than or equal to the membership degree of B.

The inclusion degree of a (fuzzy) subclass with respect to the (fuzzy) superclass can be calculated according to the inclusion degree of the attribute domains of the subclass with respect to the attribute domains of the superclass as well as the weight of attributes. The methods for evaluating the inclusion degree of fuzzy attribute domains and further evaluating the inclusion degree of a subclass with respect to the superclass can be found in Chapter 9, where the relationship between subclass and superclass with the first level of fuzziness is not discussed.

In subclass-superclass hierarchies, a critical issue is multiple inheritance of class. Ambiguity arises when more than one of the superclasses have common attributes and the subclass does not declare explicitly the class from which the attribute is inherited. At this moment, which conflicting attribute in the superclasses is inherited by the subclass dependents on their weights to the corresponding superclasses (Liu and Song, 2001; Ma, Zhang and Ma, 2004). Also it should be noted that in fuzzy multiple inheritance hierarchy, the subclass has different degrees with respect to different superclasses, not being the same as the situation in classical object-oriented database systems.

In order to represent a fuzzy generalization relation, a dashed peculiar triangular arrowhead is applied. Figure 5-2 shows a fuzzy generalization relationship. Here classes *Young Student* and *Young Faculty* are all classes with the second level of fuzziness. That means that the classes may have some instances (objects), which belong to the classes with membership degree. These two classes can be generalized into class *Youth*, a class with the second level of fuzziness.

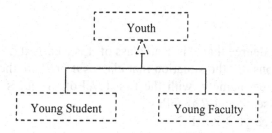

Figure 5-2. A Fuzzy Generalization Relationship in the Fuzzy UML

5.2.3   Fuzzy Aggregation

An aggregation captures a whole-part relationship between an aggregate and a constituent part and these constituent parts can exist independently. Therefore, every instance of an aggregate can be projected into a set of instances of constituent parts. Formally let A be an aggregation of constituent parts $B1$, $B2$, ..., and Bn. For $e \in A$, the projection of e to Bi is denoted by $e\downarrow_{Bi}$. Then we have $(e\downarrow_{B1}) \in B1$, $(e\downarrow_{B2}) \in B2$, ..., $(e\downarrow_{Bn}) \in Bn$.

A class aggregated from fuzzy constituent parts must be fuzzy. If the former is still called aggregate, the aggregation is fuzzy. At this point, a class is an aggregation of constituent parts with membership degree of [0, 1]. Correspondingly, we have the following method for determining fuzzy aggregation relationship:

(a) for any (fuzzy) object, if the membership degree that it belongs to the aggregate is less than or equal to the membership degree to which its projection to each constituent part belongs to the corresponding constituent part, and

(b) the membership degree that it belongs to the aggregate is great than or equal to the given threshold.

The aggregate is then an aggregation of the constituent parts with the membership degree, which is the minimum in the membership degrees to which the projections of these objects to these constituent parts belong to the corresponding constituent parts.

Formally let A be an fuzzy aggregation of fuzzy class sets $B1$, $B2$, ..., and Bn, which instance membership degrees are μ_A, μ_{B1}, $\mu_{B2, ...}$, and μ_{Bn}, respectively. Let β be a given threshold. Then

$$(\forall\ e)\ (e \in A \wedge \beta \leq \mu_A\ (e) \leq \min\ (\mu_{B1}\ (e\downarrow_{B1}), \mu_{B2}\ (e\downarrow_{B2}), ..., \mu_{Bn}\ (e\downarrow_{Bn}))).$$

That means that a fuzzy class A is the aggregate of a group fuzzy classes $B1$, $B2$, ..., and Bn if for any (fuzzy) instance object, if the membership degree that it belongs to class A is less than or equal to the member degree to which its projection to anyone of $B1$, $B2$, ..., and Bn, say Bi ($1 \leq i \leq n$), belongs to class Bi. Besides, for any (fuzzy) instance object, the membership degree that it belongs to class A is greater than or equal to the given threshold. The membership degree that A is an aggregation of class sets $B1$, $B2$, ..., and Bn should be $\min_{\mu_{Bi}\ (e\downarrow_{Bi})\ \geq\ \beta}\ (\mu_{Bi}\ (e\downarrow_{Bi}))$ ($1 \leq i \leq n$). Here, e is object instance of A.

Now let us consider the first level of fuzziness in the above-mentioned classes A, $B1$, $B2$, ..., and Bn, namely, they are the fuzzy classes with membership degrees. Let

A WITH *degree_A* DEGREE,
$B1$ WITH *degree_B1* DEGREE,
$B2$ WITH *degree_B2* DEGREE,
......
Bn WITH *degree_Bn* DEGREE.

Then A is an aggregate of $B1$, $B2$, ..., and Bn if

$$(\forall\ e)\ (e \in A \wedge \beta \leq \mu_A\ (e) \leq \min\ (\mu_{B1}\ (e\downarrow_{B1}), \mu_{B2}\ (e\downarrow_{B2}), ..., \mu_{Bn}\ (e\downarrow_{Bn})) \wedge$$
$$degree\_A \leq \min\ (degree\_B1, degree\_B2, ..., degree\_Bn)).$$

Here β is a given threshold.

It should be noted that the assessment of fuzzy aggregation relationships given above is based on the extensional viewpoint of class. Clearly these methods can not be used if the classes are defined with the intensional viewpoint because there is no any object available. In the following, we present how to determine fuzzy aggregation relationship using the inclusion degree.

Formally let *A* be an fuzzy aggregation of fuzzy class sets *B*1, *B*2, ..., and *B*n and β be a given threshold. Also let the projection of *A* to *B*i is denoted by $A\downarrow_{Bi}$. Then

$$\min (\mu (B1, A\downarrow_{B1}), \mu (B2, A\downarrow_{B2}), ..., \mu (Bn, A\downarrow_{Bn})) \geq \beta.$$

Here $\mu (Bi, A\downarrow_{Bi})$ ($1 \leq i \leq n$) means the degree to which *B*i semantically includes $A\downarrow_{Bi}$. The membership degree that *A* is an aggregation of *B*1, *B*2, ..., and *B*n is $\min (\mu (B1, A\downarrow_{B1}), \mu (B2, A\downarrow_{B2}), ..., \mu (Bn, A\downarrow_{Bn}))$.

Furthermore, the expression above can be extended for the situation that *A*, *B*1, *B*2, ..., and *B*n may have the first level of fuzziness, namely, they may be the fuzzy classes with membership degrees. Let β be a given threshold and

    A WITH *degree_A* DEGREE,

    *B*1 WITH *degree_B1* DEGREE,

    *B*2 WITH *degree_B2* DEGREE,

    ......

    *B*n WITH *degree_Bn* DEGREE.

Then *A* is an aggregate of *B*1, *B*2, ..., and *B*n if

$$\min (\mu (B1, A\downarrow_{B1}), \mu (B2, A\downarrow_{B2}), ..., \mu (Bn, A\downarrow_{Bn})) \geq \beta \wedge degree\_A \leq \min (degree\_B1, degree\_B2, ..., degree\_Bn)).$$

A dashed open diamond is used to denote a fuzzy aggregate relationship. A fuzzy aggregation relationship is shown in Figure 5-3. A car is aggregated by engine, interior, and chassis. In Figure 5-3, the engine is old and we hereby have a fuzzy class *Old Engine* with the second level of fuzziness. Class *Old Car* aggregated by classes *interior* and *chassis* and fuzzy class *old engine* is a fuzzy one with the second level of fuzziness.

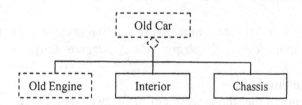

Figure 5-3. A Fuzzy Aggregation Relationship in the Fuzzy UML

5.2.4   Fuzzy Association

Two levels of fuzziness can be identified in the association relationship. The first level of fuzziness means that an association relationship fuzzily exists in two associated classes, namely, this association relationship occurs with a degree of possibility. Also it is possible that it is unknown for certain if two class instances respectively belonging to the associated classes have the given association relationship although this association relationship must occur in these two classes. This is the second level of fuzziness in the association relationship and is caused by such fact that an instance belongs to the given class with membership degree. Note that it is possible that two levels of fuzziness mentioned above may occur in association relationship simultaneously. That means that two classes have fuzzy association relationship at class level on one hand. On the other hand, the class instances of these two classes may have fuzzy association relationship at class instance level.

We can place a pair of words WITH *mem* DEGREE ($0 \leq mem \leq 1$) after the role name of an association relationship to represent the first level of fuzziness in the association relationship. We use a double line with an arrowhead to denote the second level of fuzziness in the association relationship.

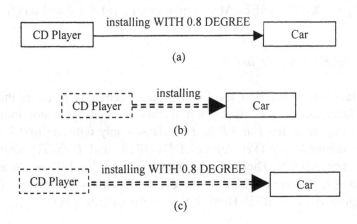

Figure 5-4. Fuzzy Association Relationships in the Fuzzy UML

Figure 5-4 shows two levels of fuzziness in fuzzy association relationships. In (a), it is uncertain if CD player is installed in car and the possibility is 0.8. So classes *CD Player* and *Car* have association relationship *installing* with 0.8 membership degree. In (b), it is certain that CD player is installed in car and the possibility is 1.0. Classes *CD Player* and *Car* have association relationship *installing* with 1.0 membership degree. But at the level of instances, there exits the possibility that the instances of classes *CD Player* and *Car* may or may not have association relationship *installing*. In (c), two kinds of fuzzy association relationship in (a) and (b) arise simultaneously.

It has been shown above that three levels of fuzziness can occur in classes. The classes with the second level of fuzziness generally result in the second level of fuzziness in the association if this association definitely exists (that means there is no first level of fuzziness in the association). Formally, let A and B be two classes with the second level of fuzziness. Then the instance e of A is one with membership degrees $\mu_A(e)$ and the instance f of B is one with membership degrees $\mu_B(f)$. Assume the association relationship between A and B, denoted *ass* (A, B), is one without the first level of fuzziness. It is clear that the association relationship between e and f, denoted *ass* (e, f), is one with the second level of fuzziness, i.e., with membership degree, which can be calculated by

$$\mu\ (ass\ (e, f)) = \min\ (\mu_A\ (e), \mu_B\ (f)).$$

The first level of fuzziness in the association relationship can be indicated explicitly by the designers even if the corresponding classes are crisp. Assume that A and B are two crisp classes and *ass* (A, B) is the association relationship with the first level of fuzziness, denoted *ass* (A, B) WITH *degree_ass* DEGREE. At this moment, $\mu_A(e) = 1.0$ and $\mu_B(f) = 1.0$. Then

$$\mu\ (ass\ (e, f)) = degree\_ass$$

The classes with the first level of fuzziness generally result in the first level of fuzziness of the association if this association is not indicated explicitly. Formally, let A and B be two classes only with the first level of fuzziness, denoted A WITH *degree_A* DEGREE and B WITH *degree_B* DEGREE, respectively. Then the association relationship between A and B, denoted *ass* (A, B), is one with the first level of fuzziness, namely, *ass* (A, B) WITH *degree_ass* DEGREE. Here *degree_ass* is calculated by

$$degree\_ass = \min\ (degree\_A, degree\_B).$$

For the instance e of A and the instance f of B, in which $\mu_A(e) = 1.0$ and $\mu_B(f) = 1.0$, we have

$$\mu\ (ass\ (e, f)) = degree\_ass = \min\ (degree\_A, degree\_B).$$

Finally, let us focus on the situation that the classes are ones with the first level and the second level of fuzziness and there is an association relationship with the first level of fuzziness between these two classes, which is explicitly indicated. Let *A* and *B* be two classes with the first level of fuzziness, denoted *A* WITH *degree_A* DEGREE and *B* WITH *degree_B* DEGREE, respectively. Let *ass* (*A, B*) be the association relationship with the first level of fuzziness between A and B, which is explicitly indicated with WITH *degree_ass* DEGREE. Also let the instance *e* of *A* be with membership degrees μ_A (*e*), and the instance *f* of *B* be with membership degrees μ_B (*f*). Then we have

$$\mu \ (ass \ (e, f)) = \min \ (\mu_A \ (e), \ \mu_B \ (f), \ degree\_A, \ degree\_B, \ degree\_a).$$

5.2.5 Fuzzy Dependency

Now let us focus on fuzzy dependency relationship between the source class and the target class. The dependency relationship is only related to the classes themselves and does not require a set of instances for its meaning. Therefore, the second level fuzziness and the third level of fuzziness in class do not affect the dependency relationship.

Fuzzy dependency relationship is a dependency relationship with degree of possibility. Just like the fuzzy association relationship above, the fuzzy dependency relationship can be indicated explicitly by the designers or be implied implicitly by the source class based on the fact that the target class is decided by the source class. Assume that the source class is a fuzzy one with the first level of fuzziness. Then the target class must be a fuzzy one with the first level of fuzziness. The degrees of possibility that the target class is decided by the source class is the same as the membership degree of source class.

For source class *Employee WITH 0.85 DEGREE*, for example, the target class *Employee Dependent* should be *Employee Dependent WITH 0.85 DEGREE*. The dependency relationship between *Employee* and *Employee Dependent* should be a fuzzy one with 0.85 degree of possibility. Notice that, not being like fuzzy association relationship, only one level of fuzziness can be identified in a dependency relationship, which is implied by first level of fuzziness of the source class if it is not given explicitly.

Since the fuzziness of dependency relationship is denoted implicitly by first level of fuzziness of the source class, a dashed line with an arrowhead can still be used to denote the fuzziness in the dependency relationship. Figure 5-5 shows a fuzzy dependency relationship.

Figure 5-5. A Fuzzy Dependency Relationship in the Fuzzy UML

In Figure 5-6, we give a simple fuzzy UML data model utilizing some notations introduced in this chapter. Class *Car* is a superclass, and *New Car* and *Old Car* are its two fuzzy subclasses, namely, they may have fuzzy instances. Similarly, class *Employee* has three fuzzy subclasses *Young Employee*, *Middle Employee*, and *Old Employee*. Classes *Employee* and *Car* have a fuzzy association relationship *using*, which fuzziness is at the second level of fuzziness. Again fuzzy classes *Young Employee* and *New Car* have a fuzzy association relationship *like*, which fuzziness is at the first level of fuzziness. In addition, class *Car* is aggregated by three classes: *Engine*, *Chassis*, and *Interior*. Class *Engine* has three attributes. The attribute *Id* and *turbo* are ones with crisp values whereas *size* is a fuzzy attribute that can take fuzzy value. Classes *Chassis* and *Interior* are all crisp classes and they have no fuzziness at the three levels.

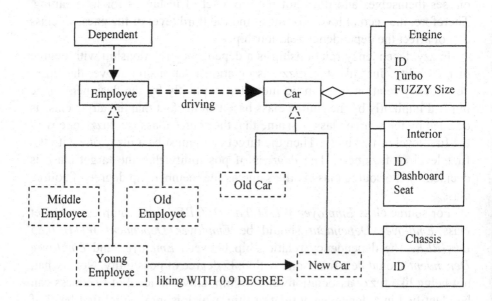

Figure 5-6. A Fuzzy UML Data Model

5.3   Summary

This chapter presents a fuzzy extended UML to cope with fuzzy as well as complex objects in the real world at a conceptual level. Different levels of fuzziness are introduced into the class diagram of the UML and the corresponding graphical representations are developed. It is not difficult to see that the classical UML is essentially a subset of the fuzzy UML. When there is not any fuzziness in the universe of discourse, the fuzzy UML can be reduced to the classical UML.

It should be noted that the focus of the chapter is on fuzzy data modeling in the UML. The issues about class operations, constraints in the fuzzy UML modeling, and mapping of the fuzzy UML data model into object-oriented databases are not discussed in this chapter.

References

Booch, G., Rumbaugh, J. and Jacobson, I., 1998, *The Unified Modeling Language User Guide*, Addison-Welsley Longman, Inc.

Chen, G. Q. and Kerre, E. E., 1998, Extending ER/EER concepts towards fuzzy conceptual data modeling, *Proceedings of the 1998 IEEE International Conference on Fuzzy Systems*, 2: 1320-1325.

Chen, P. P., 1976, The entity-relationship model: toward a unified view of data, *ACM Transactions on Database Systems*, 1 (1): 9-36.

Liu, W. Y. and Song, N., 2001, The fuzzy association degree in semantic data models, *Fuzzy Sets and Systems*, 117 (2): 203-208.

Ma, Z. M., Zhang, W. J. and Ma, W. Y., 2004, Extending object-oriented databases for fuzzy information modeling, *Information Systems*, 29 (5): 421-435.

Marín, N., Vila, M. A. and Pons, O., 2000, Fuzzy types: A new concept of type for managing vague structures, *International Journal of Intelligent Systems*, 15:1061–1085.

OMG, 2001, Unified Modeling Language (UML), version 1.4, http://www.omg.org/technology/documents/formal/uml.htm.

Parsons, S., 1996, Current approaches to handling imperfect information in data and knowledge bases, *IEEE Transactions on Knowledge Data Engineering*, 8: 353–372.

Zvieli, A. and Chen, P. P., 1986, Entity-relationship modeling and fuzzy databases, *Proceedings of the 1986 IEEE International Conference on Data Engineering*, 320-327.

Chapter 6

THE FUZZY XML MODEL

6.1 Introduction

With the wide utilization of the web and the availability of huge amount of electronic data, information representation and exchange over the web become important and XML has been the de-facto standard (Bray, Paoli and Sperberg-McQueen, 1998). XML and related standards are technologies that allow the easy development of applications that exchange data over the web such as e-commerce (EC) and supply chain management (SCM).

In real-world applications, however, information is often vague or ambiguous. There exist researches on fuzziness in EC and SCM and fuzzy set theory is used to implement web-based business intelligence (Petrovic, Roy and Petrovic, 1999; Yager, 2000; Yager and Pasi, 2001). Unfortunately, being current standard for data representation and exchange over the web, XML is not able to represent and process imprecise and uncertain data although databases with imprecise and uncertain information have extensively been discussed. Currently less research has been done in modeling and querying imperfect XML data. Only XML with incomplete information (Abiteboul, Segoufin and Vianu, 2001) and probabilistic data (Nierman and Jagadish, 2002) in XML have been proposed in research papers. More recently, Lee and Fanjiang (2003) developed a fuzzy OO modeling technique schema based on XML to model requirements specifications and incorporated the notion of stereotype to facilitate the modeling of imprecise requirements.

In this chapter, we identify multiple granularity of data fuzziness in XML. Based on possibility distribution theory, we may have possibilities associated with elements as well as attribute values of elements in XML.

Then we develop a fuzzy XML data model that addresses all of the fuzziness. Finally we focus on the conceptual design of XML using conceptual data models. We investigate the conversions from the fuzzy UML model to the fuzzy XML.

6.2   The Fuzzy XML Model

6.2.1   The Fuzziness in XML

Two kinds of fuzziness can be found in relational model: one is to associate membership degrees with individual tuples and another is to represent attribute values with possibility distributions (see Chapter 7 for details). A membership degree associated with a tuple is interpreted to mean the possibility of the tuple being a member of the corresponding relation. A possibility distribution represented an attribute value means we do not know a crisp value of the attribute but only know the range of values that the attribute may take and the possibility of each value being true.

XML data is structured and XML can represent imprecise and uncertain information naturally. In the case of XML, we may have membership degrees associated with elements. It is also possible to associate possibility distributions with attribute values of elements. XML restricts attributes to have a unique single value. We modify the schema in XML to make any attribute into a sub-element.

Now let us interpret what a membership degree associated with an element means, given that the element can nest under other elements and more than one of these elements may have an associated membership degree. The existential membership degree associated with an element should be the possibility that the state of the world includes this element and the sub-tree rooted at it. For an element with the sub-tree rooted at it, each node in the sub-tree is not treated as independent but dependent upon its root to node chain. Each possibility in the source XML document is assigned conditioned on the fact that the parent element exists certainly. In other words, this possibility is a relative one upon the assumption that the possibility the parent element exists is exactly 1.0. In order to calculate the absolute possibility, we must consider the relative possibility in the parent element. In general, the absolute possibility of an element ε can be obtained by multiplying the relative possibilities found in the source XML, along the path from ε to the root. Of course, each of these relative possibilities will be available in the source XML document. By default, relative possibilities are regarded as 1.0.

Consider a chain $A \to B \to C$ from the root node A. Assume that the source XML document contains the relative possibilities *Poss* $(C|B)$, *Poss* $(B|A)$, and *Poss* (A), associated with the nodes C, B, and A, respectively. Then we have

$Poss$ $(B) = Poss$ $(B|A) \times Poss$ (A) and

$Poss$ $(C) = Poss$ $(C|B) \times Poss$ $(B|A) \times Poss$ (A).

Here, *Poss* $(C|B)$, *Poss* $(B|A)$, and *Poss* (A) can be obtained from the source XML document.

For attribute values of elements, XML restricts attributes to have a unique single value. It is not difficult to find that this restriction does not always hold true. It is often the case that some data item is known to have multiple values – these values may be unknown completely and can be specified with a possibility distribution. For example, the e-mail address of a person may be multiple character strings because she or he has several e-mail addresses available simultaneously. In the case that we do not have complete knowledge of the e-mail address for Tom Smith, we may say that the e-mail address may be *"TSmith@yahoo.com"* with possibility 0.60, *"Tom_Smith@yahoo.com"* with possibility 0.85, *"Tom_Smith@hotmail.com"* with possibility 0.85, *"TSmith@hotmail.com"* with possibility 0.55, and *"TSmith@msn.com"* with possibility 0.45. In contrast, some data item is known to have single unique value. For instance, the age of a person in year is a unique non-negative integer. If such value is unknown so far, we can use the following possibility distribution: {0.4/23, 0.6/25, 0.8/27, 1.0/29, 1.0/30, 1.0/31, 0.8/33, 0.6/35, 0.4/37}. Based on the discussion above, it is clear to find that we have two kinds of interpretation of a fuzzy data represented by a possibility distribution: *fuzzy disjunctive data* and *fuzzy conjunctive data*.

In summary, we have two kinds of fuzziness in XML:
- the first is the fuzziness in elements and we use membership degrees associated with such elements;
- the second is the fuzziness in attribute values of elements and we use possibility distribution to represent such values.

Note that, for the latter, there exist two types of possibility distribution (i.e., disjunctive and conjunctive possibility distributions) and they may occur in child elements with or without further child elements in the ancestor-descendant chain.

Figure 6-1 gives a fragment of an XML document with fuzzy data.

1. <universities>

```
2.      <university UName = "Oakland University">
3.         <Val Poss = 0.8>
4.           <department DName = "Computer Science and Engineering">
5.             <employee FID = "85431095">
6.               <Dist type = "disjunctive">
7.                 <Val Poss = 0.8>
8.                   <fname>Frank Yager</name>
9.                   <position>Associate Professor</position>
10.                  <office>B1024</office>
11.                  <course>Advances in Database Systems</course>
12.                </Val >
13.                <Val Poss = 0.6>
14.                  <fname>Frank Yager</name>
15.                  <position>Professor</position>
16.                  <office>Y1024</office>
17.                  <course>Artificial Intelligence</course>
18.                </Val >
19.              </Dist>
20.            </employee>
21.            <student SID = "96421027">
22.              <sname>Tom Smith</name>
23.              <age>
24.                <Dist type = "disjunctive">
25.                  <Val Poss = 0.4>23</Val>
26.                  <Val Poss = 0.6>25</Val>
27.                  <Val Poss = 0.8>27</Val>
28.                  <Val Poss = 1.0>29</Val>
29.                  <Val Poss = 1.0>30</Val>
30.                  <Val Poss = 1.0>31</Val>
31.                  <Val Poss = 0.8>33</Val>
32.                  <Val Poss = 0.6>35</Val>
33.                  <Val Poss = 0.4>37</Val>
34.                </Dist>
35.              </age>
36.              <sex>Male</sex>
37.              <email>
38.                <Dist type = "conjunctive">
39.                  <Val Poss = 0.60>TSmith@yahoo.com</Val>
40.                  <Val Poss = 0.85>Tom_Smith@yahoo.com</Val>
41.                  <Val Poss = 0.85>Tom_Smith@hotmail.com</Val>
42.                  <Val Poss = 0.55>TSmith@hotmail.com</Val>
43.                  <Val Poss = 0.45>TSmith@msn.com</Val>
44.                </Dist>
45.              </email>
46.            </student>
47.          </department >
48.        </Val>
49.      </university>
50.      <university Uname = "Wayne State University">
51.      </university>
52.  </universities >
```

Figure 6-1. A Fragment of an XML Document with Fuzzy Data

6.2.2   The Representation Model

Representation of Fuzzy Data in XML Document

It is not difficult to see from the example given above that a possibility attribute, denoted Poss, should be introduced first, which takes a value in [0, 1]. This possibility attribute is applied together with a fuzzy construct called Val to specify the possibility of a given element existing in the XML document.

Consider line 3 of Figure 6-1. <Val Poss = 0.8> states that the possibility of the given element university being *Oakland University* is equal to 0.8. For an element with possibility 1.0, pair <Val Poss = 1.0> and </Val> is omitted from the XML document.

Based on pair <Val Poss> and </Val>, possibility distribution for an element can be expressed. Also possibility distribution can be used to express fuzzy element values. For this purpose, we introduce another fuzzy construct called Dist to specify a possibility distribution. Typically a Dist element has multiple Val elements as children, each with an associated possibility. Since we have two types of possibility distribution, the Dist construct should indicate the type of a possibility distribution, being *disjunctive* or *conjunctive*.

Again consider Figure 6-1. Lines 24-34 are the disjunctive Dist construct for the age of student Tom Smith. Lines 38-44 are the conjunctive Dist construct for the email of student Tom Smith. It should be pointed out that, however, the possibility distributions in line 24-34 and line 38-44 are all for leaf nodes in the ancestor-descendant chain. In fact, we can also have possibility distributions and values over non-leaf nodes. Observe the disjunctive Dist construct in lines 6-19, which express the two possible statuses for the employee with *ID 85431095*. In these two *employee* values, lines 7-12 are with possibility 0.8 and lines 13-18 are with possibility 0.6.

DTD Modification

It has been shown that the XML document must be extended for fuzzy data modeling. As a result, several fuzzy constructs have been introduced. In order to accommodate these fuzzy constructs, it is clear that the DTD of the source XML document should be correspondingly modified. In this section, we focus on DTD modification for fuzzy XML data modeling.

First we define Val element as follows:
```
<!ELEMENT Val (#PCDATA| original-definition)>
    <!ATTLIST Val Poss CDATA "1.0">
```
Then we define Dist element as follows:
```
<!ELEMENT Dist (Val+)>
    <!ATTLIST Dist type (disjunctive|conjunctive) "disjunctive">
```

Now we modify the element definition in the classical DTD so that all of the elements can use possibility distributions (Dist). For a leaf element which only contains text or #PCDATA, say leafElement, its definition in the DTD is changed from

    <!ELEMENT leafElement (#PCDATA)>

to

    <!ELEMENT leafElement (#PCDATA | Dist)>.

That is, leaf element leafElement may be crisp one (e.g., smane of student in Figure 6-1) and then can be defined as
    <!ELEMENT leafElement (#PCDATA)>.
Also it is possible that leaf element leafElement may be fuzzy one, taking a value represented by a possibility distribution (e.g., age of student in Figure 6-1). Then it should be defined as
    <!ELEMENT leafElement (Dist)>.
Furthermore we have the following definition.
    <!ELEMENT Dist (Val+)>
      <!ATTLIST Dist type (disjunctive|conjunctive) "disjunctive">
    <!ELEMENT Val (#PCDATA)>
      <!ATTLIST Val Poss CDATA "1.0">
For non-leaf element, say nonleafElement, first we should change the element definition from

    <!ELEMENT nonleafElement (*original-definition*)>

to

    <!ELEMENT nonleafElement (*original-definition*| Val+ | Dist)>,

and then add

    <!ELEMENT Val (original-definition)>.

That is, non-leaf element nonleafElement may be crisp (e.g., student in Figure 6-1) and the can be defined as
    <!ELEMENT nonleafElement (*original-definition*)>.
When non-leaf element nonleafElement is fuzzy one, we differentiate two situations: the element takes a value connected with a possibility degree (e.g., university in Figure 6-1); the element takes a set of values and each

value is connected with a possibility degree (e.g., employee in Figure 6-1). The former element is defined as follows.

```
<!ELEMENT nonleafElement (Val+)>
<!ELEMENT Val (original-definition)>
  <!ATTLIST Val Poss CDATA "1.0">
```

The later element is defined as

```
<!ELEMENT nonleafElement (Dist)>
<!ELEMENT Dist (Val+)>
  <!ATTLIST Dist type (disjunctive|conjunctive) "disjunctive">
<!ELEMENT Val (original-definition)>
  <!ATTLIST Val Poss CDATA "1.0">
```

Then the DTD of the XML document in Figure 6-1 is hereby given in Figure 6-2.

```
<!ELEMENT universities (university*)>
<!ELEMENT university (Val+)>
  <!ATTLIST university UName IDREF #REQUIRED>
<!ELEMENT Val (department*)>
  <!ATTLIST Val Poss CDATA>
<!ELEMENT department (employee*, student*)>
  <!ATTLIST department DName IDREF #REQUIRED>
<!ELEMENT employee (Dist)>
  <!ATTLIST employee FID IDREF #REQUIRED>
<!ELEMENT Dist (Val+)>
  <!ATTLIST Dist type (disjunctive)>
<!ELEMENT Val (fname?, position?, office?, course?)>
  <!ATTLIST Val Poss CDATA>
<!ELEMENT student (sname?, age?, sex?, email?)>
  <!ATTLIST student SID IDREF #REQUIRED>
<!ELEMENT fname (#PCDATA)>
<!ELEMENT position (#PCDATA)>
<!ELEMENT office (#PCDATA)>
<!ELEMENT course (#PCDATA)>
<!ELEMENT sname (#PCDATA)>
<!ELEMENT age (Dist)>
<!ELEMENT Dist (Val+)>
  <!ATTLIST Dist type (disjunctive)>
<!ELEMENT Val (#PCDATA)>
  <!ATTLIST Val Poss CDATA>
<!ELEMENT sex (#PCDATA)>
<!ELEMENT email (Dist)>
<!ELEMENT Dist (Val+)>
  <!ATTLIST Dist type (conjunctive)>
<!ELEMENT Val (#PCDATA)>
  <!ATTLIST Val Poss CDATA>
```

Figure 6-2. The DTD of the Fuzzy XML Document in Figure 6-1

6.3   Conceptual Design of the Fuzzy XML Model with the Fuzzy UML Model

Since XML lacks sufficient power in modeling real-world data and their complex inter-relationships in semantics, it is necessary to use other methods to describe data paradigms and develop a true conceptual data model, and then transform this model into an XML encoded format. There have been several proposals for conceptual data modeling of XML schema (XML DTD or XML Schema). In the following, we present the conceptual design of the fuzzy XML using the fuzzy UML model.

For our transformation approach, relevant constructs are the fuzzy extensions of those of UML's Static View, consisting of the fuzzy classes and their relationship such as fuzzy association, fuzzy generalization, and various kinds of fuzzy dependencies. We describe the transformation of these constructs into DTD fragments.

6.3.1   Transformation of Classes

UML classes are transformed into XML element type declarations (Conrad, Scheffner and Freytag, 2000). Here the class names become the names of the element types and the attributes are transformed into element content description. It is noticed that, in the UML, attribute names are mandatory whereas the attribute types are optional. In contrast, an element content only consists of type names in the XML. So it was assumed that attribute names imply their attribute type names in (Conrad, Scheffner and Freytag, 2000). When there is no class representing a suitable declaration for an attribute type, the attribute type is assumed to be an element whose content type is #PCDATA. In addition, multiplicity specifications of attributes are mapped into cardinality specifications with specifiers ?, *, and +, which are used for element content construction.

In the fuzzy UML model, four kinds of classes can be identified, which are

(a) classes without any fuzziness at the three levels,
(b) classes with the fuzziness only at the third level,
(c) classes with the fuzziness at the second level, and
(d) classes with the fuzziness at the first level.

For the classes in case (a), they can be transformed following the approach developed in (Conrad, Scheffner and Freytag, 2000). The transformation of the classes with the third and second levels of fuzziness is of particularly concern. Instead of formal definitions, in the following, we utilize examples to illustrate how to transform the classes with the third and second levels of fuzziness into XML DTD.

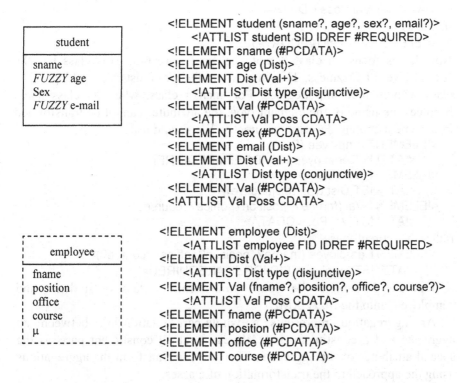

```
<!ELEMENT student (sname?, age?, sex?, email?)>
  <!ATTLIST student SID IDREF #REQUIRED>
<!ELEMENT sname (#PCDATA)>
<!ELEMENT age (Dist)>
<!ELEMENT Dist (Val+)>
  <!ATTLIST Dist type (disjunctive)>
<!ELEMENT Val (#PCDATA)>
  <!ATTLIST Val Poss CDATA>
<!ELEMENT sex (#PCDATA)>
<!ELEMENT email (Dist)>
<!ELEMENT Dist (Val+)>
  <!ATTLIST Dist type (conjunctive)>
<!ELEMENT Val (#PCDATA)>
<!ATTLIST Val Poss CDATA>
```

```
<!ELEMENT employee (Dist)>
  <!ATTLIST employee FID IDREF #REQUIRED>
<!ELEMENT Dist (Val+)>
  <!ATTLIST Dist type (disjunctive)>
<!ELEMENT Val (fname?, position?, office?, course?)>
  <!ATTLIST Val Poss CDATA>
<!ELEMENT fname (#PCDATA)>
<!ELEMENT position (#PCDATA)>
<!ELEMENT office (#PCDATA)>
<!ELEMENT course (#PCDATA)>
```

Figure 6-3. Transformation of the Classes in the Fuzzy UML to the Fuzzy XML

First let us look at class "student" in Figure 6-3. It is clear that this class has two attributes "age" and "e-mail" taking fuzzy values represented possibility distributions. In other words, the class has the third level of fuzziness. While the class name becomes the name of the element type and the attributes are transformed into element content description, these two attributes cannot be directly transformed into the element content description with content type #PCDATA. We should use

```
<!ELEMENT age (Dist)>
<!ELEMENT Dist (Val+)>
  <!ATTLIST Dist type (disjunctive)>
<!ELEMENT Val (#PCDATA)>
  !ATTLIST Val Poss CDATA>
```

rather than use

```
<!ELEMENT age (#PCDATA)>.
```

Similarly, we use

```
<!ELEMENT email (Dist)>
<!ELEMENT Dist (Val+)>
    <!ATTLIST Dist type (conjunctive)>
<!ELEMENT Val (#PCDATA)>
```

```
<!ATTLIST Val Poss CDATA>
```
in place of
```
<!ELEMENT e-mail (#PCDATA)>.
```
Now let us focus on class "employee" in Figure 6-3. This class has the second level of fuzziness. That means that the class instances belong to the class with membership degrees. For such a class, when its class name becomes the name of the element type, the attributes cannot be transformed into element content description directly. We should use
```
<!ELEMENT employee (Dist)>
    <!ATTLIST employee FID IDREF #REQUIRED>
<!ELEMENT Dist (Val+)>
    <!ATTLIST Dist type (disjunctive)>
<!ELEMENT Val (fname?, position?, office?, course?)>
    <!ATTLIST Val Poss CDATA>
```
rather than directly use
```
<!ELEMENT employee (fname?, position?, office?, course?)>
    <!ATTLIST employee FID IDREF #REQUIRED>.
```
Figure 6-3 depicts the details transforming classes "student" and "employee" into the fuzzy XML.

An aggregation represents a whole-part relationship between an aggregate and a constituent part. We can treat all constituent parts as the special attributes of the aggregate. Then we can transform the aggregations using the approach to the transformation of classes.

6.3.2   Transformation of Generalizations

The generalization in the UML defines a subclass/superclass relationship between classes: one class, called superclass, is a more general description of a set of other classes, called subclasses. Following the same transformation of classes given above, the superclass and each subclass are all transformed into the element types in the XML, respectively. Here the element type originating from the superclass is called a *superelement* and the element type originating from a subclass is called a *subelement* in (Conrad, Scheffner and Freytag, 2000). Note that a superelement must receive an additional ID attribute declared #REQUIRED and each subelement must be augmented by a #REQUIRED IDREF attribute in addition to the transformations that the class names become the names of the element types and the attributes are transformed into element content description.

Now consider the fuzziness in the generalization in the fuzzy UML model. Assume that the superclass and subclasses involved in the generalization may have fuzziness at the type/instance level (the second level) or/and at the attribute value level (the third level). The transformation of such superclass and subclasses can be finished according to the transformation of fuzzy classes developed above. Meanwhile the created superelement and each subelement must be associated with ID #REQUIRED and IDREF #REQUIRED, respectively.

Figure 6-4 depicts the transformation of the fuzzy generalization.

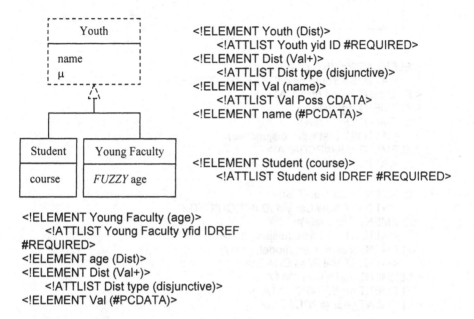

```
<!ELEMENT Youth (Dist)>
    <!ATTLIST Youth yid ID #REQUIRED>
<!ELEMENT Dist (Val+)>
    <!ATTLIST Dist type (disjunctive)>
<!ELEMENT Val (name)>
    <!ATTLIST Val Poss CDATA>
<!ELEMENT name (#PCDATA)>

<!ELEMENT Student (course)>
    <!ATTLIST Student sid IDREF #REQUIRED>
```

```
<!ELEMENT Young Faculty (age)>
    <!ATTLIST Young Faculty yfid IDREF
#REQUIRED>
<!ELEMENT age (Dist)>
<!ELEMENT Dist (Val+)>
    <!ATTLIST Dist type (disjunctive)>
<!ELEMENT Val (#PCDATA)>
```

Figure 6-4. Transformation of the Generalizations in the Fuzzy UML to the Fuzzy XML

6.3.3 Transformation of Associations

Associations are relationships that describe connections among class instances. An association is a more general relationship that aggregation or generalization. So basically we can transform the associations in the UML using the approach to the transformation of generalizations given above. That is, first the class names become the names of the element types and the attributes are transformed into element content description. Then each element transformed must be augmented by a #REQUIRED IDREF attribute (ISIS XML/EDI Project, 2001), which is an artificial one and from another class involved in the association.

Since in the fuzzy UML data model, each class involved in an association may have fuzziness at the type/instance level (the second level) or/and at the attribute value level (the third level), its transformation must be carried out according to the transformation of fuzzy classes developed above.

Utilizing the approach, Figure 6-5 depicts the transformation of the fuzzy association.

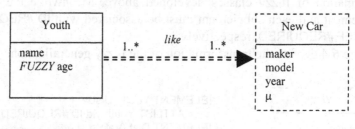

```
<!ELEMENT Youth (name, age)>
    <!ATTLIST Youth ncid IDREF #REQUIRED>
<!ELEMENT name (#PCDATA)>
<!ELEMENT age (Dist)>
<!ELEMENT Dist (Val+)>
    <!ATTLIST Dist type (disjunctive)>
<!ELEMENT Val (#PCDATA)>
    <!ATTLIST Val Poss CDATA>

<!ELEMENT New Car (Dist)>
    <!ATTLIST New Car yid ID #REQUIRED>
<!ELEMENT Dist (Val+)>
    <!ATTLIST Dist type (disjunctive)>
<!ELEMENT Val (maker, model, year)>
    <!ATTLIST Val Poss CDATA>
<!ELEMENT make (#PCDATA)>
<!ELEMENT model (#PCDATA)>
<!ELEMENT year (#PCDATA)>
```

Figure 6-5. Transformation of the Associations in the Fuzzy UML to the Fuzzy XML

6.4   Summary

Fuzzy information modeling in databases provides the foundation for intelligent information processing, while XML aims to achieving data representation and exchange over the web and has been the de-facto standard. Fuzzy databases have extensively been investigated over two decades and XML is currently a very hot topic in academic and industrial areas. While these two subjects are being studied separately, the interaction and/or integration of fuzzy data modeling and XML technologies is another step towards the development of next generation web-based intelligent information systems.

In this chapter, by using possibility distribution theory, we have identified multiple granularity of data fuzziness in the XML, which are possibilities associated with elements and possibility distributions representing attribute values of elements. A fuzzy XML data model that addresses all of the fuzziness has hereby developed. In addition, this chapter reports the conceptual design of the fuzzy XML using the fuzzy UML model.

References

Abiteboul, S., Segoufin, L. and Vianu, V., 2001, Representing and querying XML with incomplete information, *Proceedings of the 12th ACM SIGACT-SIGMOD-SIGART Symposium on Principles of Database Systems*, 150-161.

Bray, T., Paoli, J. and Sperberg-McQueen, C. M. (Eds), 1998, Extensible Markup Language (XML) 1.0, *W3C Recommendation*, http://www.w3.org/TR/1998/REC-xml-19980210.

Conrad, R., Scheffner, D. and Freytag, J. C., 2000, XML conceptual modeling using UML, *Lecture Notes in Computer Science 1920*, Springer, 558-571.

ISIS XML/EDI Project, 2001, *Mapping from UML Generalised Message Descriptions to XML DTDs*, http://palvelut.tieke.fi/edi/isis-xmledi/d2/UmlToDtdMapping05.doc.

Lee, J. and Fanjiang, Y. Y., 2003, Modeling imprecise requirements with XML, *Information and Software Technology*, 45 (7): 445-460.

Nierman, A. and Jagadish, H. V., 2002, ProTDB: Probabilistic data in XML, *Proceedings of 28th International Conference on Very Large Data Bases*, 646-657.

Petrovic, D., Roy, R. and Petrovic, R., 1999, Supply chain modeling using fuzzy sets, *International Journal of Production Economics*, 59: 443-453.

Routledge, N., Bird, L. and Goodchild, A., 2002, UML and XML schema, *Proceedings of the 2002 Australasian Database Conference on Database Technologies*.

Yager, R. R. and Pasi, G., 2001, Product category description for Web-shopping in e-commerce, *International Journal of Intelligent Systems*, 16: 1009–1021.

Yager, R. R., 2000, Targeted e-commerce marketing using fuzzy intelligent agents, *IEEE Intelligent Systems*, 15 (6): 42-45.

PART   III

FUZZY DATABASE MODELS

Chapter 7

THE FUZZY RELATIONAL DATABASES

7.1 Introduction

The relational databases have been proved to be a very useful database model in information systems and have found wide applications successfully. However, the relational database model introduced by Codd (1970) does not deal with imprecise and uncertain data well. The data that is handled has to be either precise or NULL value. NULL value is used for all types of impreciseness such as "unknown", "not-applicable" (many types of such impreciseness are cited in (ANSI/X3/SPARC, 1975). This model cannot model the real world accurately (Yazici and George, 1999).

Fuzzy data have been used to model imprecise information in databases since Zadeh introduced the concept of fuzzy sets (Zadeh, 1965), and the traditional relational databases have been thereby extended. Much of the work in the area has been in extending the basic model and query language to permit the representation and retrieval of imprecise data. A number of related issues such as data dependencies, implementation considerations and others have also been investigated in various fuzzy relational database models.

Three major extended relational models have been proposed as the fuzzy relational database models (Petry, 1996; Chen, 1999). The first one uses membership degrees of tuple belonging in [0, 1] instead of only in {0, 1} (Baldwin and Zhou, 1984; Raju and Majumdar, 1988). The second one uses the principle of replacing the ordinary equivalence among domain values by measures of nearness such as similarity relationships (Buckles and Petry, 1982) and proximity relationships (Shenoi and Melton, 1989). The third one directly uses possibility distributions for attribute values (Prade and

Testemale, 1984). Based these three fuzzy relational database models, there have also been some mixed models combining them (Rundensteiner, Hawkes, and Bandler, 1989). The extended possibility-based fuzzy relational model, for example, is typically one of the mixed models, where not only possibility distributions are allowed to appear as attribute values but also proximity (similarity or closeness) relationships are allowed to associate with the domains.

This chapter mainly focuses on the possibility-based and the extended possibility-based fuzzy relational databases. In addition to the common issues in the fuzzy relational databases such as data dependencies, this chapter particularly investigates the update of the fuzzy relational databases and the integration of fuzzy multidatabases.

7.2   The Fuzzy Relational Models

In connection to the fuzzy data representations of fuzzy relation, possibility distribution, and similarity, there exist two basic extended data models for fuzzy relational databases. One of the data models is based on similarity relations (Buckles and Petry, 1982), or proximity relation (Shenoi and Melton, 1989), or resemblance (Rundensteiner, Hawkes, and Bandler, 1989). The other one is based on possibility distribution (Prade and Testemale, 1984; Raju and Majumdar, 1988). The latter can further be classified into two categories, i.e. tuples associated with possibilities (membership degrees) and attribute values represented possibility distributions (Raju and Majumdar, 1988). The form of an n-tuple in each of the above-mentioned fuzzy relational model can be expressed, respectively, as

$$t = <p_1, p_2, ..., p_i, ..., p_n>,$$

$$t = <a_1, a_2, ..., a_i, ..., a_n, d>$$

and

$$t = <\pi_{A1}, \pi_{A2}, ..., \pi_{Ai}, ..., \pi_{An}>,$$

where $p_i \subseteq D_i$ with D_i being the domain of attribute A_i, $a_i \in D_i$, $d \in (0, 1]$, π_{Ai} is the possibility distribution of attribute A_i on its domain D_i, and $\pi_{Ai}(x)$, $x \in D_i$, denotes the possibility that x is the actual value of $t[A_i]$.

It is clear that, based on the above-mentioned basic fuzzy relational models, there should be one type of extended fuzzy relational model

(Rundensteiner, Hawkes, and Bandler, 1989; Chen, Vandenbulcke and Kerre, 1992), where possibility distribution and resemblance relation arise in a relational databases simultaneously. The focus of this Chapter is put on such fuzzy relational databases and generally it is assumed that the possibility of each tuple in a fuzzy relation is exactly 1.

Definition: A fuzzy relation *r* on a relational schema *R* (A1, A2, ..., An) is a subset of the Cartesian product of *D* (A1) × *D* (A2) × ... × *D* (An), where *D* (Ai) may be a fuzzy subset or even a set of fuzzy subset and there is the resemblance relation on the *D* (Ai). A resemblance relation *Res* on *D* (Ai) is a mapping: D (Ai) × D (Ai) → [0, 1] such that

(a) for $\forall\, x \in D$ (Ai), *Res* $(x, x) = 1$ (reflexivity)
(b) for $\forall\, x, y \in D$ (Ai), *Res* $(x, y) =$ Res (y, x) (symmetry)

Notice that the difference between a resemblance relation *Res* and a similarity relation *Sim* is that *Sim* needs transitivity in addition to reflexivity and symmetry. The transitivity means that

for $\forall\, x, y, z \in D$ (Ai), *Sim* $(x, z) \geq \max_y$ (min (*Sim* (x, y), *Sim* (y, z))).

So a similarity relation must be a resemblance relation but a resemblance relation may not be a similarity relation.

7.3 Semantic Measures and Data Redundancies

7.3.1 Existing Methods

To measure the semantic relationship between fuzzy data, some investigation results for assessing data redundancy can be found in literature.

Rundensteiner, Hawkes, and Bandler in (1989) proposed the notion nearness measure. Two fuzzy data π_A and π_B were considered α-β redundant if and only if the following inequality equations hold true:

$$\min\nolimits_{x,\, y\, \in\, \text{supp}\,(\pi A)\, \cup\, \text{supp}\,(\pi B)} (\text{Res}\,(x, y)) \geq \alpha$$

$$\min\nolimits_{z\, \in\, U} (1 - |\pi_A\,(z) - \pi_B\,(z)|) \geq \beta$$

where α and β are the given thresholds, *Res* (x, y) denotes the resemblance relation on the attribute domain, and supp (π_A) denotes the support of π_A. It is clear that a twofold condition is applied in their study. As noted in (Chen, Vandenbulcke and Kerre, 1992; Ma, Zhang and Ma, 1999), however, counterintuitive results are produced with their treatment due to the fact that two criteria are set separately for redundancy evaluation.

For two data π_A and π_B, Chen, Vandenbulcke and Kerre in (1992) defined the following approach to assess the possibility and impossibility that $\pi_A = \pi_B$.

$$E_c\,(\pi_A, \pi_B)\,(T) = \mathrm{supp}_{x,\,y\,\in U,\,c\,(x,\,y)\,\geq\,\alpha}\,(\min\,(\pi_A\,(x),\,\pi_B\,(y)))$$

$$E_c\,(\pi_A, \pi_B)\,(F) = \mathrm{supp}_{x,\,y\,\in U,\,c\,(x,\,y)\,<\,\alpha}\,(\min\,(\pi_A\,(x),\,\pi_B\,(y)))$$

where $c\ (x,\ y)$ denotes a closeness relation (being the same as the resemblance relation). It should be noted that the approach in (Chen, Vandenbulcke and Kerre, 1992) is an extension of the work in (van Schooten, 1988; Kerre, 1988). It was shown in (Ma, Zhang and Ma, 1999) that there are some inconsistencies when the approach proposed in (van Schooten, 1988; Kerre, 1988) is applied to assess the redundancy of fuzzy data represented possibility distribution.

In (Cubero and Vila, 1994), the notions of weak resemblance and strong resemblance were proposed for representing the possibility and the necessity that two fuzzy values π_A and π_B are approximately equal, respectively. Weak resemblance and strong resemblance can be expressed as follows.

$$\Pi\,(\pi_A \approx \pi_B) = \mathrm{supp}_{x,\,y\,\in U}\,(\min\,(\mathrm{Res}\,(x,\,y),\,\pi_A\,(x),\,\pi_B\,(y)))$$

$$N\,(\pi_A \approx \pi_B) = \inf_{x,\,y\,\in U}\,(\max\,(\mathrm{Res}\,(x,\,y),\,1 - \pi_A\,(x),\,1 - \pi_B\,(y)))$$

The semantic measures were employed as a basis for a new definition of fuzzy functional dependencies in (Cubero and Vila, 1994). The weak resemblance, however, appears to be too "optimistic" and strong resemblance is too severe for the semantic assessment of fuzzy data (Bosc and Pivert, 1997).

According to the situation that two criteria are set separately for the redundancy evaluation in (Rundensteiner, Hawkes, and Bandler, 1989), Bosc and Pivert (1997) gave the following function to measure the interchangeability that fuzzy value π_A can be replaced with another fuzzy data π_B, i.e., the possibility that π_A is close to π_B from the left-hand side:

$$\mu_{\mathrm{repl}}\,(\pi_A, \pi_B) = \inf_{x\,\in\mathrm{supp}\,(\pi A)}\,(\max\,(1 - \pi_A\,(x),\,\mu_S\,(\pi_A, \pi_B)\,(x))),$$

where $\mu_{S\,(\pi A,\,\pi B)}\,(x)$ is defined as

$$\mu_S\,(\pi_A, \pi_B)\,(x) = \sup_{y\,\in\mathrm{supp}\,(\pi B)}\,(\min\,(\mathrm{Res}\,(x,\,y),\,1 - |\pi_A\,(x) - \pi_B\,(y)|)).$$

It follows that an approach of Bosc and Pivert in (Bosc and Pivert, 1997) is actually an extension of the approach reported in (Rundensteiner, Hawkes, and Bandler, 1989). As shown in (Ma, Zhang and Ma, 1999), the approach in (Rundensteiner, Hawkes, and Bandler, 1989) appears to be counterintuitive. Typically the semantic relationship of inclusion, being a kind of important relationship between fuzzy data in the assessment of fuzzy data redundancy, cannot be identified. The same problem also exists in the approach in (Bosc and Pivert, 1997), which is demonstrated in Section 7.3.3.

Following the discussion above, it can be seen that the semantic measure of fuzzy data was mainly focused on equivalence relationship in the literature. To eliminate counterintuitive results in the proposed approaches and to assess the semantic relationship of fuzzy data in extended possibility-based fuzzy relational databases, including equivalence and inclusion, we define a new approach in the following.

7.3.2 Semantic Relationship between Fuzzy Data

Not being the same as precise data, fuzzy data are sets of points in space instead of points in the universe of discourse. The semantics of a fuzzy data expressed by possibility distribution corresponds to an area in space, the so-called semantic space.

Definition: For fuzzy data, its semantics correspond to an area in space, where the universe of discourse is its X-axis and possibility is its Y-axis.

The semantic relationship between two fuzzy data can be described by the relationship between their semantic spaces. Let SS (π_A) and SS (π_B) be semantic spaces of two fuzzy data π_A and π_B, respectively. If SS $(\pi_A) \supseteq$ SS (π_B) or SS $(\pi_A) \subseteq$ SS (π_B), π_A semantically includes π_B or π_A is semantically included by π_B. If SS $(\pi_A) \supseteq$ SS (π_B) and SS $(\pi_A) \subseteq$ SS (π_B), π_A and π_B are semantically equivalent to each other. It is clear that semantic equivalence is a particular case of semantic inclusion. We employ semantic inclusion degree to measure the semantic relationship of fuzzy data.

Definition: Let π_A and π_B be two fuzzy data, and their semantic spaces be SS (π_A) and SS (π_B), respectively. Let SID (π_A, π_B) denotes the degree that π_A semantically includes π_B. Then

$$\text{SID } (\pi_A, \pi_B) = (\text{SS } (\pi_B) \cap \text{SS } (\pi_A))/\text{SS } (\pi_B)$$

For two fuzzy data π_A and π_B, the meaning of SID (π_A, π_B) is the percentage of the semantic space of π_B which is wholly included in the semantic space of π_A. Following definition 2, the concept of equivalence degree can be easily drawn as follows.

Definition: Let π_A and π_B be two fuzzy data and SID (π_A, π_B) be the degree that π_A semantically includes π_B. Let SE (π_A, π_B) denote the degree that π_A and π_B are equivalent to each other. Then

$$SE\ (\pi_A, \pi_B) = min\ (SID\ (\pi_A, \pi_B),\ SID\ (\pi_B, \pi_A))$$

7.3.3   Evaluation of Semantic Measures

For two possibility distributions, the semantic inclusion degree is defined as follows.

Definition: Let $U = \{u_1, u_2, ..., u_n\}$ be the universe of discourse. Let π_A and π_B be two fuzzy data on U based on possibility distribution and $\pi_A (u_i)$, $u_i \in U$, denote the possibility that u_i is true. SID (π_A, π_B) is then defined by

$$SID\ (\pi_A, \pi_B) = \sum_{i=1}^{n} \min_{u_i \in U}\ (\pi_B\ (u_i),\ \pi_A\ (u_i)) / \sum_{i=1}^{n} \pi_B\ (u_i)$$

In the above definition, an assumption is made that only the same element in the domain is relative to each other and the relationship between different elements are not considered. However, two different elements in the same domain may be close to each other if there is a resemblance relation in the domain elements. We, therefore, give the definition for calculating the semantic inclusion degree of two fuzzy data based on possibility distribution and resemblance relations in the following paragraph.

Definition: Let $U = \{u_1, u_2, ..., u_n\}$ be the universe of discourse. Let π_A and π_B be two fuzzy data on U based on possibility distribution and $\pi_A (u_i)$, $u_i \in U$, denote the possibility that u_i is true. Let *Res* be a resemblance relation on domain U, α for $0 \leq \alpha \leq 1$ be a threshold corresponding to *Res*. SID (π_A, π_B) is then defined by

$$SID\ (\pi_A, \pi_B) = \sum_{i=1}^{n} \min_{u_i, u_j \in U, Res(u_i, u_j) \geq \alpha}\ (\pi_B\ (u_i),\ \pi_A\ (u_j)) / \sum_{i=1}^{n} \pi_B\ (u_i)$$

Example. Let $\pi_1 = \{1.0/a, 0.95/b, 0.9/c\}$ and $\pi_1 = \{0.95/a, 0.9/b, 1.0r/d, 0.3/e\}$ be two fuzzy data on domain $U = \{a, b, c, d, e, f\}$ and let *Res* be a resemblance relation on U given in Figure 7-1. Let threshold $\alpha = 0.9$. Then
SID $(\pi_1, \pi_2) = \{0.95 + 0.9 + 0.9\}/\{0.95 + 0.9 + 1.0 + 0.3\} = 0.873$,
SID $(\pi_2, \pi_1) = \{0.95 + 0.9 + 0.9\}/\{1.0 + 0.95 + 0.9\} = 0.965$,
and thus

$SE (\pi_1, \pi_2) = \min (SID (\pi_1, \pi_2), SID (\pi_2, \pi_1)) = \min (0.873, 0.965) = 0.873.$

Res	a	b	c	d	e	f
a	1.0	0.1	0.4	0.3	0.1	0.1
b		1.0	0.2	0.3	0.2	0.2
c			1.0	0.95	0.5	0.3
d				1.0	0.3	0.1
e					1.0	0.4
f						1.0

Figure 7-1. A Resemblance Relation

Now Let us consider the following two particular cases, namely, between $\pi_3 = \{1.0/a, 1.0/b, 1.0/c\}$ and $\pi_3 = \{1.0/a, 1.0/b, 1.0/d\}$ and between $\pi_5 = \{0.9/a, 1.0/b, 0.8/c\}$ and $\pi_6 = \{0.3/a, 0.4/b, 0.2/d\}$. In the similar way above, we have

$SID (\pi_3, \pi_4) = \{1.0 + 1.0 + 1.0\}/\{1.0 + 1.0 + 1.0\} = 1.0,$

$SID (\pi_4, \pi_3) = \{1.0 + 1.0 + 1.0\}/\{1.0 + 1.0 + 1.0\} = 1.0,$

and thus

$SE (\pi_3, \pi_4) = \min (SID (\pi_3, \pi_4), SID (\pi_4, \pi_3)) = \min (1.0, 1.0) = 1.0;$

$SID (\pi_5, \pi_6) = \{0.3 + 0.4 + 0.2\}/\{0.3 + 0.4 + 0.2\} = 1.0,$

$SID (\pi_6, \pi_5) = \{0.3 + 0.4 + 0.2\}/\{0.9 + 1.0 + 0.8\} = 0.333,$

and thus

$SE (\pi_5, \pi_6) = \min (SID (\pi_5, \pi_6), SID (\pi_6, \pi_5)) = \min (1.0, 0.333) = 0.333.$
It follows that π_5 semantically includes π_6 whereas π_6 does not include π_5. If we employ the approach proposed in (Bosc and Pivert, 1997), we have

$\mu_S (\pi_5, \pi_6) (a) = \sup (\min (1.0, 0.4), \min (0.1, 0.5), \min (0.3, 0.3)) = 0.4,$

$\mu_S (\pi_5, \pi_6) (b) = \sup (\min (0.1, 0.3), \min (1.0, 0.4), \min (0.3, 0.2)) = 0.4,$

$\mu_S (\pi_5, \pi_6) (d) = \sup (\min (0.3, 0.3), \min (0.3, 0.2), \min (0.95, 0.4)) = 0.4,$

$\mu_{repl} (\pi_5, \pi_6) = \inf (\max (0.1, 0.4), \max (0.0, 0.4), \max (0.7, 0.4)) = 0.4,$
and

$\mu_S (\pi_6, \pi_5) (a) = \sup (\min (1.0, 0.4), \min (0.1, 0.3), \min (0.4, 0.5)) = 0.4,$

$\mu_S (\pi_6, \pi_5) (b) = \sup (\min (0.1, 0.5), \min (1.0, 0.4), \min (0.2, 0.6)) = 0.4,$

$\mu_S (\pi_6, \pi_5) (d) = \sup (\min (0.4, 0.5), \min (0.2, 0.6), \min (0.95, 0.4)) = 0.4,$

$\mu_{repl} (\pi_6, \pi_5) = \inf (\max (0.7, 0.4), \max (0.6, 0.4), \max (0.8, 0.4)) = 0.6.$
Finally one obtains

$\mu_{EQ} (\pi_5, \pi_6) = \min (\mu_{repl} (\pi_5, \pi_6), \mu_{repl} (\pi_6, \pi_5)) = \min (0.4, 0.6) = 0.4.$
Not being the same as classical relational databases, semantic inclusion of fuzzy data is another kind of data redundancy in addition to the equivalence redundancy. It can be seen from the above evaluation that the semantic relationship of inclusion between π_5 and π_6 cannot be identified using the approaches reported in (Bosc and Pivert, 1997).

7.3.4   Fuzzy Data Redundancies and Removal

Following the semantic inclusion degree of fuzzy data, two types of fuzzy data redundancies: *inclusion redundancy* and *equivalence redundancy* can be classified and evaluated. Being different from the classical set theory, the condition SS (A) $\supseteq$ SS (B) or SS (A) $\subseteq$ SS (B) is essentially the particular case of fuzzy data due to the fuzziness of the data. In general, the threshold should be considered when evaluating the semantic relationship between two fuzzy data.

Definition: Let π_A and π_B be two fuzzy data and β be a threshold. If SID (π_A, π_B) $\geq \beta$, π_B is said to be *inclusively* redundant to π_A. If SE (π_A, π_B) $\geq \beta$, it is said that π_A and π_B are *equivalently* redundant to each other.

It is clear that equivalence redundancy of fuzzy data is a particular case of inclusion redundancy of fuzzy data. Considering the effect of resemblance relation in evaluation of semantic inclusion degree and equivalence degree, two fuzzy data π_A and π_B are considered equivalently α-β-redundant if and only if SE_α (π_A, π_B) $\geq \beta$. If SID_α (π_A, π_B) $\geq \beta$ and SID_α (π_B, π_A) $< \beta$, π_B are inclusively α-β-redundant to π_A.

If π_A and π_B are inclusively redundant or equivalently redundant, the removal of redundancy can be achieved by merging π_A and π_B and producing a new fuzzy data π_C. Following Zadeh's extension principle (Zadeh, 1975), the operation with an infix operator "θ" on π_A and π_B can be defined as follows.

$$\pi_A \, \theta \, \pi_B = \{\pi_A \, (u_i)/u_i \mid u_i \in U \wedge 1 \leq i \leq n\} \, \theta \, \{\pi_B \, (v_j)/v_j \mid v_j \in U \wedge 1 \leq j \leq n\} = \{\max \, (\min \, (\pi_A \, (u_i), \, \pi_B \, (v_j))/ \, u_i \, \theta \, v_j)|u_i, \, v_j \in U \wedge 1 \leq i, j \leq n\}$$

Assume that π_A and π_B are α-β-redundant to each other, the elimination of duplicate could be achieved by merging π_A and π_B and producing a new fuzzy data π_C, where π_A, π_B and π_C are three fuzzy data on $U = \{u1, u2, \ldots, un\}$ based on possibility distribution and there is a resemblance relation Res_U on U. Then the following three merging operations are defined:

$$\pi_C = \pi_A \cup_f \pi_B = \{\pi_C \, (w)/w \mid (\exists \, \pi_A \, (ui)/ui) \, (\exists \, \pi_B \, (vj)/vj) \, (\pi_C \, (w) = \max \, (\pi_A \, (ui), \, \pi_B \, (vj)) \wedge (w = ui|_{\pi_C \, (w) \, = \, \pi_A \, (ui)} \vee w = vj|_{\pi_C \, (w) \, = \, \pi_B \, (vj)}) \wedge Res_U \, (ui, vj) \geq \alpha \wedge ui, vj \in U \wedge 1 \leq i, j \leq n) \vee (\exists \, \pi_A \, (ui)/ui) \, (\forall \, \pi_B \, (vj)/vj) \, (\pi_C \, (w) = \pi_A \, (ui) \wedge w = ui \wedge Res_U \, (ui, vj) \geq \alpha \wedge ui, vj \in U \wedge 1 \leq i, j \leq n) \vee (\exists \, \pi_B \, (vj)/(vj) \, (\forall \pi_A \, (ui)/ui) \, (\pi_C \, (w) = \pi_B \, (vj) \wedge w = vj \wedge Res_U \, (ui, vj) \geq \alpha \wedge ui, vj \in U \wedge 1 \leq i, j \leq n)\},$$

$$\pi_C = \pi_A -_f \pi_B = \{\pi_C \ (w)/w \mid (\exists \ \pi_A \ (ui)/ui) \ (\exists \ \pi_B \ (vj)/vj) \ (\pi_C \ (w) = \max \ (\pi_A \ (ui) - \pi_B \ (vj), 0) \land w = ui \land Res_U \ (ui, vj) \geq \alpha \land ui, vj \in U \land 1 \leq i,j \leq n) \lor (\exists \ \pi_A \ (ui)/ui) \ (\forall \ \pi_B \ (vj)/vj) \ (\pi_C \ (w) = \pi_A \ (ui) \land w = ui \land Res_U \ (ui, vj) < \alpha \land ui, vj \in U \land 1 \leq i,j \leq n)\},$$

and

$$\pi_C = \pi_A \cap_f \pi_B = \{\pi_C \ (w)/w \mid (\exists \ \pi_A \ (ui)/ui) \ (\exists \ \pi_B \ (vj)/vj) \ (\pi_C \ (w) = \min \ (\pi_A \ (ui), \pi_B \ (vj)) \land (w = ui|_{\pi_C \ (w) = \pi_A \ (ui)} \lor w = vj|_{\pi_C \ (w) = \pi_B \ (vj)}) \land Res_U \ (ui, vj) \geq \alpha \land ui, vj \in U \land 1 \leq i,j \leq n)\}.$$

Example: Let $\pi_A = \{1.0/a, 0.95/b, 0.9/c, 0.2/f\}$ and $\pi_B = \{0.95/a, 0.9/b, 1.0/d, 0.3/e\}$ be two fuzzy data on domain $D = \{a, b, c, d, e, f\}$. *Res* is a resemblance relation on D given in Figure 7-1, where threshold $\alpha = 0.9$. Then

$SID_\alpha \ (\pi_A, \pi_B) = (0.95 + 0.9 + 0.9) \ / \ (0.95 + 0.9 + 1.0 + 0.3) = 0.873,$

$SID_\alpha \ (\pi_B, \pi_A) = (0.95 + 0.9 + 0.9) \ / \ (1.0 + 0.95 + 0.9 + 0.2) = 0.902,$

and thus

$SE_\alpha \ (\pi_A, \pi_B) = \min \ (SID \ (\pi_A, \pi_B), SID \ (\pi_B, \pi_A)) = \min \ (0.873, 0.902) = 0.873.$

If a threshold $\beta = 0.85$ is given, πA and πB are considered redundant to each other. Utilizing the merging operations above, one has the following results.

$\pi_A \cup_f \pi_B = \{1.0/a, 0.95/b, 1.0/d, 0.3/e, 0.2/f\},$

$\pi_A -_f \pi_B = \{0.05/a, 0.05/b, 0.2/f\},$ and

$\pi_A \cap_f \pi_B = \{0.95/a, 0.9/b, 0.9/c\}.$

The processing of fuzzy value redundancy can be extended to that of fuzzy tuple redundancy. In a similar way, fuzzy tuple redundancy can be classified into inclusion redundancy and equivalence redundancy of tuples.

Definition: Let r be a fuzzy relation on the relational schema R (A1, A2, ..., An). Let $t = (\pi_{A1}, \pi_{A1}, ..., \pi_{An})$ and $t' = (\pi_{A1}', \pi_{A2}', ..., \pi_{An}')$ be two tuples in r. Let $\alpha \in [0, 1]$ and $\beta \in [0, 1]$ be two thresholds. The tuple t' is inclusively α-β-redundant to t if and only if min $(SID_\alpha \ (\pi_{Ai}, \pi_{Ai}')) \geq \beta$ holds true $(1 \leq i \leq n)$. The tuples t and t' are equivalently α-β-redundant if and only if min $(SE_\alpha \ (\pi_{Ai}, \pi_{Ai}')) \geq \beta$ holds $(1 \leq i \leq n)$.

7.4 Data Integrity Constraints

Data dependencies play a crucial role in logical database design as well as database manipulation. Some attempts have been taken to represent data dependencies in fuzzy relational databases, such as fuzzy functional dependencies (*FFDs*) (Bosc and Pivert, 2003; Chen et al., 1994 & 1996;

Cubero and Vila, 1994; Liao, Wang and Liu, 1999; Liu, 1992, 1993 & 1997; Raju and Majumdar, 1988; Sözat and Yazici, 2001) and fuzzy multivalued dependencies (*FMVDs*) (Bhattacharjee and Mazumdar, 1998; Jyothi and Babu, 1997; Liu, 1997; Shenoi and Melton, 1989; Sözat and Yazici, 2001; Tripathy and Sakena, 1990). Among these data dependencies functional dependencies are of more interest. Being the same as classical relational databases, fuzzy functional dependencies can be used as guidelines for the design of a fuzzy relational schema that is conceptually meaningful and is free of certain update anomalies. Moreover, fuzzy functional dependencies and their inferences have been applied in database security, knowledge discovery (data mining) and reasoning currently (Dutta, 1991; Hale and Shenoi, 1996).

Fuzzy functional dependencies have received a lot of attention. It is necessary for the definition of fuzzy functional dependencies to compare the fuzzy values of the same attributes. Therefore, several definitions of fuzzy functional dependencies have been proposed on the basis of different semantic measures. In (Raju and Majumdar, 1988), a fuzzy relation EQUAL over $U \times U$ (U is a universe of discourse) is defined as a fuzzy measure. A fuzzy functional dependency $X \hookrightarrow Y$ holds in a fuzzy relation if for any pair of tuples, the resemblance on Y-values is greater than that on X-values. The proposals in (Liu, 1993) and (Liu, 1992; Liao, Wang and Liu, 1999) use the same definitions of fuzzy functional dependencies with semantic distance and semantic proximity respectively instead of the fuzzy relation EQUAL. Based on possibility distribution theory, the closeness degree of fuzzy data on a domain D is introduced by Chen et al. in (1994 & 1996). A fuzzy functional dependency $X \hookrightarrow_\Phi Y$ holds in a fuzzy relation if for any pair of tuples, the closeness degree for Y-values is at least that of X-values or over Φ. In (Cubero and Vila, 1994), a fuzzy functional dependency $X \hookrightarrow_{\alpha, \beta} Y$ holds in a fuzzy relation if for any pair of tuples, that the resemblance on X-values is greater than the threshold α implies that the resemblance on Y-values is greater than the threshold β. Regarding the issues of fuzzy functional dependencies, an overview is made by Bosc, Dubois and Prade in (Bosc, Dubois and Prade, 1998), in which different proposals for fuzzy functional dependencies are analyzed, the connection between fuzzy functional dependencies and database design are addressed, and some semantics and use of fuzzy functional dependencies are suggested. Tripathy and Sakena express fuzzy multivalued dependencies in terms of particularization and Hamming (1990). Sözat and Yazici (2001) study fuzzy functional and multivalued dependencies in similarity-based fuzzy relational database model. With semantic proximity, fuzzy functional, multivalued and join dependencies are given in (Liu, 1997). Based on the fuzzy relation EQUAL in (Raju and Majumdar, 1988) and its extension, fuzzy multivalued dependencies are also defined in (Bhattacharjee and Mazumdar, 1998) and (Jyothi and Babu, 1997), respectively.

7.4.1 Fuzzy Functional Dependencies

Fuzzy functional dependencies can reflexively represent the dependency relationships among attribute values in fuzzy relations such as "the salary almost dependents on the job position and experience". Following the notion of semantic equivalence degree introduced in Section 7.3, we give the definition of fuzzy functional dependencies as follows.

Definition: For a relation instance r (R), where R denotes the schema, its attribute set is denoted by U, and $X, Y \subseteq U$, we say r satisfies the *fuzzy functional dependency FFD*: $X \hookrightarrow Y$, if

$$(\forall t \in r)\,(\forall s \in r)\,(SE\,(t\,[X],\,s\,[X]) \leq SE\,(t\,[Y],\,s\,[Y])).$$

Consider a fuzzy relation instance r in Table 7-1. Assume that attribute domains Dom $(X) = \{a, b, c, d, e\}$ and Dom $(Y) = \{f, g, h, i, j\}$. There are two resemblance relations *Res* (X) and *Res* (Y) on X and Y shown in Figure 7-2 and Figure 7-3, respectively. Let two thresholds on *Res* (X) and *Res* (Y) be $\alpha_1 = 0.90$ and $\alpha_2 = 0.95$, respectively.

Table 7-1. Fuzzy Relation Instance r

	K	X	Y
t	1001	{0.7/a, 0.4/b, 0.5/d}	{0.9/f, 0.6/g, 1.0/h}
s	1002	{0.5/a, 0.4/c, 0.8/d}	{0.6/g, 0.9/h, 0.9/i}
u	1003	{0.3/d, 0.8/e}	{0.6/h, 0.4/i, 0.1/j}

Res	a	b	c	d	e
a	1.0	0.2	0.3	0.2	0.4
b		1.0	0.92	0.4	0.1
c			1.0	0.1	0.3
d				1.0	0.2
e					1.0

Figure 7-2. Resemblance Relation on Attribute X

Since

SE $(t\,[X],\,s\,[X]) = \min$ (SID $(t\,[X],\,s\,[X])$, SID $(s\,[X],\,t\,[X])) = \min$ (0.824, 0.875) = 0.824 and

SE $(t\,[Y],\,s\,[Y]) = \min$ (SID $(t\,[Y],\,s\,[Y])$, SID $(s\,[Y],\,t\,[Y])) = \min$ (1.0, 0.96) = 0.96,

so

SE $(t\,[X],\,s\,[X]) \leq$ SE $(t\,[Y],\,s\,[Y])$.

Similarly, we have
  SE $(t [X], u [X]) \le$ SE $(t [Y], u [Y])$ and
  SE $(s [X], u [X]) \le$ SE $(s [Y], u [Y])$.
Hence
  FFD: $X \hookrightarrow Y$ holds in r.

Res	f	g	h	i	j
f	1.0	0.3	0.2	0.96	0.2
g		1.0	0.4	0.2	0.3
h			1.0	0.3	0.1
i				1.0	0.4
j					1.0

Figure 7-3. Resemblance Relation on Attribute Y

Theorem 7.1: A classical functional dependency *FD* satisfies the definition of *FFD*.
  Proof:
  Let *FD*: $X \to Y$ be true. Then for $\forall\, t \in r$ and $\forall\, s \in r$, $t [X] = s [X] \Rightarrow t [Y] = s [Y]$. It is evident that SE $(t [X], s [X]) = \min$ (SID $(t [X], s [X])$, SID $(s [X], t [X])) = 1$ and SE $(t [Y], s [Y]) = \min$ (SID $(t [Y], s [Y])$, SID $(s [Y], t [Y])) = 1$.

7.4.2 Fuzzy Mutivalued Dependencies

Based on the notion of the semantic equivalence degree, the fuzzy multivalued dependencies are defined as follows.
  Definition: Let $r (R)$ be a fuzzy relation instance on schema R, U be the set of attributes of R, $X, Y \subseteq U$, and $Z = U - XY$. We say r satisfies the *fuzzy multivalued dependency FMVD*: $X \hookrightarrow\hookrightarrow Y$ if

$$(\forall\, t \in r)\,(\forall\, s \in r)\,(\exists\, u \in r)\,(\text{SE}\,(u [X], t [X]) \ge \text{SE}\,(t [X], s [X]) \wedge \text{SE}\,(u [Y], t [Y]) \ge \text{SE}\,(t [X], s [X]) \wedge \text{SE}\,(u [Z], s [Z]) \ge \text{SE}\,(t [X], s [X])).$$

Table 7-2. Fuzzy Relation Instance s

	K	X	Y	Z
t	1001	{0.4/a, 0.6/b, 0.7/d}	{0.6/g, 0.9/h, 0.8/i}	{0.5/a, 0.7/c, 0.4/e}
s	1002	{0.4/c, 0.5/d, 0.2/e}	{0.3/h, 0.6/i, 1.0/j}	{0.2/b, 0.5/c, 0.9/e, 0.8/f}
u	1003	{0.4/a, 0.5/b, 0.6/d}	{0.6/g, 0.7/h, 0.8/f}	{0.6/d, 1.0/e, 0.7/f}

Consider a fuzzy relation instance s in Table 7-2. Assume that attribute domains Dom $(X) = \{a, b, c, d, e\}$, Dom $(Y) = \{f, g, h, i, j\}$, and Dom $(Z) = \{a, b, c, d, e, f\}$. There are three resemblance relations *Res* (X), *Res* (Y), and *Res* (Z) on X, Y, and Z in Figure 7-2, Figure 7-3, and Figure 7-1, respectively. Let three thresholds on *Res* (*X*), *Res* (*Y*), and *Res* (*Z*) be $\alpha 1 = 0.90$, $\alpha 2 = 0.95$, and $\alpha 3 = 0.90$, respectively. Then

SE (*t* [*X*], *s* [*X*]) = min (SID (*t* [*X*], *s* [*X*]), SID (*s* [*X*], *t* [*X*])) = min (0.818, 0.529) = 0.529

SE (*t* [*X*], *u* [*X*]) = min (SID (*t* [*X*], *u* [*X*]), SID (*u* [*X*], *t* [*X*])) = min (1.0, 0.882) = 0.882 > SE (t [X], s [X])

SE (*t* [*Y*], *u* [*Y*]) = min (SID (*t* [*Y*], *u* [*Y*]), SID (*u* [*Y*], *t* [*Y*])) = min (1.0, 0.913) = 0.913 > SE (*t* [*X*], *s* [*X*])

SE (*s* [*Z*], *u* [*Z*]) = min (SID (*s* [*Z*], *u* [*Z*]), SID (*u* [*Z*], *s* [*Z*])) = min (0.913, 0.875) = 0.875 > SE (*t* [*X*], *s* [*X*])

Hence

FMVD: $X \hookrightarrow \hookrightarrow Y$ holds in *r*.

Theorem 7.2: A classical multivalued dependency *MVD* satisfies the definition of *FMVD*.

Proof:

Let relational instance *r* (*R*) satisfies *MVD*: $X \rightarrow \rightarrow Y$, where $X, Y \subseteq R$, and $Z = R - XY$. Then $\forall\ t \in r$, $\forall\ s \in r$, and $t\ [X] = s\ [X] \Rightarrow (\exists\ u \in r)\ (u\ [X] = t\ [X] \wedge u\ [Y] = t\ [Y] \wedge u\ [Z] = s\ [Z])$. Accordingly, SE (*u* [*X*], *t* [*X*]) = SE (*u* [*Y*], *t* [*Y*]) = SE (*u* [*Z*], *s* [*Z*]) = SE (*t* [*X*], *s* [*X*]) = 1.

7.4.3   Reference Rules for Fuzzy Data Dependencies

In classical relational databases, functional and multivalued dependencies satisfy the inference rules, namely, the axiom systems (Armstrong, 1974; Beeri, Fagin and Howard, 1977). According to the definitions of the fuzzy functional and multivalued dependencies based on the semantic equivalence degree, a set of the inference rules for *FFD* and *FMVD* can be derived, which are similar to that for *FD* and *MVD* in classical relational databases. We call it fuzzy axiom systems. It can be proven that the fuzzy axiom systems are sound and complete.

The reference rules for *FFDs*:

FA1 (Reflexivity): If $Y \subseteq X \subseteq U$, then $X \hookrightarrow Y$.

FA2 (Augmentation): If $X \hookrightarrow Y$ and $Z \subseteq U$, then $XZ \hookrightarrow YZ$.

FA3 (Transitivity): If $X \hookrightarrow Y$ and $Y \hookrightarrow Z$, then $X \hookrightarrow Z$.

FA9 (Union): If $X \hookrightarrow Y$ and $X \hookrightarrow Z$, then $X \hookrightarrow YZ$.

FA10 (Decomposition): If $X \hookrightarrow YZ$, then $X \hookrightarrow Y$ and $X \hookrightarrow Z$.

FA11 (Pseudotransitivity): If $X \hookrightarrow Y$ and $YW \hookrightarrow Z$, then $XW \hookrightarrow Z$.

Theorem 7.3: The inference rules FA1-FA3 and FA9-FA11 are sound.

Proof:

(1) Since $Y \subseteq X$, we have SE (*t* [*X*], *s* [*X*]) ≤ SE (*t* [*Y*], *s* [*Y*]) for $\forall\ t \in r$ and $\forall\ s \in r$ from the definition of the semantic equivalence of tuples.

(2) Since *FFD*: $X \hookrightarrow Y$ holds in a relation r, SE $(t\,[X], s\,[X]) \leq$ SE $(t\,[Y], s\,[Y])$ for $\forall\, t \in r$ and $\forall\, s \in r$, we have min (SE $(t\,[X], s\,[X])$, SE $(t\,[Z], s\,[Z])$) $\leq$ min (SE $(t\,[Y], s\,[Y])$, SE $(t\,[Z], s\,[Z])$), i. e., SE $(t\,[XZ], s\,[XZ]) \leq$ SE $(t\,[YZ], s\,[YZ])$.

(3) If $X \hookrightarrow Y$ and $Y \hookrightarrow Z$, then SE $(t\,[X], s\,[X]) \leq$ SE $(t\,[Y], s\,[Y])$ and SE $(t\,[Y], s\,[Y]) \leq$ SE $(t\,[Z], s\,[Z])$ for $\forall\, t \in r$ and $\forall\, s \in r$, thus SE $(t\,[X], s\,[X]) \leq$ SE $(t\,[Z], s\,[Z])$, that is, $X \hookrightarrow Z$.

(4) The decomposition rule and the pseudotransitivity rule follow easily from FA1-FA3

(5) Now we prove the union rule. Since $X \hookrightarrow Y$, so we may augment X to $X \hookrightarrow XY$ by FA2. Also for $X \hookrightarrow Z$, we may augment Y to $XY \hookrightarrow YZ$ by FA2. By transitivity, $X \hookrightarrow XY$ and $XY \hookrightarrow YZ$ imply $X \hookrightarrow YZ$.

The reference rules for *FMVDs*:

FA4 (Complementation): If $X \hookrightarrow\hookrightarrow Y$, then $X \hookrightarrow\hookrightarrow (U - XY)$.

FA5 (Augmentation): If $X \hookrightarrow\hookrightarrow Y$ and $V \subseteq W$, then $WX \hookrightarrow\hookrightarrow VY$.

FA6 (Transitivity): If $X \hookrightarrow\hookrightarrow Y$ and $Y \hookrightarrow\hookrightarrow Z$, then $X \hookrightarrow\hookrightarrow (Z - Y)$.

FA12 (Union): If $X \hookrightarrow\hookrightarrow Y$ and $X \hookrightarrow\hookrightarrow Z$, then $X \hookrightarrow\hookrightarrow YZ$.

FA13 (Decomposition): If $X \hookrightarrow\hookrightarrow Y$ and $X \hookrightarrow\hookrightarrow Z$, then $X \hookrightarrow\hookrightarrow Y \cap Z$ and $X \hookrightarrow\hookrightarrow (Y - Z)$.

FA14 (Pseudotransitivity): If $X \hookrightarrow\hookrightarrow Y$ and $YW \hookrightarrow\hookrightarrow Z$, then $XW \hookrightarrow\hookrightarrow (Z - YW)$.

Theorem 7.4: The inference rules FA4-FA6 and FA12-FA14 are sound.

Proof:

Proofs of FA4, FA6, and FA12 follow directly from the proofs in (Beeri, Fagin and Howard, 1977; Bhattacharjee and Mazumdar, 1998; Tripathy and Sakena, 1990). The decomposition rule follows easily from FA4 and FA12 and the pseudotransitivity rule follows easily from FA5 and FA6.

We prove FA5 in the following. Since *FMVD*: $X \hookrightarrow\hookrightarrow Y$ hold in a relation r, SE $(u\,[X], t\,[X]) \geq$ SE $(t\,[X], s\,[X])$, SE $(u\,[Y], t\,[Y]) \geq$ SE $(t\,[X], s\,[X])$, and SE $(u\,[U - XY], s\,[U - XY]) \geq$ SE $(t\,[X], s\,[X])$ for t, s, and $u \in r$. We have min (SE $(u\,[X], t\,[X])$, SE $(u\,[W], t\,[W])$) $\geq$ min (SE $(t\,[X], s\,[X])$, $(t\,[W], s\,[W])$) and min (SE $(u\,[Y], t\,[Y])$, SE $(u\,[V], t\,[V])$) $\geq$ min (SE $(t\,[X], s\,[X])$, SE $(u\,[V], t\,[V])$) $\geq$ min (SE $(t\,[X], s\,[X])$, $(t\,[W], s\,[W])$) because of $V \subseteq W$. Besides, SE $(u\,[U - XYWV], s\,[U - XYWV]) \geq$ SE $(u\,[U - XY], s\,[U - XY]) \geq$ SE $(t\,[X], s\,[X]) \geq$ SE $(t\,[WX], s\,[WX])$. So $WX \hookrightarrow\hookrightarrow VY$ holds in r.

The mixed reference rules for *FFDs* and *FMVDs*:

FA7: If $X \hookrightarrow Y$, then $X \hookrightarrow\hookrightarrow Y$.

FA8: If $X \hookrightarrow\hookrightarrow Y$, $Z \subseteq Y$, $W \cap Y = \Phi$, and $W \hookrightarrow Z$, then $X \hookrightarrow Z$.

Theorem 7.5: The inference rules FA7-FA8 are sound.

Proof:

(1) Suppose $X \hookrightarrow\hookrightarrow Y$ not hold in r. Then SE $(u\,[Y], t\,[Y]) <$ SE $(t\,[X], s\,[X])$ or SE $(u\,[Z], s\,[Z]) <$ SE $(t\,[X], s\,[X])$ when SE $(u\,[X], t\,[X]) \geq$ SE $(t\,[X],$

s [X]). Since $X \hookrightarrow Y$ hold in r, we have SE (t [X], s [X]) $\leq$ SE (t [Y], s [Y]), SE (u [X], t [X]) $\leq$ SE (u [Y], t [Y]), and SE (u [X], s [X]) $\leq$ SE (u [Y], s [Y]). If SE (u [Y], t [Y]) < SE (t [X], s [X]), then we have SE (t [X], s [X]) $\leq$ (u [X], t [X]) $\leq$ SE (u [Y], t [Y]) < SE (t [X], s [X]). There is a contradictory. Similarly, using FA2 (Augmentation) and Proposition 1, we can draw that there exists a contradictory if SE (u [Z], s [Z]) < SE (t [X], s [X]).

(2) Suppose that $X \hookrightarrow\hookrightarrow Y$ and $W \hookrightarrow Z$ hold in a relation r (R), where $W \cap Y = \Phi$ and $Z \subseteq Y$, but $X \hookrightarrow Z$ does not hold in r. Then there are tuple t and s in r such that SE (t [X], s [X]) > SE (t [Z], s [Z]). By $X \hookrightarrow\hookrightarrow Y$ applied to t and s, there is a tuple u in r such that SE (u [X], t [X]) $\geq \alpha$, SE (u [Y], t [Y]) $\geq \alpha$, and SE (u [$R - XY$], s [$R - XY$]) $\geq \alpha$, where SE (t [X], s [X]) $= \alpha$. Since $W \cap Y = \Phi$ and $W \subseteq X(R - XY)$, hence SE (u [W], s [W]) $\geq$ SE (u [$X(R - XY)$], s [$X(R - XY)$]) = min (SE (u [X], s [X]), SE (u [$R - XY$], s [$R - XY$])) $\geq \alpha$. As $Z \subseteq Y$, SE (u [Z], t [Z]) $\geq$ SE (u [Y], t [Y]) $\geq \alpha$. Hence SE (u [Z], s [Z]) < SE (t [X], s [X]), and then SE (u [W], s [W]) > SE (u [Z], s [Z]). This contradicts $W \hookrightarrow Z$. So we can conclude that $X \hookrightarrow Z$ holds in r.

Theorem 7.6: The inference rules FA1-FA14 are complete.
Proof[(Liu, 1997)]:

Let F, G be the sets of *FFD*s and *FMVD*s on the universe of discourse U, respectively. The theorem means that any *FFD*: $f = A \hookrightarrow B$ and *FMVD*: $g = C \hookrightarrow\hookrightarrow D$, which are logically implied by F and G, can be deduced from F and G by FA1-FA14.

Let (F, G)+ be the closures of F and G. For a give *FFD*: $f = A \hookrightarrow B$ or *FMVD*: $g = C \hookrightarrow\hookrightarrow D$ that not belong to (F, G)+, there exists an instance r on U such as all dependencies in F and G are valid in r but $A \hookrightarrow B$ or $C \hookrightarrow\hookrightarrow D$ is invalid in r.

Let F', G' be two sets of classical dependencies, which correspond to F, G, namely, $F' = \{X \to Y | X \hookrightarrow Y \in F\}$, $G' = \{X \to\to Y | X \hookrightarrow\hookrightarrow Y \in G\}$. Let *FD*: $f' = A \to B$ and *MVD*: $g' = C \to\to D$. We can construct a relational instance r', which satisfies F' and G' but does not satisfy f' and g'. By Theorem 7.1 and Theorem 7.2, we know that r' satisfies F and G but does not satisfy f and g. This problem transformed into the correspondence classical problem (Beeri, Fagin and Howard, 1977).

Theorem 7.7: The inference rules FA1-FA14 are sound and complete.

The soundness of inference rules follow from Theorem 7.4 and Theorem 7.5 and the completeness of inference rules follow from Theorem 7.6.

7.5   Fuzzy Algebra Operations

7.5.1   Fuzzy Relational Algebra

Union: Let r and s be two union-compatible fuzzy relations on the scheme R (A1, A2, ..., An). Let $\alpha = \{\alpha i | \alpha i \in [0, 1] \wedge 1 \leq i \leq n\}$ be the threshold of the resemblance relations on attribute domains and $\beta \in [0, 1]$ be a given threshold. Then the union of these two relations is defined as follows. It is clear that fuzzy union is essentially a α-β-union.

$$r \cup s = \{t \mid (\forall v) (v \in s \wedge t \in r \Rightarrow \text{SE}\alpha (t, v) < \beta) \vee (\forall u) (u \in r \wedge t \in s$$
$$\Rightarrow \text{SE}\alpha (t, u) < \beta) \vee ((\exists u) (\exists v) (u \in r \wedge v \in s \Rightarrow \text{SE}\alpha (u, v) \geq \beta \wedge t = u$$
$$\cup_f v)\}$$

Let r and s be two fuzzy relations shown respectively in Table 7-3 and Table 7-4, where there is a resemblance relation on attribute "*Age*" given in Figure 7-3 and its threshold is given as $\alpha = 0.9$. Another threshold is given as $\beta = 0.8$ (the same is in the following examples).

Table 7-3. Fuzzy Relation r

	ID	Dept	Age
$u1$	9106	CS	{0.3/19, 0.8/20, 0.7/21}
$u2$	9107	CS	{0.6/30, 0.9/31, 0.7/32}
$u3$	9711	EE	{0.5/32, 0.7/33, 0.6/34}

Table 7-4. Fuzzy Relation s

	ID	Dept	Age
$v1$	9106	CS	{0.8/20, 0.7/21}
$v2$	9108	CS	{0.5/32, 0.8/33, 0.6/34}
$v3$	9711	EE	{0.8/32, 0.6/33, 0.7/34}

Res	30	31	32	33	34	35
30	1.0	0.5	0.4	0.3	0.2	0.2
31		1.0	0.6	0.5	0.4	0.3
32			1.0	0.7	0.6	0.5
33				1.0	0.8	0.7
34					1.0	0.95
35						1.0

Figure 7-4. Resemblance Relation on Attribute Age

It is clear that tuple $u2$ in r and tuple $v2$ in s are not redundant. Now let us look at the semantics between $u1$ and $v1$ as well as $u3$ and $v3$.

$SE_{0.9}$ ($u1$ (Age), $v1$ (Age)) = min ($SID_{0.9}$ ($u1$ (Age), $v1$ (Age)), $SID_{0.9}$ ($v1$ (Age), $u1$ (Age))) = min ((0.8 + 0.7)/(0.8 + 0.7), (0.8 + 0.7)/(0.3 + 0.8 + 0.7)) = min (1.0, 0.83) = 0.83 $\geq \beta$,

and

$SE_{0.9}$ ($u3$ (Age), $v3$ (Age)) = min ($SID_{0.9}$ ($u3$ (Age), $v3$ (Age)), $SID_{0.9}$ ($v3$ (Age), $u3$ (Age))) = min ((0.5 + 0.6 + 0.6)/(0.8 + 0.6 + 0.7), (0.5 + 0.6 + 0.6)/(0.5 + 0.7 + 0.6)) = min (0.81, 0.94) $\geq \beta$.

Therefore,

$SE_{0.9}$ ($u1$, $v1$) = min ($SE_{0.9}$ ($u1$ ($Card$), $v1$ ($Card$)), $SE_{0.9}$ ($u1$ ($Dept$), $v1$ ($Dept$)), $SE_{0.9}$ ($u1$ (Age), $v1$ (Age))) = min (1, 1, 0.83) = 0.83 $\geq \beta$,

and

$SE_{0.9}$ ($u3$, $v3$) = min ($SE_{0.9}$ ($u3$ ($Card$), $v3$ ($Card$)), $SE_{0.9}$ ($u3$ ($Dept$), $v3$ ($Dept$)), $SE_{0.9}$ ($u3$ (Age), $v3$ (Age))) = min (1, 1, 0.81) = 0.81 $\geq \beta$.

One can conclude that tuple u1 in r and tuple v1 in s are redundant and tuple u3 in r and tuple v3 in s are redundant. According to the definitions of fuzzy union and "f", the result relation of union of r and s is shown in Table 7-5.

Table 7-5. The Union Operation $r \cup s$

ID	Dept	Age
9106	CS	{0.3/19, 0.8/20, 0.7/21}
9107	CS	{0.6/30, 0.9/31, 0.7/32}
9108	CS	{0.5/32, 0.8/33, 0.6/34}
9711	EE	{0.8/32, 0.7/33, 0.7/34}

Difference: Let r and s be the same as the above. Their difference is defined as follows.

$$r - s = \{t \mid (\forall v)\,(v \in s \wedge t \in r \wedge SE_\alpha\,(t, v) < \beta) \vee ((\exists u)\,(\exists v)\,(u \in r \wedge v \in s \wedge SE_\alpha\,(u, v) \geq \beta \wedge t = u -_f v)\}$$

The fuzzy difference is also an α-β-difference. The difference of the fuzzy relations in Table 7-3 and Table 7-4 is shown in Table 7-6.

Table 7-6. The Difference Operation $r - s$

ID	Dept	Age
9106	CS	{0.3/19}
9107	CS	{0.6/30, 0.9/31, 0.7/32}
9711	EE	{0.1/33}

Cartesian Product: The Cartesian product of fuzzy relations is the same as one under classical relational databases. Let r and s be two fuzzy relations on schema R and S, respectively. Then

$$r \times s = \{t\,(R \cup S) \mid (\forall\, u)\,(\forall\, v)\,(u \in r \wedge v \in s \wedge t\,[R] = u\,[R] \wedge t\,[S] = v\,[S])\}$$

Selection: Let r (R) be a fuzzy relation and P be a predicate denoted selection condition. In classical relational databases, a predicate is formed through combining the basic clause $X\,\theta\,Y$ as operands with operators $\neg$, $\wedge$, and $\vee$, where $\theta \in \{>, <, =, \neq, \geq, \leq\}$, and X and Y may be constants, attributes, or expressions which are formed through combining constants, attributes or expressions with arithmetic operations. Under a fuzzy relational database environment, the predicate P may be fuzzy, denoted P_f, to implement fuzzy query for fuzzy databases. In P_f, the constants and attributes may be fuzzy, so the expressions may also be fuzzy. The evaluation of a fuzzy expression can be conducted by using Zadeh's extension principle. Based on the same consideration, the "θ" should be fuzzy comparison operations $\succ_\beta$, $\prec_\beta$, $\succeq_\beta$, $\preceq_\beta$, $\approx_\beta$, and $\not\approx_\beta$, in P_f, where β is a threshold. Let π_A and π_B be two fuzzy data over $U = \{u1, u2, \ldots, un\}$ and α be the threshold of the resemblance relation on U. Then

(a) $\pi_A \approx_\beta \pi_B$ if $SE_\alpha\,(\pi_A, \pi_B) \geq \beta$,

(b) $\pi_A \not\approx_\beta \pi_B$ if $SE_\alpha\,(\pi_A, \pi_B) < \beta$,

(c) $\pi_A \succ_\beta \pi_B$ if $\pi_A \not\approx_\beta \pi_B$ and max (supp (π_A)) > max (supp (π_B)),

(d) $\pi_A \succeq_\beta \pi_B$ if $\pi_A \approx_\beta \pi_B$ or $\pi_A \succ_\beta \pi_B$,

(e) $\pi_A \prec_\beta \pi_B$ if $\pi_A \not\approx_\beta \pi_B$ and max (supp (π_A)) < max (supp (π_B)), and

(f) $\pi_A \preceq_\beta \pi_B$ if $\pi_A \not\approx_\beta \pi_B$ or $\pi_A \prec_\beta \pi_B$.

Then the selection on r for P_f is defined as follows.

$$\sigma_{Pf}\,(r) = \{t \mid t \in r \wedge P_f\,(t)\}$$

A fuzzy relation r is shown in Table 7-7. Now let us retrieve such information that the age is about 25-26 and the department is *IS*, where fuzzy condition "about 25-26" is represented by the possibility distribution $\{1.0/25, 0.9/26, 0.3/27\}$. Then

$SE_{1.0}$ (t4 (Age), $\{1.0/25, 0.9/26, 0.3/27\}$) = min (0.82, 0.86) = 0.82 $\geq \beta$, so t (Age) $\approx_\beta$ $\{1.0/25, 0.9/26, 0.3/27\}$.

Table 7-7. Fuzzy Relation *r*

	ID	Dept	Age	Degree	Nationality	Office
t1	9106	CS	$\{0.5/18, 0.9/19, 0.7/20\}$	M. Phil	USA	Y1101
t2	9107	CS	$\{0.4/20, 0.8/21, 0.6/22\}$	M. Phil	Canada	Y1101
t3	9705	IS	$\{0.2/24, 0.9/25, 1.0/26\}$	M. Phil	France	B6280
t4	9706	IS	$\{0.1/28, 0.7/29, 0.6/30\}$	Ph.D.	Italy	B6280
t5	9707	IS	$\{0.6/29, 0.7/30, 0.1/31\}$	Ph.D.	France	B6280

It is easy to see that tuple $t3$ satisfies the selection condition. The other tuples in r do not satisfy the condition. The result relation of the selection is shown in Table 7-8.

Table 7-8. Selection Operation $\sigma_{\text{Dept} = \text{"IS"} \wedge \text{Age} \approx \text{"}\{1.0/25., 0.9/26, 0.3/27\}\text{"}}$ (r)

ID	Dept	Age	Degree	Nationality	Office
9705	IS	{0.2/24, 0.9/25, 1.0/26}	M. Phil	France	B6280

Projection: Let r (R) be a fuzzy relation and attribute subset $S \subset R$. The projection of r on S is defined as follows.

$$\Pi_S (r) = \{t (S)| (\forall u) (u \in r (R) \wedge t = \cup_f u [R])\}$$

Considering redundancy removal in a result relation, fuzzy projection is a α-β-projection. The projection of a fuzzy relation in Table 7-7 is shown in Table 7-9. Here, there are no data redundancies after projecting tuples $t1$, $t2$, and $t3$ and the first three tuples in Table 7-9. But there exists data redundancy after projecting tuples $t4$ and $t5$. The result of removing redundancy forms that last tuple in Table 7-9.

Table 7-9. Projection Operation $\Pi_{\{\text{Dept, Age}\}}$ (r)

Dept	Age
CS	{0.5/18, 0.9/19, 0.7/20}
CS	{0.4/20, 0.8/21, 0.6/22}
IS	{0.2/24, 0.9/25, 1.0/26}
IS	{0.1/28, 0.7/29, 0.7/30, 0.1/31}

The five operations above are called primitive operations in relational databases. There are three additional operation intersection, join, and division, which can be defined by the primitive operations.

Intersection: Let r and s be two union-compatible fuzzy relations. Then fuzzy intersection of these two relations can be defined in terms of fuzzy difference operation as:

$$r \cap s = r - (r - s).$$

Join: Let r (R) and s (S) be any two fuzzy relations. Pf is a conditional predicate in the form of $A \theta B$, where $\theta \in \{\succ_\beta, \prec_\beta, \succeq_\beta, \preceq_\beta, \approx_\beta, \not\approx_\beta\}$, $A \in R$, and $B \in S$. Then fuzzy join of these two relations can be defined in terms of fuzzy selection operation as:

$$r \bowtie_{Pf} s = \sigma_{Pf} (r \times s).$$

When attributes A and B are identical and "θ" takes $\approx_\beta$, the fuzzy join becomes the fuzzy natural join, denoted $r \bowtie s$. Being the special case of fuzzy join, fuzzy natural join can be evaluated with the definition above. In the following, the definition of fuzzy natural join is given directly. Let $Q = R \cap S$. Then

$$r \bowtie s = \{t((R - Q) \cup S) \mid (\exists\, u)\,(\exists\, v)\,(u \in r \wedge v \in s \wedge \mathrm{SE}_\alpha\,(u\,[Q], v\,[Q]) \geq \beta \wedge t\,[R - Q] = u\,[R - Q] \wedge t\,[S - Q] = v\,[S - Q] \wedge t\,[Q] = u\,[Q]\cap_f v\,[Q])\}$$

The natural join of the fuzzy relations in Table 7-10 and in Table 7-11 is shown in Table 7-12. Here, there is a resemblance relation *Res* on Age shown in Figure 7-4 on the attribute *Age*. In fuzzy relation r and s, only $u2$ [*Age*] $\approx_\beta v2$ [*Age*] and $u4$ [*Age*] $\approx_\beta v4$ [*Age*] hold.

Table 7-10. Fuzzy Relation r

	ID	Dept	Age
$u1$	9106	CS	{0.3/19, 0.8/20, 0.7/21}
$u2$	9107	EE	{0.8/21, 0.7/22}
$u3$	9711	IS	{0.6/27, 0.9/28, 0.7/29}
$u4$	9712	EE	{0.8/32, 0.9/33, 0.6/34}

Table 7-11. Fuzzy Relation s

	First Name	Age	Degree	Nationality	Office
$v1$	Mary	{0.9/19, 0.7/20, 0.2/21}	M. Phil	USA	Y1101
$v2$	Tom	{1.0/21, 0.7/22}	Ph.D.	Canada	Y1101
$v3$	John	{0.6/24, 1.0/25, 0.7/26}	M. Phil	France	B6280
$v4$	Jack	{0.7/32, 1.0/33, 0.7/34}	Ph.D.	Italy	B6280

Table 7-12. Natural Join Operation $r \bowtie s$

ID	First Name	Dept	Age	Degree	Nationality	Office
9107	Tom	EE	{0.8/21, 0.7/22}	Ph.D.	Canada	Y1101
9712	Jack	EE	{0.7/32, 0.9/33, 0.6/34}	Ph.D.	Italy	B6280

Division: Division, referred to quotient operation sometimes, is used to find out the sub-relation $r \div s$ of a relation r, containing sub-tuples of r which have for complements in r all the tuples of a relation s. In classical relational databases, the division operation is defined by

$$r \div s = \{t \mid (\forall\, u)\,(u \in s \wedge (t, u) \in r)\},$$

where u is a tuple of s and t is a sub-tuple of r such that (t, u) is a tuple of r. Let $r\,(R)$ and $s\,(S)$ be two fuzzy relations, where $S \subset R$. Let $Q = R - S$. Then the fuzzy division of r and s can be defined as:

$r \div s = \Pi_Q(r) - \Pi_Q(r(Q) \times s - r)$.

The rename and outerunion are the other relational operations in addition to the eight operation defined above. Their definitions are given as follows.

Rename: This operation is used to change the names of some attributes of a relation. Let $r(R)$ be a fuzzy relation, and let A and B be two attributes satisfying $A \in R$ and $B \notin R$, where A and B have the same domain. Let $S = (R - \{A\}) \cup \{B\}$. Then r with A renamed to B is defined as

$$\rho_{A \leftarrow B}(r) = \{t[S] \mid (\forall y)(y \in r \wedge t[S - B] = y[R - A] \wedge t[B] = y[A])\}.$$

Outerunion: The common union operation requires two source relations be union-compatible. In order to integrate heterogeneous multiple relations, outerunion operation has widely been used in relational databases. Here, the definition of fuzzy outerunion operation is given so that heterogeneous fuzzy data resources can be integrated.

Let $r(K, A, X)$ and $s(K, A, Y)$ be two fuzzy relations, where K is primary key. The outerunion of r and s, denoted by $r \cup s$, is defined as

$$r \cup s = \{t[KAXY] \mid (\exists u)(\exists v)(u \in r \wedge v \in s \wedge t[K] = u[K] = v[K] \wedge$$
$$(\forall S)(S \in A \wedge t[S] = u[S] \cup_f v[S]) \wedge t[X] = u[X] \wedge t[Y]) = v[Y]) \vee$$
$$((\exists u)(\forall v)(u \in r \wedge v \in s \wedge t[K] = u[K] \wedge t[A] = u[A] \wedge t[X] = u$$
$$[X] \wedge t[Y] = \varphi \wedge v[K] \neq t[K]) \vee ((\exists v)(\forall u)(v \in s \wedge u \in r \wedge t[K] = v$$
$$[K] \wedge t[A] = v[A] \wedge t[X] = v[Y] \wedge t[X] = \varphi \wedge u[K] \neq t[K])\}.$$

It can be seen from the definition above that fuzzy values are not permitted to appear in primary key in fuzzy outerunion. The outerunion of fuzzy relations in Table 7-13 and Table 7-14 is shown in Table 7-15

Table 7-13. Fuzzy Relation r

ID	Office	Age
9106	Y1415	{0.3/19, 0.8/20, 0.7/21}
9107	B6280	{0.6/30, 0.9/31, 0.7/32}

Table 7-14. Fuzzy Relation s

ID	Degree	Age
9106	{0.7/BE, 0.5/MPh}	{0.3/19, 0.8/20, 0.7/21}
9108	{0.6/M.Ph, 0.8/Ph.D}	{0.6/30, 0.9/31, 0.7/32}

Table 7-15. Outerunion Operation $r \cup s$

ID	Office	Age	Degree
9106	Y1415	{0.3/19, 0.8/20, 0.7/21}	{0.7/BE, 0.5/MPh}
9107	B6280	{0.6/30, 0.9/31, 0.7/32}	φ
9108	φ	{0.6/30, 0.9/31, 0.7/32}	{0.6/M.Ph, 0.8/Ph.D}

7.5.2   Properties of Fuzzy Relational Algebra

Being similar to the conventional relational databases, the proposed fuzzy relational algebra is sound. In other words, it is closed. It means that the results of all operations are valid relations. In detail, the result relations produced by fuzzy relational operations satisfy the following three criteria:

(a) the attribute values must come from an appropriate attribute domain,

(b) there are no duplicate tuples in a relation, and

(c) the relation must be a finite set of tuples.

Projection, division, and selection take out a part from the source relation in either column direction or row direction. Because the attribute values in source relation must belong to the appropriate attribute domain, the attribute values in these three result relations must come from the appropriate attribute domain. Union, difference, and intersection operations are conducted under union-compatible condition, which satisfies the first criterion. In join and Cartesian product, the attribute values in result relations come from two source relations, respectively, and they must be within the appropriate attribute domains. It is clear that rename operation satisfies the first criterion. As to outerunion operation, it is similar to natural join and thus the first criterion can also be satisfied.

For selection and rename, if there are no redundant tuples in ordinary relation, there are no redundant tuples in the result relations. There exist no redundant tuples in the result relations of union, difference, intersection, join, Cartesian product, division, projection, and outerunion. This can be ensured by the definitions of those operations because the removal of redundancies has been considered. Therefore, the second criterion is satisfied.

Now let us look at the satisfactory situation of the third criterion. Let r and s be two fuzzy relations, and let $|r|$ and $|s|$ denote the numbers of tuples in r and s, respectively. It is easy to see that $0 \leq |\sigma_{Pf}(r)| \leq |r|$ for fuzzy selection. This implies that when no any tuple in r satisfies the selection condition, the tuple number in the result relation is 0, and that when all tuples in r satisfy the selection condition, one obtains $|\sigma_{Pf}(r)| = |r|$. When part of the tuples in r satisfy the selection condition, $|\sigma_{Pf}(r)|$ must be greater than 0 and less than $|r|$. For projection $\Pi_S(r)$, if all tuples in r are redundant after projecting, then $|\Pi_S(r)| = 1$; if there is not any redundancy in r after projecting, then $|\Pi_S(r)| = |r|$. In the other situations, $|\Pi_S(r)|$ must be greater than 1 and less than $|r|$, i.e., $1 \leq |\Pi_S(r)| \leq |r|$. Additionally, $|r \cup s|$ must not be greater than $|r| + |s|$, $|r - s|$, $|r \cap s|$ and $|r \div s|$ must not be greater than $|r|$, and $|r \bowtie_{Pf} s|$ and $|r \times s|$ must not be greater than $|r| \times |s|$. In addition, $|\rho_{A \leftarrow B}$

$(r)| = |r|$ and $|r \mathbin{\hat{\cup}} s| \le |r| + |s|$. Since the number of tuples in the result relation is closely related with the source relations and the source relations are finite, the result relations must be finite.

In addition, fuzzy set operations in relational algebra have the same properties as those of classical set operations. Let r, s, and u be three union-compatible fuzzy relations. Then

(a) $r \cup s = s \cup r$ and $r \cap s = s \cap r$,   (commutativity)

(b) $r \cup r = r$ and $r \cap r = r$,   (idempotence)

(c) $r \cap (r \cup s) = r$ and $r \cup (r \cap s) = r$,   (absorption)

(d) $(r \cup s) \cup u = r \cup (s \cup u)$ and $(r \cap s) \cap u = r \cap (s \cap u)$,

                                       (associativity)

(e) $r \cap (s \cup u) = (r \cap s) \cup (r \cap s)$ and $r \cup (s \cap u) = (r \cup s) \cap (r \cup s)$, and   (distributivity)

(f) $r \cup s = r \cup (s - r)$ and $r \cap s = r - (r - s)$.

The following properties are also held in fuzzy operations in relational algebra. Let r and s be two fuzzy relations on schema R and u be a fuzzy relation on schema Q. Let P_f be a selection predicate involving attributes of R. Then

(a) $u \bowtie (r \cup s) = (u \bowtie r) \cup (u \bowtie s)$ and $u \bowtie (r - s) = (u \bowtie r) - (u \bowtie s)$,

(b) $\sigma_{Pf}(r \cup s) = \sigma_{Pf}(r) \cup \sigma_{Pf}(s)$ and $\sigma_{Pf}(r - s) = \sigma_{Pf}(r) - \sigma_{Pf}(s)$, and

(c) $\sigma_{Pf}(u \bowtie r) = u \bowtie \sigma_{Pf}(r)$.

These properties can be proven by the definitions of fuzzy operations in relational algebra.

7.6   Flexible Query with SQL

Query processing in relational databases refers to such procedure that the tuples satisfying a given selection condition is selected and then they are delivered to the user according to the required formats. These format requirements include which attributes appear in the result relation and if the result relation is grouped and ordered over the given attribute(s). So a query can be seen as comprising two components, namely, a Boolean selection condition and some format requirements. For the sake of the simple illustration, some format requirements are ignored in the following discussion. Then, utilizing a well-known relational query language, i.e., SQL (Structured Query Language), a basic query is represented as

SELECT <attribute list> *FROM* <relation name> *WHERE* <selection condition>, where *<attribute list>* is the list of attributes separated by commas: *Attribute₁, Attribute₂, ..., Attributeₙ*. At least one attribute name must be specified in *<attribute list>*. Attributes that take place in *<attribute list>* are selected from the associated relation which is specified in the **FROM** statement. *<relation name>* is specified with **FROM**, which specifies the relation name from which the attributes are selected with the **SELECT** statement.

Classical relational databases suffer from a lack of flexibility to query. The given selection condition and the contents of the relation are all crisp. In this context, a tuple will either definitely or definitely not satisfy the condition. In incomplete relational databases, however, a tuple may satisfy with a certain possibility and a certain necessity degree the selection condition even if the condition is crisp due to the fact that tuples are incomplete. On the other hand, imprecise information may exist in the selection condition and the situation that a tuple may more or less satisfy the selection condition may also occur. For classical relational databases, however, the query with imprecise selection condition is also useful in order to satisfy the requirement of decision making. The classical query processing is obviously too rigid for two cases. A query is flexible if the following conditions can be satisfied (Bosc and Pivert, 1992; Bosc and Pivert, 1995):

(a) A qualitative distinction between the selected tuples is allowed.
(b) Imprecise conditions inside queries are introduced when the user cannot define his/her needs in a definite way, or when a prespecified number of responses are desired and therefore a margin is allowed to interpret the query.

Typically, the case in (a) occurs when the queried relational databases contain incomplete information and the query conditions are crisp. In a relation of product design, for example, it is supposed that there are four products A, B, C and D which lengths are respectively interval values [5, 8], [7, 9], [10, 14] and [11, 14]. Now let us query this relation with the condition "length = 8". Then A and B may satisfy the condition whereas C and D must not satisfy the condition. The case (b) typically occurs when the query conditions are imprecise even if the queried relational databases do not contain incomplete information. For example, there are four products E, F, G and H which lengths are respectively crisp values 8, 9, 12 and 14. Now let us query this relation with the condition *"length is between 10 and 15"*. Then G and H should satisfy the condition whereas E and F must not satisfy the condition. It can be seen that flexible queries permit users to provide incomplete query conditions and the query results include the tuples satisfying the conditions definitely as well as the tuples satisfying the conditions indefinitely.

For fuzzy relational databases, just like the definition of fuzzy selection operation given above, a basic query condition with form of X θ Y may consist of fuzzy comparison operations $\succ_\beta$, $\prec_\beta$, $\succeq_\beta$, $\preceq_\beta$, $\approx_\beta$, and $\not\approx_\beta$ for "θ" and fuzzy constants for "Y", where β is a threshold. Then under a given threshold, a tuple either satisfies the condition if the condition is true or does not satisfy the condition if the condition is false. Since the basic conditions are only evaluated true or false, complex query conditions comprised of basic conditions and logical operations can be evaluated true or false by means of 2VL. So based on the given threshold, all tuples in fuzzy relation are divided into two parts for a query, namely, answer part and no answer part. Compared with the queries for relational databases containing partial values and null values (Lipski, 1979), the query answers for fuzzy relational databases are only sure answers. There are no possible answers to be included. The reason that this situation occurs is because of the usage of threshold. The basic conditions with which evaluations of semantic relationship are less than the threshold are regarded false. Therefore, depending on the different thresholds that are values in [0,1], the same query for the same fuzzy relation may have different query answers. The queries for fuzzy relational databases are concerned with the number choices of threshold. Therefore, the following syntax of SQL is used to represent the select sentence:

SELECT <attribute list> FROM <relation name> WHERE <selection condition> [WITH POSSIBILITY <threshold>],

where *<attribute list>* and *<relation name>* are the same as the SQL in classical relational, *<selection condition>* is a fuzzy select condition, and *<threshold>* is a crisp threshold in [0, 1]. Utilizing such SQL, one can get such tuples that satisfy the given select condition and the given threshold. Note that the item **WITH POSSIBILITY** *<threshold>* can be omitted. The default of *<threshold>* is exactly 1 at this moment.

Here, a problem exists in fuzzy queries, i.e., the strength of query answers to the queries is not known. Such information is useful sometimes. Let us look at an example in Table 7-16.

Table 7-16. Fuzzy Relation *r*

Sensor Name	Temperature
A	{0.2/254, 0.7/256, 0.9/258, 0.6/260}
B	{0.8/256, 0.9/258, 0.6/260, 0.3/262}

One makes a query:

SELECT Sensor Name FROM r WHERE Temperature $\approx$ {0.7/256, 0.9/258, 0.6/260, 0.3/262} *WITH POSSIBILITY 0.85.*

Then
   SE ({0.2/254, 0.7/256, 0.9/258, 0.6/260}, {0.7/256, 0.9/258, 0.6/260,
      0.3/262}) = 0.88 > 0.85
   SE ({0.8/256, 0.9/258, 0.6/260, 0.3/262}, {0.7/256, 0.9/258, 0.6/260,
      0.3/262}) = 0.96 > 0.85

So sensors A and B all satisfy the condition and become the query answers. It is clear that sensor B more satisfies the condition than sensor A. However, in query answers, they cannot be identified with respect to the satisfaction degrees.

In order to estimate the strength of query answers to the queries, such restriction is relaxed that the basic query conditions are only evaluated true or false according to the threshold. Here a multivalued logic (MVL) system is introduced, in which each logical value is a number in [0, 1]. Based on the MVL, two basic query conditions $X = Y$ and $X > Y$ are defined as follows.

   (a) $X = Y$ is evaluated to be a logical value $\mu (X = Y) = SE (X, Y)$;
   (b) $X > Y$ is evaluated to be a logical value $\mu (X > Y)$, where

$$\mu(X,Y) = \begin{cases} 0 : \text{if min (supp (X))} \leq \text{min (supp (Y)) and max (supp (X))} \leq \text{max (supp (Y))} \\ 1 - SE(X,Y) : \text{otherwise} \end{cases}$$

The logical operations *AND*, *OR*, and *NOT* under MVL are defined as min (), max () and complementation, respectively. Let $\mu1$ and $\mu2$ be logical values under MVL. It is clear that $\mu1$ and $\mu2$ are all in [0, 1]. Then

   (a) $\mu1$ *AND* $\mu2$ = min $(1, \mu2)$,
   (b) $\mu1$ *OR* $\mu2$ = max $(1, \mu2)$, and
   (c) *NOT* $\mu1 = 1 - \mu1$.

For a query with complex query condition, the logical value that each tuple in the fuzzy relation satisfies the condition can be evaluated according to the comparison operations and logical operations under MVL. This logical value can be seen as the strength that the tuple matches the condition. In general, the tuples whose strength is zero are ignored. Only the tuples whose strengths are larger than zero are permitted in query answers and these tuples can be ranked by the descent of the strengths. When a threshold is given, the tuples that strengths are less than the threshold can be cut. Since the tuples in query answers are connected with the strengths matching the query, one can choose the tuple with the maximum strength from the query answers. After introducing MVL, the query answers can be measured through the matching strengths.

In the example in Table 7-16, the matching strengths of sensors A and B to the given condition are 0.88 and 0.96, respectively. Such results demonstrate that sensor B more satisfies the condition than sensor A.

7.7   Updating Fuzzy Relational Databases

One of the major tasks of database management systems (DBMS) is to update databases. Three kinds of update operations can be identified in relational databases, which are *Insertion, Deletion,* and *Modification.* Insertion operation is to insert a valid tuple into a given relation and deletion operation is to remove the tuples that satisfy the given condition(s) from a given relation. As to modification operation, the tuples that satisfy the given condition(s) are modified to meet another given condition(s). So modification operation can be viewed as a synthesis of deletion operation and insertion operation, where we first remove the tuples that satisfy the given condition(s) from the given relation, then modify these removed tuples to meet another given condition(s), and finally the modified tuples are inserted into the original relation.

Fuzzy relational databases have extensively investigated for last two decades. However, less research has been done in updating fuzzy relational databases. It is hard to update fuzzy relational databases because of information fuzziness. In this section, we discuss these three update operations for fuzzy relational databases. We investigate the update strategies and develop the algorithm to implement the update of fuzzy relational databases.

7.7.1   Insertion Operation

Only valid tuples can be inserted into a fuzzy relation. So when a tuple is to be inserted in to a given fuzzy relation, it must be validated before conducting insertion operation. A valid inserting tuple means that it must satisfy the followings:

(a) its key value(s) must be crisp,
(b) it is not redundant with any tuple in the given fuzzy relation, and
(c) it must satisfy the data integrity constraints of the given fuzzy relation.

The key of tuples is used to identify tuples uniquely. If the inserting tuple has fuzzy key value, the insertion operation is rejected. The tuple whose key value is crisp is sound. Of course, the insertion operation is rejected if the inserting tuple is redundant with a tuple in the given fuzzy relation.

Now let us focus on the situation that the inserting tuple does not satisfy the data integrity constraints of the given fuzzy relation. In the classical relational databases, data integrity constraints (functional and multivalued dependencies) are "hard". But the functional and multivalued dependencies in the fuzzy relational databases are a kind of "soft" constraints. Here the "soft" constraints do not mean that they can be broken by the inserting tuple but mean that it is possible to make the inserting tuple satisfy the fuzzy functional and/or multivalued dependencies when it does not satisfy such constraints. The reason that we can do that is because of information imperfection of attribute values.

In (Chang and Chen, 1998; Liao, Wang and Liu, 1999; Ma, Zhang and Mili, 2002), the fuzzy functional and/or multivalued dependencies of fuzzy relational databases have been used to compress (refine) fuzzy data. The idea behind these methods is that the data dependencies do not hold because some attribute values are inconsistent, but we can eliminate the inconsistency. For example, let t and s be two tuples in a classical relation r (R) and $FD: X \rightarrow Y$, where R denotes the schema, its attribute set is denoted by U, and $X, Y \subseteq U$ (here we assume that X and Y are all single attributes). We say $t [Y]$ and $s [Y]$ are inconsistent if $t [X] = s [X]$ and $t [Y] \neq s [Y]$. To eliminate the inconsistency, $t [Y]$ and s $[Y]$ are modified into $t [Y] = s [Y]$ or t $[X]$ and $s [X]$ are modified into t $[X] \neq s [X]$. In the fuzzy relational databases, the attribute values may be fuzzy data. So there are more spaces to make inconsistent attribute values consistent. Unnecessary elements in fuzzy data can be eliminated and a fuzzy value can be compressed into more informative one. Similarly, we can use the method of compressing fuzzy data by fuzzy data integrity constraints for our purpose. As a result, some fuzzy attribute values either in the inserting tuple or in the tuples of the relation are compressed according to the fuzzy data integrity so that the inserting tuple can satisfy the fuzzy data integrity constraints of the given fuzzy relation, if it does not.

In the following, we give an example to show how we can compress fuzzy data so that the inserting tuple satisfies the data dependencies. Let r $(X,$ $Y, Z)$ be a fuzzy relation and $FFD: Y \hookrightarrow Z$ be a fuzzy functional dependency in r. Here X is the key of r. Assume that r only contains a tuple $s = (1001,$ $\{0.7/a, 0.4/b, 0.5/d\}, \{0.9/f, 0.6/g, 1.0/h\})$ and there are two resemblance relations on X and Y shown in Figure 7-2 and Figure 7-3, respectively. Let two thresholds on the two resemblance relations be $\alpha_1 = 0.90$ and $\alpha_2 = 0.95$, respectively.

Now we would like to insert tuple $t = (1002, \{0.5/a, 0.4/c, 0.8/d\}, \{0.6/g,$ $0.9/h, 0.9/i, 0.6/j\})$ into r. We have

SE $(t [Y], s [Y]) = $ min (SID $(t [Y], s [Y])$, SID $(s [Y], t [Y])) = $ min $(0.875,$
0.824) $= 0.824$

and

SE $(t [Z], s [Z])) = $ min (SID $(t [Z], s [Z])$, SID $(s [Z], t [Z])) = $ min $(0.8,$
0.96) $= 0.8.$

It is clear that SE $(t [Y], s [Y]) \leq$ SE $(t [Z], s [Z])$ is not true. At this point, inserting t into r directly is not allowed because $FFD: Y \hookrightarrow Z$ will not hold in r. But we can make $t [Z]$ and $s [Z]$ closer in semantics so that SE $(t [Z], s [Z])$

$\geq$ SE (t [Y], s [Y]). For this purpose, we should reduce the possibility of element j in t [Z] from 0.6 to x. According to SE (t [Z], s [Z]) $\geq$ 0.824, we get a unique $x \geq 0.513$. Then instead of tuple t, tuple (1002, {0.5/a, 0.4/c, 0.8/d}, {0.6/g, 0.9/h, 0.9/i, 0.513/j}) can make *FFD*: $Y \hookrightarrow Z$ hold in r and hereby can be inserted into r. It should be noticed that when we compress t [Z] and s [Z], we have the following principles:

(a) We should try to reduce the possibilities of such elements in t [Z] and s [Z] that are not common with other elements. First we can select any one from these elements to reduce its possibility. If its possibility is reduced down to less than 0, the element must be eliminated from the corresponding fuzzy data and then we have to select another one from these elements to repeat the processing above. If the last element is processed and its possibility is still reduced down to less than 0, the element must be eliminated from the corresponding fuzzy data and we have to have the following processing in (b).

(b) We should try to increase the possibilities of such elements in t [Z] and s [Z] that are common each other but their possibilities are different. First, for any pair of common elements, we select the element which possibility is less than the possibility of another element to increase its possibility. If its possibility is increased up to greater than the possibility of another element in the pair, the possibility of this element is only the possibility of another element in the corresponding fuzzy data and we have to select another pair of common elements to repeat the processing above. If the last pair of common element is processed and the possibility is still increased up to the possibility of another element in the pair, the possibility of this element is the possibility of another element in the corresponding fuzzy data and we have to compress t [Y] and s [Y].

Generally speaking, we can only compress t [Y] and s [Y] rather than t [Z] and s [Z] if SE (t [Z], s [Z])) = 0 and SE (t [Y], s [Y]) < 1; if 0 < SE (t [Z], s [Z])) < 1 and SE (t [Y], s [Y]) = 1, we can only compress t [Z] and s [Z] rather than t [Y] and s [Y]; If 0 < SE (t [Z], s [Z])) < SE (t [Y], s [Y]) < 1, we can compress t [Z] and s [Z], or t [Y] and s [Y] to satisfy *FFD*: $Y \hookrightarrow Z$. But it should be noticed that when we compress t [Y] and s [Y], the principles we should follow are very different from that used in compressing t [Z] and s [Z]. At this moment, we try to make t [Y] and s [Y] farther in semantics so that SE (t [Z], s [Z]) $\geq$ SE (t [Y], s [Y]). So we have the following principles when we compress t [Y] and s [Y]:

(c) We should try to reduce the possibilities of such elements in t [Y] and s [Y] that are common each other. First, for any pair of common elements, if their possibilities are different, we select the element which possibility is less than the possibility of another element to reduce its possibility. But if their possibilities are identical, we should reduce their possibilities simultaneously. If the possibility of any element in the pair is reduced down to less than 0, the element must be eliminated from the corresponding fuzzy data and then we have to select another pair of common elements to repeat the processing above. If the last pair of common element is processed and the possibility of any element in the pair is reduced down to less than 0, the element must be eliminated from the corresponding fuzzy data and we have to have the following processing in (d).

(d) We should try to increase the possibilities of such elements in t [Y] and s [Y] that are not common with other elements. First we can select any one from these elements to increase its possibility. If its possibility is increased up to greater than 1, the possibility of this element is only 1 in the corresponding fuzzy data and we have to select we have to select another one from these elements to repeat the processing above. If the last element is processed and its possibility is still increased up to greater than 1, it is indicated that t and s cannot be compressed by $FFD: Y \hookrightarrow Z$.

In the above, we discuss fuzzy data compression based on fuzzy functional dependencies so that the inserting tuple can satisfy this integrity constraint. Similarly we can do that by fuzzy multivalued dependencies. The strategies and approaches for compressing fuzzy data by fuzzy data dependencies have been developed in (Ma, Zhang and Mili, 2002), where fuzzy data are represented by the interval number description rather than the possibility distribution. So the fuzzy data compression here is completely different from that of (Ma, Zhang and Mili, 2002) in the implementation but they refer to the similar strategies. We do not give the detailed principles for fuzzy data compression by fuzzy multivalued dependencies here.

If the inserting tuple, say t, still breaks the fuzzy data dependencies after fuzzy data compression, we say t can not be compressed against the fuzzy relation and the insertion operation must be rejected. For this case, the fuzzy relation must be recovered from the original state of no data compression. Only when the inserting tuple can be compressed against the fuzzy relation, the compression then takes effect.

The inserting tuple that satisfies the above-mentioned requirements, i.e., it is sound, no redundancy, and compressible, can be inserted into the given fuzzy relation. It has been shown that the insertion operation in the fuzzy relational databases is relevant to the issues of fuzzy data dependencies, and fuzzy data redundancies. So we cannot simply use the union operation of the fuzzy relational operations in Section 7.5 to carry out the insertion. We must define the insertion operation in context of the fuzzy relational databases.

Based on the discussion above, the insertion operation must achieve the following procedures.

(a) Validating the inserting tuple to see if it is sound;
(b) Determining if tuple redundancies exist;
(c) Validating the data integrity of the inserting tuple in the original relation.

Figure 7-5 shows the relationships among these procedures. Let t be the tuple that is to be inserted into the given fuzzy relation r.

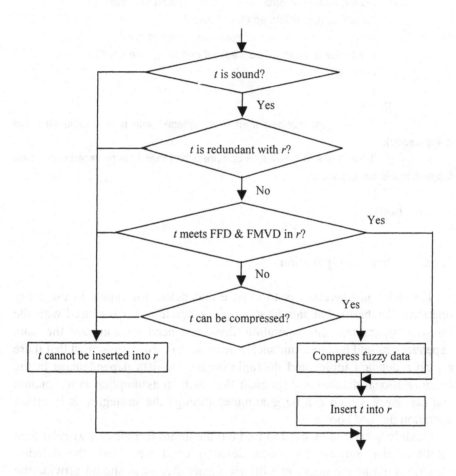

Figure 7-5. Insertion Process in the Fuzzy Relational Databases

Based on the insertion strategies discussed above, the implementation algorithm of the insertion operation is developed as follows.

Insertion (r, t)

Input: the inserting tuple t, the original fuzzy relation r, and a set of fuzzy data dependencies FFD/FMVD;

Output: the fuzzy relation *r* after insertion operation;
   If *s* is not sound then return (*r*);
   For any tuple *s* in *r*, repeat to do {
      If (SED (*s*, *t*) > a *given threshold*) then return (*r*);
      (/*t is redundant with *s**/)
      }
   *r*1:= *r*,   (/*backing up *r* to *r*1*/)
   For any data dependency, repeat to do
      If (*t* does not make the data dependency holding in *r*) then
         If (*t* is not compressible against *r*) then {
            r:= *r*1;   (/*restoring *r* from *r*1*/)
            Print ("Tuple *t* cannot be inserted into fuzzy relation *r*");
            return (*r*);
         }
         Else {
            If (*t* is compressible) then (*t* is replaced with a new tuple after *t* is
compressed);
            If (any tuple in *r*, say *s*, is compressible) then (*s* is replaced with a new
tuple after *s* is compressed);
         }
   r. = *r* ∪ {*t*};

7.7.2   Deletion Operation

The deletion operation is to choose and delete the tuples in the fuzzy
relational databases that satisfy some given conditions. Compared with the
insertion operation, this operation does not need to consider the data
dependencies and tuple redundancies because it is always assumed that there
are no redundant tuples and no tuple breaks the data dependencies in the
fuzzy relational databases. It is clear that such an assumption is reasonable
and necessary, which can be guaranteed through the strategies of Insertion
operation defined above.

Flexible query can be used to find out the tuples from the fuzzy relational
databases that satisfy the given deletion condition. Here the deletion
conditions act as the query conditions. Generally, users should provide the
condition that the deleted tuples should satisfy. Of course, the relation
deletion should be supported, which means that all tuples are deleted. When
the deletion condition is omitted, all tuples of the relation are deleted.

The implementation algorithm of the deletion operation is as follows.
Deletion (*r*, *P*ₜ)
Input: fuzzy relation *r* and a given deletion condition *P*ₜ;

Output: the fuzzy relation r after deletion operation;

    If $P_f = \Phi$ then $s := r$ else $s := \sigma_{Pf}(r)$;

    If $s = \Phi$ then return (r);

    $r := r - s$;

    return (r);

7.7.3   Modification Operation

In the relational databases, modification operation means that some attribute values of tuples are replaced with new attribute values. As a result, the contents of these tuples in the relational databases change. In order to perform such operations, users should provide two aspects of conditions: one is the condition that the modifying tuples should satisfy; the other one is the condition that the modified tuples should satisfy. The modification is done through locating the tuples that satisfying the first condition, and then the attribute values of these tuples are replaced with the corresponding attribute values given in the second condition. It can be seen that the modification is essentially performed through the deletion and the insertion jointly. Note that the first condition can be omitted. It means that all tuples should be modified according to the second condition. The second condition cannot be omitted.

Also it should be noticed that, however, the modification operation that changes the contents of some tuple cannot be finished sometimes. If the modification operation results in that the tuples break the data dependencies, the modification operation does not succeed and is rejected. If we use the deletion operation and the insertion operation to carry out the modification operation, we have to recover the relational databases when the modification operation cannot be finished.

The implementation algorithm of the modification operation is given as follows.

    Modification (r, P_{f1}, P_{f2})

    Input: fuzzy relation r, two given condition P_{f1} and P_{f2};

    Output: the fuzzy relation r after modification operation;

      If $P_{f1} = \Phi$ then $s := r$ else $s := \sigma_{Pf1}(r)$;

      If $s = \Phi$ then return (r);

      $r := r - s$;

      For each tuple $t \in s$, repeat to do {

         modifying t to t' according to P_{f2};

         If (t' cannot be inserted into r) then Insert (r, t);

      }

      return (r);

7.8   Integration of Multiple Fuzzy Relational Databases

Sharing and exchanging information across multiple databases in different sites have become an essential requirement in distributed application environments such as the development of global/cooperative information systems and data warehousing applications (Mena *et al.*, 2000; Wiederhold, 2000). It should be noticed that current research of database integration mainly focus on integrating crisp component databases. On the other hand, the fuzzy relational databases have extensively being investigated for two decades under single database environment. While multidatabase systems and fuzzy relational databases have received increasing attentions and have respectively made significant progress, data sharing among multidatabses and knowledge-based intelligent system development put an essential requirement on integration of fuzzy multidatabases (Zhang, Laun and Meng, 1997) accompanying the extensive application of computer technologies in data and knowledge intensive areas as well as the rapid advance in networking technologies. However, little has been reported on integrating fuzzy component databases to develop fuzzy multidatabase systems.

The only effort that we are aware of in the area of fuzzy relational database integration in a multidatabase system is by Zhang, Laun and Meng (1997). In their work, several kinds of conflicts that may occur in fuzzy multidatabases were identified, including missing membership degree attribute, inconsistent (membership degree) attribute values, and attribute domain inconsistency, and the resolutions were proposed in a procedural manner. In particular, their paper focused on the conversion of fuzzy terms and fuzzy-probabilistic relational models are resulted in for the integrated target databases. It should be noted that missing attributes, attribute name conflicts and entity identification were not proposed in (Zhang, Laun and Meng, 1997). In addition, the fuzzy data in (Zhang, Laun and Meng, 1997) is represented by the membership function whose curve is a trapezoidal shape.

7.8.1   Background

There are several approaches to implement schema integration of heterogeneous multiple databases. The *first* approach is to merge individual schemas of component databases into a single global conceptual schema for all independent databases (Breitbart, Olson and Thompson, 1987; Deen, Amin and Taylor, 1987; Motro, 1987). This approach requires that all local schemas are mapped to the global schema. The *second* approach is to adopt a so-called federated database system (Heimbigner and McLeod, 1985). Being not the same as the first approach, there is not a global schema for all component databases in a federated database system and only a schema describing data that the application may access to is created in the local databases, which is called "partial schema". This approach only requires a partial integration. Notice that the target databases based on global schema and federal databases are physical databases. There are a solid mapping among component databases and target databases. Because the small change of component databases can cause the large change of target databases, maintaining these mapping is difficult. Generally there are some restricts on the component databases. The *third* approach is to dynamically create the target databases by providing users a multiple-database query language (Czejdo, Rusinkiewicz and Embley, 1987; Litwin et al., 1987 & 1990). The global or partial schemas are not needed in this approach and the target databases are essentially the databases based on the view. In other words, they are logical databases or virtual databases. Being different from the view in traditional relational databases, the view relation here should resolve the possible conflicts. Because this approach has no restricts on component databases, it is widely adopted to integrate heterogeneous multiple-database systems.

In database integration, a core problem is to identify the same real-world object from component databases and then resolve a large number of incompatibilities that exist in different component databases (Kim *et al.*, 1995; Parent and Spaccapietra, 1998). It is a difficult and interesting issue to identify if tuples from component databases describe the same real-world object. If component relations have a common key, the component tuples with the same key values must describe the same real-world object. Otherwise, it is necessary to identify entity (object).

First, let's focus on the component relations with common keys. Let r and s be component relations from different component databases, and t_r and t_s be their tuples, called component tuples, respectively. If t_r and t_s describe the same real-world object, namely, they have the same attribute values on the common key, then t_r and t_s can be integrated to produce a single tuple t, called *target tuple* with outerjoin (Breitbart, Olson and Thompson, 1987; Chen, 1990) or outerunion (Tseng, Chen and Yang, 1993) operation after resolving the conflicts. According to the semantic relationship between t_r [Ai] and t_s [Aj], four types of important conflicts are generalized as follows (DeMichiel, 1989; Tseng, Chen and Yang, 1993).

(a) *Naming conflicts.* This type of conflict can be divided into two aspects. One is that semantically related data items are named differently, and the other is that semantically unrelated data items are named equivalently.

(b) *Data type conflicts.* This occurs when semantically related data items are represented in different data types.

(c) *Data scaling conflicts.* This occurs when semantically related data items are represented in different databases using different units of measure.

(d) *Missing data.* This occurs when the schemas of component databases have different attribute sets.

The conflict of missing data can be resolved by using outerunion operation and null values (Codd, 1986) in target tuples. For the other three types of conflicts, the mappings of attribute values from the attributes of component tuples to the *virtual attributes* (DeMichiel, 1989) of target tuples are necessary. There are three types of mappings: one-to-one, many-to-one, and one-to-many. The naming conflicts and data type conflicts can be resolved with the one-to-one mapping. The data scaling conflicts can be resolved with either many-to-one mapping or one-to-many mapping, depending on particular application situations. For the mappings of the one-to-one and many-to-one, the result is still an atomic value in a virtual attribute of a target relation. For the mapping of one-to-many, however, the result is that a special value of a virtual attribute, called the partial value, will be produced (DeMichiel, 1989; Grant, 1979), in which exactly one of the values is a true value.

Concerning incompatible keys in multidatabases, typically, we have the following situations:

Case 1: the two tables might use different identifiers to identify the same real world entity, and

Case 2: the tables might use the same identifier to identify different real world entity.

Case 1 is called *entity heterogeneity* in (Dey, Sarkar and De, 1998). In fact, two kinds of cases concern *entity identification*, or *entity matching* (Ahmed *et al.*, 1991; Chatterjee and Segev, 1991; Chatterjee and Segev, 1995; Chen, Tsai and Koh, 1996; Dey, Sarkar and De, 1998; Lim et al., 1996; Pu, 1991; Wang and Zhang, 1996).

There are the following approaches to entity identification. The first one is to require the user to specify equivalence between tuples, i.e., the responsibility to matching the entities is assigned to the user (Ahmed *et al.*, 1991). The second one is to match entities using a portation of the key values in the restricted domain (Pu, 1991), which results in probabilistic key equivalence. The third one is to use all common attributes (including key attributes) to help determine equivalent entities (Chatterjee and Segev, 1991; Chen, Tsai and Koh, 1996; Dey, Sarkar and De, 1998). The last one is to use knowledge (rules) or integrity constraints to identify equivalent entities (Chatterjee and Segev, 1995; Wang and Zhang, 1996) on the basis of the third approach. For the second and third approaches, since it is not completely determined if two tuples from different relations refer to the same real world entity, a probabilistic data model is presented to estimate the accuracy of the comparison. It can be seen that necessary semantic information and domain knowledge are required and are assumed available for the identification in the first, second and last approaches. However, they may not be easy to acquire all time (Chen, Tsai and Koh, 1996). So in the following, we use the third approach for the entity identification in fuzzy multidatabases.

Here *fuzzy multidatabases* refer to the integration of more than two fuzzy relational databases. These fuzzy relational databases may be created and maintained by different individuals and are probably based on different fuzzy relational models presented in Section 7.2. In the following, we only focus on the fuzzy relational model where non-key attribute values may take possibility distributions and tuples may or may not be associated with membership degrees.

7.8.2 Conflicts and Resolutions in Fuzzy Multidatabases with Compatible Keys

In this section, we identify the conflicts in integrating multiple fuzzy relational databases and develop the resolutions. Here the fuzzy relational databases are with compatible keys.

Conflict Identifications
Since fuzzy relational databases exist in multiple relational databases and crisp relational databases are essentially the special forms of fuzzy relational databases, there are new types of conflicts, which should be resolved in schema integration together with the conflicts identified above. In this section, we identify various conflicts that may occur in the schema of fuzzy multidatabase systems.

Let r and s be two fuzzy component relations with common key from different component databases and t_r and t_s be their tuples, called component tuples, respectively. Assume there is no any fuzzy value for the key and the key values of t_r and t_s are identical.

Membership Degree Conflicts
Membership degree conflicts occur at the level of tuples, which can be classified into two classes as follows:

(a) *Missing membership degree.* Among t_r and t_s, one is associated with a membership degree attribute, i.e., the tuple is fuzzy, but another is not, i.e., the tuple is crisp.

(b) *Inconsistent membership degree.* Although t_r and t_s have degree memberships $t_r [pD]$ and $t_s [pD]$, respectively, $t_r [pD] \neq t_s [pD]$.

Example: Consider three fuzzy relations r_1, r_2 and r_3 in Figure 7-6, which have common key *ID*.

Fuzzy relation r_1		Fuzzy relation r_2			Fuzzy relation r_3		
ID	*Name*	*ID*	*Name*	*pD*	*ID*	*Name*	*pD*
9540	John	9540	John	0.8	9540	John	0.5

Figure 7-6. Fuzzy Relations with Membership Degree Conflicts

It can be seen that tuple <9540, John> in r_1, denoted t_{r1}, tuple <9540, John, 0.8> in r_2, denoted t_{r2}, and <9540, John, 0.5> in r_3, denoted t_{r3}, have the same key value. That means that they denote the same real-world entity. But there is not membership degree attribute in r_1. So compared with t_{r2} and t_{r3}, the conflict of missing membership degree occurs in t_{r1}. Besides, t_{r2} [*pD*] and t_{r3} [*pD*] are different although r_2 and r_3 all have membership degree attribute *pD*. The conflict of inconsistent membership degree occurs in t_{r2} and t_{r3}.

Attribute Value Conflicts in Identical Attribute Domains

In addition to the conflicts at the level of tuples, there may exist conflicts at levels of attribute domains and attribute values. First, let us focus on attribute value conflicts, where the attributes with conflicts have the same domains.

Let A_r and A_s be attributes with the same domains in r and s, respectively, and t_r [A_r] and t_s [A_s] are semantically related to each other.

(a) *Inconsistent crisp attribute values.* t_r [A_r] and t_s [A_s] are all crisp but t_r [A_r] $\neq t_s$ [A_s].

(b) *Missing fuzzy attribute values.* Among t_r [A_r] and t_s [A_s], one is fuzzy whereas another is crisp.

(c) *Inconsistent fuzzy attribute values.* t_r [A_r] and t_s [A_s] are all fuzzy but t_r [A_r] $\neq t_s$ [A_s].

Example: Consider two fuzzy relations r and s in Figure 7-7, which have common key *Name*.

Fuzzy relation r		Fuzzy relation s	
Name	*Age*	*Name*	*Age*
Tom	25	Tom	27
John	24	John	about 25
Mary	about 21	Mary	about 23

Figure 7-7. Fuzzy Relations with Attribute Value Conflicts in Identical Attribute Domains

Tuple <Tom, 25> in r and tuple <Tom, 27> in s have the same key value and they hereby denote the same real-world entity. But their values on attribute *Age* are crisp values 25 and 27, respectively. The conflict of inconsistent crisp attribute values occurs in attribute *Age* of these two tuples. Similarly, tuple <John, 24> in *r* and tuple <John, about 25> denote the same real-world entity. But their values on attribute *Age* are crisp value 24 and fuzzy value *about 25*, respectively. The conflict of missing fuzzy attribute values occurs in attribute *Age* of these two tuples. Again, tuple <Mary, about 21> in *r* and tuple <Mary, about 23> denote the same real-world entity. But their values on attribute *Age* are fuzzy values *about 21* and *about 23*, respectively. The conflict of inconsistent fuzzy attribute values occurs in attribute *Age* of these two tuples.

Missing Attributes

Missing attributes mean that *r* and *s* have different attribute sets. In other words, an attribute in a component relation is not semantically related to any attribute in another component relation.

Example: Consider two relations *r* and *s*, which are on schema {*ID, Name, Age*} and on schema {*ID, Name, Major*}, respectively. It is clear that there is no any attribute in *s* that is semantically related to attribute *Age* in *r*. Also there is no any attribute in *r* that is semantically related to attribute *Major* in *s*. Therefore, attribute *Age* in *r* is a missing attribute of relation *s* and attribute *Major* in *s* is a missing attribute of relation *r*.

Attribute Name Conflicts

Attribute name conflicts are the naming conflicts. Let A_r and A_s be attributes in *r* and *s*, respectively. This type of conflict can be divided into two aspects:

    (a) Semantically related attributes are named differently, i.e., synonyms.

    (b) Semantically unrelated data items are named equivalently, i.e., homonyms.

It should be noticed that the conflicts of missing attributes and attribute names are not concerned with if component relations are fuzzy.

Example: Consider two relations *r* and *s*, which are on schema {*ID, Last Name, Position*} and on schema {*ID, Family Name, Position*}, respectively. Here attribute *Last Name* in *r* and attribute *Family Name* in *s* are named differently. But they are semantically related to each other. That means that they indicate the same things. Concerning attribute *Position*, it means academic position in *r*, professor, associate professor, etc. But in *s*, it means office location. So attribute *Position* in *r* and attribute *Position* in *s* are named equivalently but they are semantically unrelated to each other. In other words, they indicate different things.

Attribute Domain Conflicts

Data type conflict and data scaling conflict mentioned above are caused by inconsistent attribute domains. When there are fuzzy attribute values in component tuples, the attribute domain conflicts become more complicated.

It is noticed that there is no attribute domain conflict in membership degree attributes.

Let A_r and A_s be attributes with different domains in r and s, respectively. Assume that t_r [A_r] and t_s [A_s] are semantically related to each other.

   (a) *Data format conflicts.* Although A_r and A_s have the same data type and data unit, they have different expressive formats.

      For example, t_r [A_r] and t_s [A_s] are all date data, but t_r [A_r] is 22/05/98 with format "*dd/mm/yy*" while t_s [A_s] is 05/22/98 with format "*mm/dd/yy*".

   (b) *Data unit conflicts.* Attributes A_r and A_s have the same data type, but their measure units are different.

      For example, t_r [A_r] and t_s [A_s] are all real, but t_r [A_r] is 22.4 with unit "*kilogram*" while t_s [A_s] is "22.9 with unit "*pound*".

   (c) *Data type conflicts.* Attributes A_r and A_s have different data type.

      For example, t_r [A_r] is integer 22 and t_s [A_s] is real 21.9.

Since attribute domains have the above-mentioned conflicts, attribute values must have conflicts. Considering fuzziness of attribute values, we differentiate the following cases.

Case 1: t_r [A_r] and t_s [A_s] are all crisp.

Case 2:   Among t_r [A_r] and t_s [A_s], one is fuzzy based on possibility distribution whereas another is crisp.

Case 3: t_r [A_r] and t_s [A_s] are all fuzzy.

Example: Consider two fuzzy relations r and s in Figure 7-8, which have common key *Name*.

	Fuzzy relation r				Fuzzy relation s	
Name	*Birth Date*	*Weight*		*Name*	*Birth Date*	*Weight*
Tom	28/12/70	70.6		Tom	12/28/70	150
John	01/10/62	82.7		John	10/01/62	about 180
Chris	22/05/58	about 88.5		Chris	05/22/58	about 192

Figure 7-8. Fuzzy Relations with Attribute Domain Conflicts

Here, attribute *Birth Date* in r and attribute *Birth Date* in s are with form "*dd/mm/yy*" and format "*mm/dd/yy*", respectively. So there exists data format conflict between them. Attribute *Weight* in r is real type with unit kilogram whereas attribute *Weight* in s is integer type with unit pound. So there exist data unit conflict and data type conflict between them simultaneously. Viewed from attribute values, among tuple <Tom, 28/12/70, 70.6> in r and tuple <Tom, 12/28/70, 150> in s, their values on attribute *Weight* are crisp real 70.6 kilogram and crisp integer 150 pound, respectively. But among tuple <John, 01/10/62, 82.7> in r and tuple <John, 10/01/62, about 180> in s, their values on attribute *Weight* are crisp real 82.7 kilogram and fuzzy integer *about 180* pound, respectively, and among tuple <Chris, 22/05/58, about 88.5> in *r* and tuple <Chris, 05/22/58, about 192> in *s*, their values on attribute *Weight* are fuzzy real *about 88.5* kilogram and fuzzy integer *about 192*, respectively.

Conflicts Resolutions

Among the above-mentioned conflicts, some, including missing attributes, attribute name conflicts, inconsistent crisp attribute values on identical attribute domains and inconsistent crisp attribute values on different attribute domains, have been investigated and resolved (Deen, Amin and Taylor, 1987; Heimbigner and McLeod, 1985). In this section, we focus on some new types of conflicts concerned with fuzzy databases.

Let *r* and *s* be fuzzy component relations from different component databases. Let t_r and t_s be component tuples belonging to *r* and *s*, respectively, and t_r and t_s have the same crisp key values, namely, they describe the identical object in the real world. Now, we integrate t_r and t_s to form a tuple *t*. It is clear that *t* has the same key and key values as t_r (or t_s). The other attribute values of *t* are formed after resolving the conflicts between semantically related attribute values. Here, we assume that there is no attribute name conflicts in *r* and *s* because they can be resolved before.

Resolving Membership Degree Conflicts

First, consider the situation of missing membership degree. Let t_r and t_s be tuples in *r* (K, X) and *s* (K, X, pD), respectively, where *K* is key, *X* is a set of common attribute, and *pD* is membership degree attribute. Let t_r $[K]$ and t_s $[K]$ are crisp and t_r $[K] = t_s$ $[K]$. Then t_r and t_s denote the same real-world object. Assume that there is no any conflict in t_r $[X]$ and t_s $[X]$. It is clear that the conflict of missing membership degree emerges in t_r and t_s. Tuple *t* formed by integrating t_r and t_s is on schema $\{K, X, pD\}$, in which *t* $[K] = t_r$ $[K] = t_s$ $[K]$ and *t* $[X] = t_r$ $[X] = t_s$ $[X]$. It is clear that *t* $[pD] = $ max $(1.0, t_s$ $[pD]) = 1.0$.

Now let us focus on the situation of inconsistent membership degree. Let *r* and *s* be *r* (K, X, pD) and *s* (K, X, pD), respectively, where *K*, *X* and *pD* have the same meanings as the above. Let t_r $[K]$ and t_s $[K]$ are crisp and t_r $[K]$ $= t_s$ $[K]$. Assume that t_r $[X]$ and t_s $[X]$ are crisp or fuzzy simultaneously. If t_r $[X]$ and t_s $[X]$ are fuzzy, then they must be equivalent to each other. Assume t_r $[pD] \neq t_s$ $[pD]$. It can be seen that t_r and t_s denote the same real-world object and there is the conflict of inconsistent membership degree between t_r and t_s. For tuple *t*, its schema is $\{K, X, pD\}$, and *t* $[K] = t_r$ $[K] = t_s$ $[K]$, *t* $[X] = t_r$ $[X] = t_s$ $[X]$, and *t* $[X] = $ max $(t_r$ $[pD], t_s$ $[pD])$.

Example: Consider the relations in Figure 7-6. Utilizing the methods to resolving membership degree conflicts given above, we have the integrated relations shown in Figure 7-9.

The fuzzy relation after integrating r_2 and r			The fuzzy relation after integrating r_1, r_2 and r_3		
ID	Name	pD	ID	Name	pD
9540	John	0.8	9540	John	1.0

Figure 7-9. Integrated Fuzzy Relations After Resolving Membership Degree Conflicts

Resolving Attribute Value Conflicts in Identical Attribute Domains

Let t_r and t_s be component tuples in r (K, X) and s (K, X), respectively, where K is key and X is a set of common attribute. In order to simplify the discussion, here, membership degree attributes are not considered. If they are included, the potential conflicts can be resolved by applying the methods above. Assume t_r [K] and t_s [K] are crisp and t_r [K] = t_s [K]. At this moment, the schema of integrated target relation is {K, X} and t [K] = t_r [K] = t_s [K]. Let A $\in$ X, then

(a) When t_r [A] and t_s [A] are crisp and t_r [A] $\neq$ t_s [A], the conflict of inconsistent crisp attribute values occurs and t [A] = [t_r [A], t_s [A]], being a partial value (Chen, Tsai and Koh, 1996). Of course, if t_r [A] = t_s [A], t [A] = t_r [A] = t_s [A].

(b) When t_r [A] and t_s [A] are crisp and fuzzy, respectively, the conflict of missing fuzzy attribute values occurs. Assume t_r [A] is crisp and t_s [A] is fuzzy. Then t [A] = t_r [A].

(c) When both t_r [A] and t_s [A] are fuzzy and t_r [A] $\neq$ t_s [A], the conflict of inconsistent fuzzy attribute values occurs and t [A] = t_r [A] $\cup_f t_s$ [A], where "$\cup_f$" is a fuzzy union operation defined Section 7.3.4. Of course, if t_r [A] = t_s [A], t [A] = t_r [A] = t_s [A]. That fuzzy union operation is adopted, not being intersection operation, difference operation and so on, is to avoid information missing in the integration. The union of two fuzzy values on the same universe of discourse U, say A and B with the possibility functions π_A and π_B, is still a fuzzy set on U with the possibility function $\pi_{A \cup_f B}$: $U \rightarrow$ [0, 1], where

$$\forall u \in U, \pi_{A \cup_f B} (u) = \max (\pi_A (u), \pi_B (u)).$$

Example: Consider the relations in Figure 7-7. Assume the domain of attribute *Age* is integer interval [5, 50] and three fuzzy values "about 21", "about 23", and "about 25" are represented as possibility distributions {0.6/19, 0.8/20, 1.0/21, 0.9/22, 0.8/23, 0.6/24}, {0.6/20, 0.8/21, 1.0/22, 1.0/23, 0.9/24, 0.7/25}, and {0.6/22, 0.7/23, 0.8/24, 1.0/25, 0.7/26, 0.5/27}, respectively. Then we have the relation in Figure 7-10 after integrating r and s.

The fuzzy relation after integrating r and s

Name	Age
Tom	{25, 27}
John	{0.6/22, 0.7/23, 1.0/24, 1.0/25, 0.7/26, 0.5/27}
Mary	{0.6/19, 0.8/20, 1.0/21, 1.0/22, 1.0/23, 0.9/24, 0.7/25}

Figure 7-10. Integrated Fuzzy Relation After Resolving Attribute Value Conflicts in Identical Attribute Domains

Resolving Attribute Value Conflicts in Inconsistent Attribute Domains

In order to resolve attribute value conflicts in inconsistent attribute domain, the conflicts of attribute domains should be resolved firstly. For this purpose, the component relations are converted into other relations, called virtual component relations. The attributes in virtual component relations are called *virtual attributes* (DeMichiel, 1989; Tseng, Chen and Yang, 1993). Note that there are no attribute domain conflicts in virtual component relations because they have been resolved by mapping an attribute concerned with domain conflicts in an original component relation to the corresponding virtual attribute. It is clear that such mappings must also been done between a tuple in original component relation and the corresponding tuple in virtual component relation, called *virtual tuple*, or more precisely between an attribute value and the value of corresponding virtual attribute. Instead of integrating original component relations, their virtual component relations are integrated to form the target relation.

One-to-One Mapping. According to different types of attribute domain conflicts, the above-mentioned mappings can be classified into one-to-one mapping, many-to-one mapping, and one-to-many mapping. The one-to-one mapping produces a certain result for one data item to be mapped. Therefore, a crisp attribute value in original component relation is mapped into another crisp value of the corresponding virtual attribute. In addition, a fuzzy attribute value in original component relation is mapped into another fuzzy value of the corresponding virtual attribute. The difference between these two fuzzy values represented by possibility distributions is only their supports but they have the one-to-one relationships. A pair of values with one-to-one relationship has the same possibility.

Example: Let an original component tuple be t_r and the corresponding virtual component tuple be t_r'. Let A be an attribute in the schema of t_r and A' be the corresponding virtual attribute. They have domains of integer with units "*cm*" and "*mm*", respectively. Utilizing one-to-one mapping, we have the result shown in Figure 7-11.

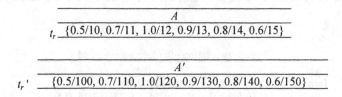

	A
t_r	{0.5/10, 0.7/11, 1.0/12, 0.9/13, 0.8/14, 0.6/15}

	A'
t_r'	{0.5/100, 0.7/110, 1.0/120, 0.9/130, 0.8/140, 0.6/150}

Figure 7-11. Fuzzy Attribute Value Conversion via One-to-One Mapping

Many-to-One Mapping. The many-to-one mapping also produces a certain result for one data item to be mapped. A crisp attribute value in original component relation is mapped into another crisp value of the corresponding virtual attribute. A fuzzy attribute value in original component relation is mapped into another fuzzy value of the corresponding virtual attribute. However, since there is a many-to-one mapping relationship, several elements in the support of the former are mapped into one element in the support of the later, which possibility should be the maximum one in the possibilities of these elements.

Example: Let t_r, t_r', *A*, and *A'* be the same as Figure 7-11. But *A*, and *A'* have domains of real and integer, respectively. Utilizing many-to-one mapping, we have Figure 7-12.

	A
t_r	{0.4/10.4, 0.5/10.8, 0.6/11.2, 0.7/11.6, 0.8/12.0, 0.9/12.4, 1.0/12.8, 0.9/13.2, 0.8/13.6, 0.7/14.0, 0.6/14.4, 0.5/14.8, 0.4/15.2}

	A'
t_r'	{0.4/10, 0.6/11, 0.9/12, 1.0/13, 0.8/14, 0.5/15}

Figure 7-12. Fuzzy Attribute Value Conversion via Many-to-One Mapping

Data format conflicts, data type conflicts, and some data unit conflicts can be resolved by utilizing one-to-one and many-to-one mappings. Since the virtual component relations should be integrated to form the target relation instead of original component relations and they have no attribute domain conflicts, attribute value conflicts are that in identical attribute domains. At this moment, we can use the methods of resolving attribute value conflicts in identical attribute domains to resolve them.

One-to-Many Mapping. It should be noticed that some data unit conflicts can been only resolved by utilizing one-to-many mapping. The one-to-many mapping produces a list or set of value for one data item to be mapped. A crisp attribute value in original component relation is mapped into a partial value of the corresponding virtual attribute (DeMichiel, 1989; Tseng, Chen and Yang, 1993). A partial value can be regarded as a special case of fuzzy value, in which the possibility of each element is one. A fuzzy attribute value in original component relation is mapped into another fuzzy value of the corresponding virtual attribute. However, since there is a one-to-many mapping relationship, one element in the support of the former is mapped into several elements in the support of the later, where the possibility of each element should be the possibility of the original element.

Example: Let t_r be original component tuple and A be an attribute, denoted transport forms, in the schema of t_r. Assume the domain of A is {Land, Air, Water} and t_r $[A]$ = {0.4/Air, 0.7/Land, 0.9/Water}. If the domain of the virtual attribute A' which corresponds to A is {Train, Truck, Plane, Ship}, utilizing one-to-many mapping, we have Figure 7-13.

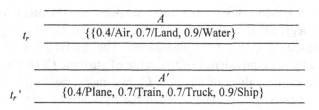

	A
t_r	{{0.4/Air, 0.7/Land, 0.9/Water}

	A'
t_r'	{0.4/Plane, 0.7/Train, 0.7/Truck, 0.9/Ship}

Figure 7-13. Fuzzy Attribute Value Conversion via One-to-Many Mapping

Utilizing one-to-many mapping, some data unit conflicts can be resolved. Therefore, the virtual component relations to be integrated have no attribute domain conflicts. At this moment, attribute value conflicts in the virtual component relations are that in identical attribute domains, which can be resolved by using the methods of resolving attribute value conflicts in identical attribute domains.

7.8.2   Entity Identification in Fuzzy Multidatabases with Incompatible Keys

In the above-mentioned discussion of multidatabase integration, there is an assumption made; i.e., there is not any conflict on the keys. In other words, the keys can be used to identify if two tuples from different relations refer to the same real-world entity. However, the keys may be incompatible.

Equivalence of Two Entities

Let r (A1, A2, ..., An) and s (B1, B2, ..., Bm) be two relations from different databases, which are to be integrated. Assume {C1, C2, ..., Ck} = {A1, A2, ..., An} ∩ {B1, B2, ..., Bm} and the candidate keys of r and s are not included in {C1, C2, ..., Ck} simultaneously. That means that r and s

have incompatible keys. At this point, for two tuples from r and s respectively, determining if they refer to the same real world entities is the key of implementing multidatabase integration. As no common key, the compatible non-key attributes have to be used to help determine equivalent entities (Chatterjee and Segev, 1991; Chen, Tsai and Koh, 1996; Dey, Sarkar and De, 1998).

Different non-key attributes play different roles in entity identification. Some may be dominant and some may be non-dominant. For example, the name of a product is more important than the length of the product in entity identification. Therefore, a weight wi is assigned to each compatible attribute Ci according to its importance such that

$$0 \leq wi \leq 1 \text{ and } \Sigma \, wi = 1 \, (i = 1, 2, ..., k).$$

Let t_r and t_s be tuples from r and s respectively. In order to denote the possibility degree that t_r and t_s refer to the same real world entity, the notion of equivalence of t_r and t_s is introduced. The equivalence of t_r and t_s is determined by the equivalence of the value of attribute Ci ($0 \leq i \leq 1$). Let the equivalence of the values of attribute Ci in t_r and t_s be Ei ($t1$ [Ci], $t2$ [Ci]), where $0 \leq Ei$ (t_r [Ci], t_s [Ci]) ≤ 1. Then the equivalence of t_r and t_s, denoted $P_{equivalence}$ (t_r, t_s), is expressed as follows.

$$P_{equivalence} \, (t_r, t_s) = \Sigma \, (Ei \, (t_r \, [Ci], t_s \, [Ci]) \times wi) \, (i = 1, 2, ..., k).$$

If $P_{equivalence}$ (t_r, t_s) = 0, t_r and t_s do not refer to the same real world entity and they will not be integrated. If $P_{equivalence}$ (t_r, t_s) = 1, t_r and t_s refer to the same real world entity and they will definitely be integrated into a new tuple. If $0 < P_{equivalence}$ (t_r, t_s) < 1, however, it is uncertain whether t_r and t_s refer to the same real world entity or not and the new tuple integrated should be attached to by $P_{equivalence}$ (t_r, t_s). Such a tuple denotes uncertain probability information and a probabilistic data model is hereby presented.

The above-mentioned approach for identifying entities without incompatible key attributes was first introduced in (Chatterjee and Segev, 1991) for multidatabase integration. But some conflicts at instance level such as missing data and mismatch domain were not considered. So the computation of the equivalence of two attribute values was discussed under the consideration of these conflicts (Chen, Tsai and Koh, 1996). It should be noted that the conflict of missing data is caused by different attribute sets of schema and missing attributes must not appear in common non-key attributes. Therefore, the issue on missing data should not be considered in estimating the equivalence. In addition, some new semantic conflicts introduced in fuzzy multidatabases are not considered in (Chatterjee and

Segev, 1991; Chen, Tsai and Koh, 1996; Dey, Sarkar and De, 1998) since the component relations are assumed to be crisp in their work. In the following, the computation of the equivalence of two attribute values is investigated under fuzzy multidatabases. Here, membership degree conflicts and attribute name conflicts are ignored because they are assumed to be resolved.

Evaluating the Equivalence of Attribute Values

Let $\{C1, C2, ..., Ck\}$ be common non-key attribute set of fuzzy component relations r and s. Let t_r and t_s be two tuples from r and s respectively. We evaluate the equivalence of attribute values t_r [Ci] and t_s [Ci], where $Ci \in \{C1, C2, ..., Ck\}$ and let Dom (Ci) = $\{v1, v2, ..., vl\}$.

Attribute Value Conflicts in Identical Attribute Domains

As attribute domains are identical, t_r [Ci] and t_s [Ci] can directly be compared. The following four cases can be identified during the evaluation of the equivalence.

Case 1: *consistent crisp attribute values.*

t_r [Ci] and t_s [Ci] are all crisp and t_r [Ci] = t_s [Ci]. Then Ei (t_r [Ci], t_s [Ci]) = 1.

Case 2: *inconsistent crisp attribute values.*

t_r [Ci] and t_s are all crisp but t_r [Ci] $\neq$ t_s [Ci]. Then Ei (t_r [Ci], t_s [Ci]) = 0.

Case 3: *missing fuzzy attribute values.*

Among t_r [Ci] and t_s, one is fuzzy based on a possibility distribution whereas the other is crisp. At this point, the crisp attribute value is regarded as a special form of fuzzy value, where there is only one element in its support and the possibility of this element is one. The equivalence of t_r [Ci] and t_s [Ci] is essentially the equivalence degree of fuzzy data defined in Section 7.3. Then

$$Ei\ (t_r\ [Ci],\ t_s\ [Ci]) = SE\ (t_r\ [Ci],\ t_s\ [Ci]) = \min\ (SID\ (t_r\ [Ci],\ t_s\ [Ci]),\ SID\ (t_s\ [Ci],\ t_r\ [Ci])).$$

Case 4: *inconsistent fuzzy attribute values.*

t_r [Ci] and t_s [Ci] are all fuzzy. Being the same as the above, the equivalence of t_r [Ci] and t_s [Ci] is the equivalence degree of fuzzy data and

$$Ei\ (t_r\ [Ci],\ t_s\ [Ci]) = SE\ (t_r\ [Ci],\ t_s\ [Ci]) = \min\ (SID\ (t_r\ [Ci],\ t_s\ [Ci]),\ SID\ (t_s\ [Ci],\ t_r\ [Ci])).$$

Attribute Domain Conflicts

When there exist data format conflicts, data type conflicts, or data unit conflicts, t_r [Ci] and t_s [Ci] cannot be directly compared. In order to estimate the equivalence of t_r [Ci] and t_s [Ci], they should be converted into the values of virtual attributes by using one-to-one mapping, many-to-one mapping, or one-to-many mapping, which are comparable. Then the equivalence of original attribute values is evaluated by estimating that of corresponding values of virtual attributes.

Assume that t_r [Ci] is mapped into t_r' [Ci'], where Ci' is a virtual attribute of Ci and t_r [Ci] may be a crisp value or a fuzzy value. Applying the mapping approaches (one-to-one, many-to-one, or one-to-many), t_r [Ci] can be mapped into t_r' [Ci']. t_r' [Ci'] and t_s [Ci] can be comparable and t_s [Ci] may be a crisp value or a fuzzy value also. Applying the evaluation approaches given above, we can evaluate

$$Ei\ (t_r\ [Ci],\ t_s\ [Ci]) = Ei\ (t_r'\ [Ci'],\ t_s\ [Ci]).$$

Example. Considering the fuzzy relations describing virtual enterprise information in Figure 7-14, it is clear that there is no common key in r and s. Therefore, we cannot directly know if two tuples from r and s refer to the same real world entity.

The set of compatible attributes is {*Name, Lead-time, Weight, Transport*}. Attribute *Name* plays a crucial role in entity identification, so w_{Name} is designated 1/2. $w_{Lead-time}$, w_{Weight} and $w_{Transport}$ are designated 1/6, respectively. It can be seen that there is a domain conflict between *Lead-time* in r and *Lead-time* in s. The same situations can also be found in *Weight* and *Transport*. In order to evaluate the equivalence of two tuples from r and s respectively, say t_r = <00061, Engine, 3, 40.2, Land> and t_s = <0605, Engine, about 21, 40, Train, John>, we assume that t_r is mapped into a virtual tuple t_r', which is compatible with t_s. Then t_r' [*Lead-time* (Days)] = 21, t_r' [*Weight* (kg)] = 40, and t_r' [*Transport*] = {Train, Truck}.

Fuzzy relation r

Part ID	Name	Lead-time (weeks)	Weight (kg)	Transport
00061	Engine	3	40.2	Land
00062	Gearbox	2	about 54.8	Water

Fuzzy relation s

Part ID	Name	Lead-time (days)	Weight (kg)	Transport	Responsibility
0605	Engine	about 21	40	Train	John
0628	Gearbox	about 14	55	Vessel	Tom

Figure 7-14. Fuzzy Database Relations with Incompatible Keys for Integration

Let fuzzy value "about 21" be represented by a possibility distribution {0.5/18, 0.7/19, 0.9/20, 1.0/21, 0.8/22, 0.6/23, 0.4/24}. Then we have

$Ei\ (t_r\ [Name],\ t_s\ [Name]) = Ei\ (Engine,\ Engine) = 1,$

Ei (t_r [*Lead-time*], t_s [*Lead-time*]) = Ei (t_r' [*Lead-time*], t_s [*Lead-time*]) =
Ei (21, {0.5/18, 0.7/19, 0.9/20, 1.0/21, 0.8/22, 0.6/23, 0.4/24}) = SE
({1/21}, {0.5/18, 0.7/19, 0.9/20, 1.0/21, 0.8/22, 0.6/23, 0.4/24}) =
10/49,

Ei (t_r [*Weight*], t_s [*Weight*]) = Ei (40, 40) = 1, and
Ei (t_r [*Transport*], t_s [*Transport*]) = Ei (t_r' [*Transport*], t_s [*Transport*]) =
Ei ({Train, Truck}, Train) = SE ({1/Train, 1/Truck}, {1/Train}) = 1/2.
Therefore,

$P_{equivalence}$ (t_r, t_s) = Ei (t_r [*Name*], t_s [*Name*]) × w_{Name} + Ei (t_r [*Lead-time*], t_s
[*Lead-time*]) × $w_{Lead-time}$ + Ei (t_r [*Weight*], t_s [*Weight*]) × w_{Weight} + Ei
(t_r [*Transport*], t_s [*Transport*]) × $w_{Transport}$ = 1 × 1/2 + 10/49 × 1/6 + 1
× 1/6 + 1/2 × 1/6 = 0.954.

If a threshold is given, say 0.95, tuples t_r and t_s from r and s respectively
are considered to refer to the same real world entity and is integrated into a
new tuple <00061, 0605, Engine, 21, 40, Land, John>. In order to represent
the uncertainty that t_r may be equivalent to t_s, the equivalence $P_{equivalence}$ (t_r,
t_s) should be attached to the integrated tuple, a tuple with probability.
Generally speaking, some attribute values of the tuple can be fuzzy since
component relations are fuzzy. Therefore, a data model for fuzzy
multidatabase integration is fuzzy attribute-based probabilistic one.
Similarly, tuples <00062, Gearbox, 2, about 54.8, Water> and <0628,
Gearbox, about 14, 55, ship, Tom> from r and s, respectively, can be
evaluated and integrated.

7.9   Summary

Focusing on the possibility-based fuzzy relational databases, in
particular, the extended possibility-based fuzzy relational databases, this
chapter investigated some major issues related to fuzzy relational databases
such as the database models, data redundancy, data integrity constraints,
relational algebra, database update, and multidatabases. Among these issues,
the update and integration of the fuzzy relational databases are rarely
discussed in the context of the fuzzy relational databases.

It should be noticed that, however, classical relational database model
and its extension of imprecision and uncertainty do not satisfy the need of
modeling complex objects with imprecision and uncertainty. So many
researches have been concentrated on the development of some database
models to deal with complex objects and uncertain data together. In next two
chapters (Chapter 8 and Chapter 9), the fuzzy nested relational databases and
the fuzzy object-oriented databases are presented, respectively.

References

Ahmed, R., De Smedt, P., Du, W., Kent, W., Ketabchi, M. A., Litwin, W., Rafii, A. and Shan, M. C., 1991, The pegasus heterogeneous multidatabase system, *IEEE Computer*, 24 (12): 19-27.

ANSI/X3/SPARC, 1975, Study group on database management systems: interim report, FDT (7) 2, Bulletin of ACM SIGFIDET.

Armstrong, W. W., 1974, Dependency structures of data base relationships, *Proceedings of the IFIP Congress*, 580- 583.

Baldwin, J. F. and Zhou, S. Q., 1984, A fuzzy relational inference language, *Fuzzy Sets and Systems*, 14: 155-174.

Beeri, C., Fagin, R. and Howard, J. H., 1977, A complete axiomatization for functional and multivalued dependencies in database relations, *ACM SIGMOD Conference*, 47-61.

Bhattacharjee, T. K. and Mazumdar, A. K., 1998, Axiomatisation of fuzzy multivalued dependencies in a fuzzy relational data model, *Fuzzy Sets and Systems*, 96 (3): 343-352.

Bosc, P. and Pivert, O., 1992, Some approaches for relational databases flexible querying, *Journal of Intelligent Information Systems*, 1: 323-354.

Bosc, P. and Pivert, O., 1997, On the comparison of imprecise values in fuzzy databases, *Proceedings of the 1997 IEEE International Conference on Fuzzy Systems*, 2: 707-712.

Bosc, P. and Pivert, O., 2003, On the impact of regular functional dependencies when moving to a possibilistic database framework, *Fuzzy Sets and Systems*, 140 (1): 207-227.

Bosc, P. and Pivert, O., 1995, SQLf: A Relational Database Language for Fuzzy Querying, *IEEE Transactions on Fuzzy Systems*, 3 (1): 1-17.

Bosc, P., Dubois, D. and Prade, H., 1998, Fuzzy functional dependencies and redundancy elimination, *Journal of the American Society for Information Science*, 49 (3): 217-235.

Breitbart, Y., Olson, P. L. and Thompson, G. R., 1987, Database integration in a distributed heterogeneous database System, *Proceedings of IEEE International Conference on Data Engineering*, 301-310.

Buckles, B. P. and Petry, E. F., 1982, A fuzzy representation of data for relational database, *Fuzzy Sets and Systems*, 7 (3): 213-226.

Chang, C. S. and Chen, A. L. P., 1998, Efficient refinement of uncertain data by fuzzy integrity constraints, *Information Sciences*, 104 (3-4): 191–211.

Chatterjee, A. and Segev, A., 1991, Data manipulation in heterogeneous databases, *SIGMOD Record*, 20 (4): 64-68.

Chatterjee, A. and Segev, A., 1995, Rule based joins in heterogeneous databases, *Decision Support Systems*, 13 (3-4): 313-333.

Chen, A. L. P., 1990, Outerjoin optimization in multidatabase Systems, *Proceedings of IEEE International Symposium on Databases in Parallel and Distributed Systems*, 211-218.

Chen, A. L. P., Tsai, P. S. M. and Koh, J. L., 1996, Identifying object isomerism in multidatabase systems, *Distributed and Parallel Databases*, 4 (2): 143-168.

Chen, G. Q., 1999, *Fuzzy Logic in Data Modeling; Semantics, Constraints, and Database Design*, Kluwer Academic Publisher.

Chen, G. Q., Kerre, E. E. and Vandenbulcke, J., 1994, A computational algorithm for the FFD closure and a complete axiomatization of fuzzy functional dependency (FFD), *International Journal of Intelligent Systems*, 9: 421-439.

Chen, G. Q., Kerre, E. E. and Vandenbulcke, J., 1996, Normalization based on functional dependency in a fuzzy relational data model, *Information Systems*, 21 (3): 299-310.

Chen, G. Q., Vandenbulcke, J. and Kerre, E. E., 1992, A general treatment of data redundancy in a fuzzy relational data model, *Journal American Society of Information Sciences*, 43 (3): 304-311.

Codd, E. F., 1970, A relational model of data for large shared data banks, *Communications of The ACM*, 13 (6): 377-387.

Codd, E. F., 1986, Missing information (applicable and inapplicable) in relational databases, *SIGMOD Record*, 15: 53-78.

Cubero, J. C. and Vila, M. A., 1994, A new definition of fuzzy functional dependency in fuzzy relational databases, *International Journal of Intelligent Systems*, 9 (5): 441-448.

Czejdo, B., Rusinkiewicz, M. and Embley, D. W., 1987, An approach to schema integration and query formulation in federated database systems, *Proceedings of IEEE International Conference on Data Engineering*, 477-484.

Deen, S. M., Amin, R. R. and Taylor, M. C., 1987, Data Integration in Distributed Databases, *IEEE Transactions on Software Engineering*, 13: 860-864.

DeMichiel, L. G., 1989, Resolving database incompatibility: an approach to performing relational operations over mismatched domains, *IEEE Transactions on Knowledge and Data Engineering*, 1: 485-493.

Dey, D., Sarkar, S. and De, P., 1998, A probabilistic decision model for entity matching in heterogeneous databases, *Management Science*, 44 (10): 1379-1395.

Dutta, S., 1991, Aroximate Reasoning by Analogy to Answer Null Query, *International Journal of Proximate Reasoning*, 5: 373-398.

Fagin, R., 1977, Multivalued Dependencies and a New Normal Form for Relational Databases, *ACM Transactions on Database Systems*, 2 (3): 262-278.

Flach, P. A. and Savnik, I., 1999, Database dependency discovery: a machine learning approach, *AI Communications*, 12 (3): 139-160.

Grant, J., 1979, Partial values in a tabular database model, *Information Processing Letters*, 9: 97-99.

Hale, J. and Shenoi, S., 1996, Analyzing FD inference in relational databases, *Data & Knowledge Engineering*, 18 (2): 167-183.

Heimbigner, D. and McLeod, D., 1985, A federated architecture for information management, *ACM Transactions on Office Information Systems*, 3: 253-278.

Jyothi, S. and Babu, M. S., 1997, Multivalued dependencies in fuzzy relational databases and lossless join decomposition, *Fuzzy Sets and Systems*, 88 (3): 315-332.

Kerre, E. E., 1988, Fuzzy sets and approximate reasoning, *Lecture notes for the course special topics in computer sciences*, Lincoln, NB: University of Nebraska.

Kim, W. Choi, I., Gala, S. and Scheevel, M., 1995, On resolving schematic heterogeneity in multidatabase systems, *Modern Database Systems: the Object Model, Interoperability, and Beyond*, Addison-Wesley ACM Press, 521-550.

Liao, S. Y., Wang, H. Q. and Liu, W. Y., 1999, Functional dependencies with null values, fuzzy values, and crisp values, *IEEE Transactions on Fuzzy Systems*, 7 (1): 97-103.

Lim, E. P., Srivastava, J. Prabhakar, A. and Richardson, J., 1996, Entity identification in database integration, *Information Sciences*, 89 (1-2): 1-38.

Lipski, W., 1979, On semantic issues connected with incomplete information databases, *ACM Transactions on Database Systems*, 4 (3): 262-296.

Litwin, W., Abdellatif, A., Nicolas, B., Vigier, P. and Zeronnal, A., 1987, MSQL: a multi-database manipulation language, *Information Science*, 49: 59-101.

Litwin, W., Mark, L. and Roussopoulos, N., 1990, Interoperability of multiple autonomous databases, *ACM Computing Surveys*, 22: 267-293.

Liu, W. Y., 1992, The reduction of the fuzzy data domain and fuzzy consistent join, *Fuzzy Sets and Systems*, 51 (1): 89-96.

Liu, W. Y., 1993, Extending the relational model to deal with fuzzy values, *Fuzzy Sets and Systems*, 60 (2): 207-212.

Liu, W. Y., 1997, Fuzzy data dependencies and implication of fuzzy data dependencies, *Fuzzy Sets and Systems*, 92 (3): 341-348.

Ma, Z. M., Zhang, W. J. and Ma, W. Y., 1999, Assessment of data redundancy in fuzzy relational databases based on semantic inclusion degree, *Information Processing Letters*, 72 (1-2): 25-29.

Ma, Z. M., Zhang, W. J. and Mili, F., 2002, Fuzzy data compression based on data dependencies, *International Journal of Intelligent Systems*, 17 (4): 409-426.

Mena, E., Illarramendi, A., Kashyap, V. and Sheth, A., 2000, OBSERVER: an approach for query processing in global information systems based on interoperation across pre-existing ontologies, International Journal Distributed and Parallel Databases, 8 (2): 223-271.

Motro, A., 1987, Super-views: virtual integration of multiple databases, *IEEE Transactions on Software Engineering*, 13: 785-798.

Parent, C. and Spaccapietra, S., 1998, Issues and approaches of database integration, *Communications of the ACM*, 41 (5): 166-178.

Petry, F. E., 1996, *Fuzzy Databases: Principles and Applications*, Kluwer Academic Publisher.

Prade, H. and Testemale, C., 1984, Generalizing database relational algebra for the treatment of incomplete or uncertain information and vague queries, *Information Sciences*, 34: 115-143.

Pu, C., 1991, Key equivalence in heterogenerous databases, *Proceedings of International Workshop on Interoperability in Multidatabase Systems*, 314-316.

Raju, K. V. S. V. N. and Majumdar, A. K., 1988, Fuzzy functional dependencies and lossless join decomposition of fuzzy relational database system, *ACM Transactions on Database Systems*, 13 (2): 129-166.

Rundensteiner, E. A., Hawkes, L. W. and Bandler, W., 1989, On nearness measures in fuzzy relational data models, *International Journal Approximate Reasoning*, 3: 267-298.

Savnik, I. and Flach, P. A., 2000, Discovery of Multivalued Dependencies from Relations, *Intelligent Data Analysis*, 4 (3-4): 195-211.

Shenoi, S. and Melton, A., 1989, Proximity relations in the fuzzy relational databases, *Fuzzy Sets and Systems*, 31 (3): 285-296.

Sözat, M. I. and Yazici, A., 2001, A Complete axiomatization for fuzzy functional and multivalued dependencies in fuzzy database relations, *Fuzzy Sets and Systems*, 117 (2): 161-181.

Takahashi, Y, 1993, Fuzzy database query languages and their relational completeness theorem, *IEEE Transactions on Knowledge and Data Engineering*, 5 (1): 122-125.

Tripathy, R. C. and Sakena, P. C., 1990, Multivalued dependencies in fuzzy relational databases, *Fuzzy Sets and Systems*, 38 (3): 267-279.

Tseng, F. S. C., Chen, A. L. P. and Yang W. P., 1993, Answering heterogeneous database queries with degrees of uncertainty, *Distributed and Parallel Databases: An International Journal*, 1: 281-302.

Umano, M. and Fukami, S., 1994, Fuzzy relational algebra for possibility-distribution-duzzy-relational model of fuzzy data", *Journal of Intelligent Information Systems*, 3: 7-27.

van Schooten, A., 1988, Design and implementation of a model for the presentation and manipulation of uncertainty and imprecision in databases and expert systems, *Ph.D. thesis in Dutch*, Belgium: University of Gent, 1988.

Wang, K. and Zhang, W., 1996, Detecting data inconsistency for multidatabases, *Proceedings of the 1996 International Conference on Parallel and Distributed Computing Systems*, 2: 657-663.

Wiederhold, G., 2000, Future needs in integration of information, *International Journal of Cooperative Systems*; 9 (4): 449-772.

Yan, M. H. and Fu, A. W.-C., 2001, Algorithm for discovering multivalued dependencies, *Proceedings of the2001 ACM International Conference on Information and Knowledge Management*, 556-558.

Yazici, A. and George, R., 1999, *Fuzzy Database Modeling*, Physica-Verlag.

Zadeh, L. A., 1965, Fuzzy sets, *Information & Control*, 8 (3): 338-353.

Zadeh, L. A., 1975, The concept of a linguistic variable and its application to approximate reasoning, *Information Sciences*, 8: 119-249, 301-357; 9: 43-80.

Zhang, W. N., Laun, E. and Meng, W. Y., 1997, A methodology of integrating fuzzy relational databases in a multidatabase systems, *Proceedings of the 5th International Conference on Database Systems for Advanced Applications*, 401-410.

Chapter 8

THE FUZZY NESTED RELATIONAL DATABASES

8.1   Introduction

The normalization, being one kind of constraints, is proposed in traditional relational databases. Among various normalized forms, first normal form (1NF) is the most fundamental one, which assumes that each attribute value in a relational instance must be atomic. As we know, the real-world applications are complex, and data types and their relationships are rich as well as complicated. The 1NF assumption limits the expressive power of traditional relational database model. Therefore, some attempts to relax 1NF limitation are made and one kind of data model, called non-first normal (or nested) relational database model have been introduced, where attribute values may be atomic or set-valued and even relations themselves (Colby, 1990; Makinouchi, 1977; Ozsoyoglu, Ozsoyoglu and Matos, 1987; Roth, Korth and Batory, 1987; Schek and Scholl, 1986). Such database model is also called NF^2 one simply. NF^2 data models based on relational data model can model complex structures of objects and the relationship among them.

A NF^2 data model containing fuzzy information accommodates uncertainty and complexity of the real-world objects simultaneously. Therefore, some researches have concentrated on introducing imprecise and uncertain information into NF^2 relational databases. In (Levene, 1992; Roth, Korth and Silberschatz, 1989), a NF^2 database model with null values is presented. In (Yazici $et\ al$, 1999), uncertain null values, set values, range values (partial values and value intervals), and fuzzy values are all modeled in NF^2 data model and the extended NF^2 algebra is given. It should be noted that, however, the operations for the extended NF^2 relational algebra in (Yazici *et al*, 1999) mainly focus on two restructuring operations: *Merge* and *Unmerge*. The definitions for basic set operations are brief that fuzzy data redundancies and their removals are not investigated fully. In particular, fuzzy data in the extended NF^2 data model of (Yazici *et al*, 1999) are similarity-based (Buckles and Petry, 1982). In this chapter, we focus on extended possibility-based representation of fuzzy data, where the fuzziness of data comes from possibility distributions (Kerre, 1988; Prade and Testemale, 1984) over universes of discourse as well as similarity (Buckles and Petry, 1982; Yazici *et al*, 1999) (proximity or resemblance (Rundensteiner, Hawkes and Bandler, 1989) relations. We introduce extended possibility-based fuzzy data into nested relational databases and define fuzzy nested algebra.

8.2   The Fuzzy Nested Relational Models

An extended possibility-based fuzzy NF^2 relational schema is a set of attributes (A1, A2, ..., An, *pM*) and their domains are D1, D2, ..., Dn, D0, respectively, where Di ($1 \leq i \leq n$) can be one of the following:

(a) The set of atomic values. For any an element ai $\in$ Di, it is a typical simple crisp attribute value.

(b) The set of null values, denoted *ndom*, where null values may be *unk*, *inap*, *nin*, and *onul*.

(c) The set of fuzzy subset. The corresponding attribute value is an extended possibility-based fuzzy data.

(d) The power set of the set in (1). The corresponding attribute value, say ai, is multivalued one with the form of {ai1, ai2, ..., aik}.

(e) The set of relation values. The corresponding attribute value, say ai, is a tuple of the form <ai1, ai2, ..., aim> which is an element of Di1 $\times$ Di2 $\times$ ... $\times$ Dim (m > 1 and $1 \leq i \leq n$), where each Dij ($1 \leq j \leq m$) may be a domain in (a), (b), (c), and (d) and even the set of relation values.

The domain D_0 is a set of atomic values and each value is a crisp one from the range [0, 1], representing the possibility that the correspond tuple is true in the NF^2 relation. We assume that the possibilities of all tuples are precisely one in the thesis. Then for an attribute $A_i \in R$ ($1 \leq i \leq n$), its attribute domain is formally represented as follows:

$$\tau_i = dom \mid ndom \mid fdom \mid sdom \mid <B_1 : \tau_{i1}, B_2 : \tau_{i2}, ..., B_m : \tau_{im}>$$

where B1, B2, ..., Bm are attributes.

A relational instance r over fuzzy NF^2 schema $(A_1 : \tau_1, A_2 : \tau_2, ..., A_n : \tau_n)$ is a subset of Cartesian product $\tau_1 \times \tau_2 \times ... \times \tau_n$. A tuple in r with the form of <a1, a2, ..., an> consists of n components. Each component ai $(1 \le i \le n)$ may be an atomic value, null value, set value, fuzzy value, or another tuple.

An example of fuzzy NF^2 relation is shown in Table 8-1. It can be seen that *Tank_Id* and *Start_data* are crisp atomic-valued attributes, *Tank_body* is a relation-valued attribute, and *Responsibility* is a set-valued attribute. In attribute *Tank_body*, two component attributes *Volume* and *Capacity* are fuzzy ones.

Table 8-1. Pressured Air Tank Relation

Tank_ ID	Tank_body				Start_ Date	Responsi bility
	Body_ID	Material	Volume	Capacity		
TA1	BO01	Alloy	about 2.5e+03	about 1.0e+06	01/12/99	John
TA2	BO02	Steel	about 2.5e+04	about 1.0e+07	28/03/00	{Tom, Mary}

Now let us concentrate on the redundancies of tuples in a fuzzy NF^2 relation. First, let us look at two values on a structured attribute $a_j = $ (Aj1: π_{Aj1}, Aj2: π_{Aj2}, ..., Ajm: π_{Ajm}) and $a_j' = $ (Aj1: π_{Aj1}', Aj2: π_{Aj2}', ..., Ajm: π_{Ajm}'), which consist of simple attribute values, crisp (atomic and set-valued) or fuzzy, on the schema R (Aj1, Aj2, ..., Ajm). There is a resemblance relation on each attribute domain Djk $(1 \le k \le m)$ and $\alpha jk \in [0, 1]$ $(1 \le k \le m)$ is the threshold on the resemblance relation. Let $\beta \in [0, 1]$ be a given threshold. a_j and a_j' are α-β-redundant if and only if for $k = 1, 2, ..., m$, min $(SE_{\alpha jk} (\pi_{Ajk}, \pi_{Ajk}')) \ge \beta$ holds true. min $(SE_{\alpha jk} (\pi_{Ajk}, \pi_{Ajk}'))$ $(1 \le k \le m)$ is called the equivalence degree of structured attribute values.

Consequently, the notion of equivalence degree of structured attribute values can be extended for the tuples in fuzzy nested relations to assess tuple redundancies. Informally, any two tuples in a nested relation are redundant, if, for pair of the corresponding attribute values, the equivalence degree is greater than or equal to the threshold value. If the pair of the corresponding attribute values is simple, the equivalence degree is one for two values. For two values of structured attributes, however, the equivalence degree is one for structured attributes. Two redundant tuples t and t' are written $t \equiv t'$.

8.3 Algebra Operations

Based on the NF^2 database model without imprecision and uncertainty, the ordinary relational algebra has been extended. In addition, two new restructuring operators, called the Nest and Unnest (Ozsoyoglu, Ozsoyoglu and Matos, 1987; Paredaens and Gucht, 1992; Roth, Korth and Batory,

1987) (as well as Pack and Unpack in (Ozsoyoglu, Ozsoyoglu and Matos, 1987)), have been introduced. The Nest operator can obtain the nested relation including complex-valued attributes. The Unnest operator is used to flatten the nested relation. That is, it takes a relation nested on a set of attributes and desegregates it, creating a "flatter" structure. In the following, we define relational operations for fuzzy nested relational databases.

8.3.1   Traditional Relational Operations

Union and *Difference*: Let r and s be two union-compatible fuzzy nested relations. Then

$$r \cup s = min\,(\{t \mid t \in r \lor t \in s\})$$

and

$$r - s = \{t \mid t \in r \land (\forall v \in s)\,(t \not\equiv v)\}$$

Here, the operation *min* () means to remove the fuzzy redundant tuples in r and s. Of course, the threshold value should be provided for the purpose.

Cartesian Product. Let r and s be two fuzzy nested relations on schemas R and S, respectively. Then $r \times s$ is a fuzzy nested relation with the schema $R \cup S$. The formal definition of Cartesian product operation is as follows.

$$r \times s = \{t \mid t\,(R) \in r \land t\,(S) \in s\}$$

Projection. Let r be a fuzzy nested relation on the schema R and $S \subset R$. Then the projection of r on the schema S is formally defined as follows.

$$\Pi_S\,(r) = min\,(\{t \mid (\forall\,v \in r)\,(t = v\,(S)\})$$

Here, an attribute in S may be of the form $B.C$, in which B is a structured attribute and C is its component attribute. Being the same as union operation, projection operation also needs to remove fuzzy redundant tuples in the result relation after the operation.

Selection. In classical relational databases, the selection condition is of the form $X\,\theta\,Y$, where X is an attribute, Y is an attribute or a constant value, and $\theta \in \{=, \neq, >, \geq, <, \leq\}$. In order to implement fuzzy query for fuzzy relational databases, "θ" should be fuzzy, denoting $\approx, \not\approx, \succ, \prec, \succeq,$ and $\preceq$. In addition, X is only a simple attribute or the simple attribute of a structured attribute but Y may be one of the following.

(a) A constant, crisp or fuzzy one;

(b) A simple attribute;

(c) The simple component attribute of a structured attribute, having the form A. B, where A is a structured attribute and B is its simple component attribute.

Assume that there is a resemblance relation on the universe of discourse and α is the threshold on it. Then the fuzzy comparison operations are defined as follows:

(a) $X \approx Y$ iff $SE_\alpha (X, Y) \geq \beta$, where β is a selected cut (the followings are the same).

(b) $X \not\approx Y$ iff $SE_\alpha (X, Y) < \beta$.

(c) $X \succ Y$ iff $X \not\approx Y$ and min (Supp (X)) > min (Supp (Y)).

(d) $X \succeq Y$ iff $X \approx Y$ or $X \succ Y$.

(e) $X \prec Y$ iff $X \not\approx Y$ and min (Supp (X)) < min (Supp (Y)).

(f) $X \preceq Y$ iff $X \approx Y$ or $X \prec Y$.

Depending on Y, the following situations can be identified for the selection condition $X \theta Y$. Let X be the attribute A_i: τ_i in a fuzzy nested relation.

(a) $A_i \theta c$, where c is a crisp constant. According to τ_i, the definition of $A_i \theta c$ is as follows:

if τ_i is *dom*, $A_i \theta c$ is a traditional comparison and $\theta \in \{=, \neq, >, <, \geq, \leq\}$;

if τ_i is *fdom*, $A_i \theta c$ is a fuzzy comparison and $\theta \in \{\approx, \not\approx, \succ, \prec, \succeq, \preceq \}$;

if τ_i is *ndom*, $A_i \theta c$ is a null comparison and regarded as the special fuzzy comparison;

if τ_i is *sdom*, $A_i \theta c$ is a element-set comparison. Then $A_i \theta c$ if c and any element in the value of Ai of a tuple satisfy the "θ".

(b) $A_i \theta f$, where f is a fuzzy value.

if τ_i is *dom*, *fdom*, or *ndom*, $A_i \theta f$ is a fuzzy comparison and $\theta \in \{\approx, \not\approx, \succ, \prec, \succeq, \preceq \}$;

if τ_i is *sdom*, $A_i \theta f$ is a fuzzy set comparison. Then $A_i \theta f$ if f and any element in the value of Ai of a tuple satisfy the fuzzy "θ", where $\theta \in \{\approx, \not\approx, \succ, \prec, \succeq, \preceq \}$.

(c) $A_i \theta A_j$, where A_j: τ_j is a simple attribute and $i \neq j$.

if τ_i and τ_j are all *dom*, $A_i \theta A_j$ is a traditional comparison;

if τ_i and τ_j are *dom* and *fdom*, *fdom* and *fdom*, or *ndom* and *fdom*, $A_i \theta A_j$ is a fuzzy comparison;

if τ_i and τ_j are *dom* and *ndom*, $A_i \theta A_j$ is a null comparison;

if τ_i and τ_j are *dom* and *sdom*, $A_i \theta A_j$ is a element-set comparison;

if τ_i and τ_j are *fdom* and *sdom*, $A_i \theta A_j$ is a fuzzy set comparison;

if τ_i and τ_j are all *ndom*, $A_i \theta A_j$ is a null-null comparison. Then $A_i \theta A_j$ if they have the same null values on the same universe of discourse;

if τ_i and τ_j are *ndom* and *sdom*, $A_i \theta A_j$ is a null-set comparison and regarded as the special element-set comparison;

if τ_i and τ_j are *sdom* and *sdom*, A_i θ A_j is a set-set comparison and regarded as the special element-set comparison.

(d) A_i θ A_j. B, where A_j is a structured attribute ($i \neq j$) and B is a simple attribute. The situations are the same as those in above case (c).

In fuzzy nested relational databases, the selection condition is similar to that in fuzzy relational databases except that the attribute may be of the form $B.C$, where B is a structured attribute and C is its component attribute. Let Q be a predicate denoting the selection condition. The selection operation for a fuzzy nested relation r is defined as follows.

$$\sigma_Q(r) = \{t \mid t \in r \wedge Q(t)\}$$

8.3.2   Nest and Unnest Operations

In addition to some traditional relational operations, two restructuring, called *Nest* and *Unnest* (called *Pack* and *Unpack*, *Merge* and *Unmerge* also in literature), are also crucial for fuzzy nested relational databases. The Nest operator can gain the nested relation including structured attributes. The Unnest operator is used to flatten the nested relation. That is, it takes a nested relation on a set of attributes and desegregates it, creating a "flatter" structure.

Let r be a fuzzy nested relation with the schema $R = \{A_1, A_2, ..., A_i, ..., A_k, ..., A_n\}$, where $1 \leq i, k \leq n$. Now $Y = \{A_i, ..., A_k\}$ is merged into a structured attribute B and a new fuzzy nested relation s is formed, which schema is $S = \{A_1, A_2, ..., A_{i-1}, B, A_{k+1}, ..., A_n\}$. The following notation is used to represent the Nest operation above.

$$s(S) = \Gamma_{Y \to B}(r(R)) = \{\omega [(R - Y) \cup B] \mid (\exists u)(\forall v)(u \in r \wedge v \in r \wedge SE$$
$$(u[R - Y], v[R - Y]) < \beta \wedge \omega[R - Y] = u[R - Y] \wedge \omega[B] = u[Y]) \vee$$
$$(\forall u)(\forall v)(u \in r \wedge v \in r \wedge SE(u[R - Y], v[R - Y]) \geq \beta \wedge \omega[R - Y] = u$$
$$[R - Y] \cup_f v[R - Y] \wedge \omega[B] = u[Y] \cup v[Y])\}$$

It can be seen that in the process of the Nest operation on attribute sets Y to B, multiple tuples in r which are fuzzily equivalent on the attribute set R – Y are merged to form a tuples of s. Such merging operation is respectively completed on attribute sets R – Y and Y. On the R – Y, fuzzy union $\cup_f$ is used and for an attribute $C \in R - Y$, the value of C of the created tuple is an atomic value, crisp or fuzzy. The value of an attribute B. C $\in$ Y of the created tuple, however, is a set value and the common union is used.

Example 8.1. Consider the fuzzy nested relation shown in Table 8-2. We want to implement the Nest operation for the relation by grouping attributes

B and C under a structured attribute X. Let the given threshold $\beta = 0.85$. The resulting relation will be the fuzzy nested relation shown in Table 8-3.

Table 8-2. Fuzzy Relation *r*

A	B	C	D
a1	b1	c1	{0.2/d1, 0.5/d2, 0.8/d3}
a1	b2	c2	{0.5/d2, 0.9/d3}
a1	b3	c3	{0.1/d1, 0.5/d2, 0.9/d3}

Table 8-3. Fuzzy Nested Relation $\Gamma_{\{B, C\} \rightarrow X}(r)$

A	X		D
	B	C	
a1	{b1, b2, b3}	{c1, c2, c3}	{0.2/d1, 0.5/d2, 0.9/d3}

Another restructuring operation, called *Unnest*, is an inverse of *Nest* under certain conditions. In a classical nested relation, this condition is that the nested relation is in Partitioned Normal Form (PNF) (Thomas and Fischer, 1986). A relation is in PNF if and only if

(a) all of a subset of the simple attributes forms a relation key and

(b) every sub-relation is in PNF.

Let *s* be a fuzzy nested relation with the schema $S = \{A_1, A_2, ..., A_{i-1}, B, A_{k+1}, ..., A_n\}$, where B is a structured attribute and B : $\{A_i, ..., A_k\}$. Unnest operation products a new fuzzy nested relation *r*, which schema is $R = \{A_1, A_2, ..., A_{i-1}, A_i, ..., A_k, A_{k+1}, ..., A_n\}$, i.e., $R = S - B \cup \{A_i, ..., A_k\}$. The following notation is used to represent the Unnest operation above.

$$r(R) = \Xi_B(s(S)) = \{t[(R - B) \cup \{A_i, ..., A_k\}] \mid (\forall u)(u \in s \wedge t[R - B] = u[R - B] \wedge t[A_i ... A_k] \in u[B])\}$$

8.3 Summary

The requirement of modeling complex objects as well as information imprecision and uncertainty has challenged current database technology. Classical relational databases and their extensions of processing imprecise and uncertain data do not satisfy such need. So fuzzy extensions of post-relational data models have been proposed and their fuzzy extensions have recently received increasing attention (de Caluwe, 1998; Ma, 2005).

This chapter introduces fuzzy data into nested relational database model. The fuzzy data here is the more general form, namely, extended possibility-based fuzzy data, which is represented by possibility distribution over a universe of discourse and meanwhile a resemblance relation on the universe is in effect. We give the structure of fuzzy nested relational model and the approach for assessing fuzzy data redundancies. On the basis, the algebra is defined for manipulating fuzzy and complex data in the chapter.

References

Buckles, B. P. and Petry, F. E., 1982, A fuzzy representation of data for relational database, *Fuzzy Sets and Systems*, 7 (3): 213-226.

Colby, L. S., 1990, A recursive algebra for nested relations, *Information Systems*, 15 (5): 567–662.

de Caluwe, R. (editor), 1998, *Fuzzy and Uncertain Object-Oriented Databases: Concepts and Models*, World Scientific Pub Co.

Kerre, E. E., 1988, *Fuzzy Sets and Approximate Reasoning*. Lecture Notes for the Course (Special Topics in Computer Sciences). Lincoln, NB: University of Nebraska.

Levene, M., 1992, *The Nested Universal Relation Database Model*, Lecture Notes in Computer Science No. 595, Springer-Verlag, Berlin.

Ma, Z. M. (editor), 2004, *Advances in Fuzzy Object-Oriented Databases: Modeling and Applications*, Idea Group Publishing.

Makinouchi, A., 1977, A consideration on normal form of not-necessarily normalized relations in the relational data model, *Proceedings of Third International Conference on Very Large Databases*, Tokyo, Japan, October, 447–453.

Ozsoyoglu, G., Ozsoyoglu, Z. M. and Matos, V., 1987, Extending relational algebra and relational calculus with set-valued attributes and aggregate functions, *ACM Transactions on Database Systems*, 12 (4): 566-592.

Paredaens, J. and Gucht, D. V., 1992, Converting nested algebra expressions into flat algebra expressions, *ACM Transactions on Database Systems*, 17 (1): 65-93.

Prade, H. and Testemale, C., 1984, Generalizing database relational algebra for the treatment of incomplete or uncertain Information and vague queries, *Information Sciences*, 34: 115-143.

Roth, M. A., Korth, H. F. and Batory, D. S., 1987, SQL/NF: A query language for non-1NF relational databases, *Information Systems*, 12: 99-114.

Roth, M. A., Korth, H. F. and Silberschatz, A., 1989, Null values in nested relational databases, *Acta Informatica*, 26: 615-642.

Rundensteiner, E. A., Hawkes, L. W. and Bandler, W., 1989, On nearness measures in fuzzy relational data models, *International Journal of Approximate Reasoning*, 3: 267-98.

Schek, H. J. and Scholl, M. H., 1986, The relational model with relational-valued attributes, *Information Systems*, 11 (2): 137-147.

Thomas, S. J. and Fischer, P. C., 1986, Nested relational structures, *Advances in Computing Research*, 3: 269-307.

Yazici, A., Soysal, A., Buckles, B. P. and Petry, F. E., 1999, Uncertainty in a nested relational database model, *Data & Knowledge Engineering*, 30: 275-301.

Chapter 9

THE FUZZY OBJECT-ORIENTED DATABASES

9.1   Introduction

Classical relational database model and its extension of imprecision and uncertainty do not satisfy the need of modeling complex objects with imprecision and uncertainty. So many researches have been concentrated on the development of some database models to deal with complex objects and uncertain data together. In (Yazici et al., 1999), an extended nested relational data model (also known as an NF^2 data model) was introduced for representing and manipulating complex and uncertain data in databases and the extended algebra and the extended SQL-like query language were hereby defined. Also physical data representation of the model and the core operations that the model provides were also introduced in (Yazici et al., 1999). It should be pointed out that, being the extension of relational data model, NF^2 data model is able to handle complex-valued attributes and may be better suited to some complex applications such as office automation systems, information retrieval systems and expert database systems (Yazici et al., 1999). But it is difficult for NF^2 data model to represent complex relationships among objects and attributes. Some advanced abstracts in data modeling (e.g., class hierarchy, inheritance, superclass/subclass, and encapsulation) are not supported by NF^2 data model, which are needed by many real applications. Therefore, in order to model uncertain data and complex-valued attributes as well as complex relationships among objects, current efforts have being focused on conceptual data models and object-oriented databases (*OODB*) with imprecise and uncertain information.

Regarding modeling imprecise and uncertain information in object-oriented databases, Zicari and Milano in (1990) first introduced incomplete information, namely, null values, where incomplete schema and incomplete objects can be distinguished. From then on, the incorporation of imprecise and uncertain information in object-oriented databases has increasingly received the attentions, where fuzziness is witnessed at the levels of object instances and class hierarchies. Based on similarity relationship, in (George *et al.*, 1996), the range of attribute values is used to represent the set of allowed values for an attribute of a given class. Depending on the inclusion of the actual attribute values of the given object into the range of the attributes for the class, the membership degrees of an object to a class can be calculated. The weak and strong class hierarchies were defined based on monotone increase or decrease of the membership of a subclass in its superclass. Based on the extension of a graphs-based model object model, a fuzzy object-oriented data model was defined in (Bordogna, Pasi and Lucarella, 1999). The notion of strength expressed by linguistic qualifiers was proposed, which can be associated with the instance relationship as well as an object with a class. Fuzzy classes and fuzzy class hierarchies were thus modeled in the *OODB*. An *UFO* (uncertainty and fuzziness in an object-oriented) databases model was proposed in (Gyseghem and de Caluwe, 1998) to model fuzziness and uncertainty by means of fuzzy set theory and generalized fuzzy set, respectively. That the behaviour and structure of the object are incompletely defined results in a gradual nature for the instantiation of an object. The partial inheritance, conditional inheritance, and multiple inheritances are permitted in fuzzy hierarchies. Based on possibility theory, vagueness and uncertainty were represented in class hierarchies in (Dubois, Prade and Rossazza, 1991), where the fuzzy ranges of the subclass attributes defined restrictions on that of the superclass attributes and then the degree of inclusion of a subclass in the superclass was dependent on the inclusion between the fuzzy ranges of their attributes. Based on the concept of the semantic proximity, an evaluated method of the fuzzy association degree was given in semantic data models (Liu and Song, 2001). Recent efforts have been paid on the establishment of consistent framework for a fuzzy object-oriented model based on the standard for the Object Data Management Group (*ODMG*) object data model (Cross, de Caluwe and Vangyseghem, 1997; Cross and Firat, 2000).

9.2   Fuzzy Objects and Fuzzy Classes

9.2.1   Fuzzy Objects

Objects model real world entities or abstract concepts. Objects have properties that may be attributes of the object itself or relationships also known as associations between the object and one or more other objects. An object is fuzzy because of a lack of information. For example, an object representing a part in preliminary design for certain will also be made of *stainless steel, moulded steel,* or *alloy steel* (each of them may be connected with a possibility, say, 0.7, 0.5 and 0.9, respectively). Formally, objects that have at least one attribute whose value is a fuzzy set are fuzzy objects.

9.2.2 Fuzzy Classes

The objects having the same properties are gathered into classes that are organized into hierarchies. Theoretically, a class can be considered from two different viewpoints (Dubois, Prade and Rossazza, 1991):
   (a) an extensional class, where the class is defined by the list of its object instances, and
   (b) an intensional class, where the class is defined by a set of attributes and their admissible values.
In addition, a subclass defined from its superclass by means of inheritance mechanism in the *OODB* can be seen as the special case of (b) above.

Therefore, a class is fuzzy because of the following several reasons. First, some objects are fuzzy ones, which have similar properties. A class defined by these objects may be fuzzy. These objects belong to the class with membership degree of [0, 1]. Second, when a class is intensionally defined, the domain of an attribute may be fuzzy and a fuzzy class is formed. For example, a class *Old equipment* is a fuzzy one because the domain of its attribute *Using period* is a set of fuzzy values such as *long, very long,* and *about 20 years.* Third, the subclass produced by a fuzzy class by means of specialization and the superclass produced by some classes (in which there is at least one class who is fuzzy) by means of generalization are also fuzzy.

The main difference between fuzzy classes and crisp classes is that the boundaries of fuzzy classes are imprecise. The imprecision in the class boundaries is caused by the imprecision of the values in the attribute domain. In the fuzzy *OODB*, classes are fuzzy because their attribute domains are fuzzy. The issue that an object fuzzily belongs to a class occurs since a class or an object is fuzzy. Similarly, a class is a subclass of another class with membership degree of [0, 1] because of the class fuzziness. In the *OODB*, the above-mentioned relationships are certain. Therefore, the evaluations of fuzzy object-class relationships and fuzzy inheritance hierarchies are the cores of information modeling in the fuzzy *OODB*. In the following discussion, we assume that the fuzzy attribute values of fuzzy objects and the fuzzy values in fuzzy attribute domains are represented by possibility distribution.

9.2.3   Fuzzy Object-Class Relationships

In the fuzzy *OODB*, the following four situations can be distinguished for object-class relationships.

(a) Crisp class and crisp object. This situation is the same as the *OODB*, where the object belongs or not to the class certainly. For example, the objects *Car* and *Computer* are for a class *Vehicle*, respectively.

(b) Crisp class and fuzzy object. Although the class is precisely defined and has the precise boundary, an object is fuzzy since its attribute value(s) may be fuzzy. In this situation, the object may be related to the class with the special degree in [0, 1]. For example, the object which *position* attribute may be *graduate, research assistant*, or *research assistant professor*, is for the class *Faculty*.

(c) Fuzzy class and crisp object. Being the same as the case in (b), the object may belong to the class with the membership degree in [0, 1]. For example, a Ph.D. student is for *Young student* class.

(d) Fuzzy class and fuzzy object. In this situation, the object also belongs to the class with the membership degree in [0, 1].

The object-class relationships in (b), (c) and (d) above are called *fuzzy object-class relationships*. In fact, the situation in (a) can be seen the special case of fuzzy object-class relationships, where the membership degree of the object to the class is one. It is clear that estimating the membership of an object to the class is crucial for fuzzy object-class relationship when classes are instantiated.

In the *OODB*, determining if an object belongs to a class depends on if its attribute values are respectively included in the corresponding attribute domains of the class. Similarly, in order to calculate the membership degree of an object to the class in a fuzzy object-class relationship, it is necessary to evaluate the degrees that the attribute domains of the class include the attribute values of the object. However, it should be noted that in a fuzzy object-class relationship, only the inclusion degree of object values with respect to the class domains is not accurate for the evaluation of membership degree of an object to the class. The attributes play different role in the definition and identification of a class (Liu and Song, 2001). Some may be dominant and some not. Therefore, a weight w is assigned to each attribute of the class according to its importance by designer. Then the membership degree of an object to the class in a fuzzy object-class relationship should be calculated using the inclusion degree of object values with respect to the class domains, and the weight of attributes.

Let C be a class with attributes $\{A_1, A2, ..., A_n\}$, o be an object on attribute set $\{A_1, A2, ..., A_n\}$, and $o(A_i)$ denote the attribute value of o on A_i ($1 \leq i \leq n$). In C, each attribute A_i is connected with a domain denoted *dom*

(A$_i$). The inclusion degree of o (A$_i$) with respect to *dom* (A$_i$) is denoted ID (*dom* (A$_i$), o (A$_i$)). In the following, we investigate the evaluation of ID (*dom* (A$_i$), o (A$_i$)). As we know, *dom* (A$_i$) is a set of crisp values in the *OODB* and may be a set of fuzzy subsets in fuzzy databases. Therefore, in a uniform *OODB* for crisp and fuzzy information modeling, *dom* (A$_i$) should be the union of these two components, *dom* (A$_i$) = *cdom* (A$_i$) $\cup$ *fdom* (A$_i$), where *cdom* (A$_i$) and *fdom* (A$_i$) respectively denote the sets of crisp values and fuzzy subsets. On the other hand, o (A$_i$) may be a crisp value or a fuzzy value. The following cases can be identified for evaluating ID (*dom* (A$_i$), o (A$_i$)).

Case 1: o (A$_i$) is a fuzzy value. Let *fdom* (A$_i$) = $\{f_1, f_2, ..., f_m\}$, where f_j ($1 \leq j \leq m$) is a fuzzy value, and *cdom* (A$_i$) = $\{c_1, c_2, ..., c_k\}$, where c_l ($1 \leq l \leq k$) is a crisp value. Then

ID (*dom* (A$_i$), o (A$_i$)) = max (ID (*cdom* (A$_i$), o (A$_i$)), ID (*fdom* (A$_i$), o (A$_i$))) = max (SID ($\{1.0/c_1, 1.0/c_2, ..., 1.0/c_k\}$, o (A$_i$)), max$_j$ (SID (f_j, o (A$_i$)))),

where SID (x, y), as shown in Section 7.2, is used to calculate the degree that fuzzy value x include fuzzy value y.

Case 2: o (A$_i$) is a crisp value. Then

ID (*dom* (A$_i$), o (A$_i$)) = 1 if o (A$_i$) $\in$ *cdom* (A$_i$)

else

ID (*dom* (A$_i$), o (A$_i$)) = ID (*fdom* (A$_i$), $\{1.0/o$ (A$_i$)$\}$).

Consider a fuzzy class *Young students* with attributes *Age* and *Height*, and two objects $o1$ and $o2$. Assume *cdom* (*Age*) = $\{5 - 20\}$, *fdom* (*Age*) = $\{\{1.0/20, 1.0/21, 0.7/22, 0.5/23\}, \{0.4/22, 0.6/23, 0.8/24, 1.0/25, 0.9/26, 0.8/27, 0.6/28\}, \{0.6/27, 0.8/28, 0.9/29, 1.0/30, 0.9/31, 0.6/32, 0.4/33, 0.2/34\}\}$, and *dom* (*Height*) = *cdom* (*Height*) = [60, 210]. Let $o1$ (*Age*) = 15, $o2$ (*Age*) = $\{0.6/25, 0.8/26, 1.0/27, 0.9/28, 0.7/29, 0.5/30, 0.3/31\}$, and $o2$ (*Height*) = 182. According to the definition above, we have
ID (*dom* (*Age*), $o1$ (*Age*)) = 1,
ID (*dom* (*Height*), $o2$ (*Height*)) = 1,
ID (*cdom* (*Age*), $o2$ (*Age*)) = SID ($\{1.0/5, 1.0/6, ..., 1.0/19, 1.0/20\}$, $o2$ (*Age*)) = 0, and
ID (*fdom* (*Age*), $o2$ (*Age*)) = max (SID ($\{1.0/20, 1.0/21, 0.7/22, 0.5/23\}$, $o2$ (*Age*)), SID $\{0.4/22, 0.6/23, 0.8/24, 1.0/25, 0.9/26, 0.8/27, 0.6/28\}$, $o2$ (*Age*)), SID ($\{0.6/27, 0.8/28, 0.9/29, 1.0/30, 0.9/31, 0.6/32, 0.4/33, 0.2/34\}$, $o2$ (*Age*))) = max (0, 0.58, 0.60) = 0.60.

Therefore,

ID (*dom* (*Age*), *o2* (*Age*)) = max (ID (*cdom* (*Age*), *o2* (*Age*)), ID (*fdom* (*Age*), *o2* (*Age*))) = 0.60.

Now, we define the formula to calculate the membership degree of the object o to the class C as follows, where w (A_i (C)) denotes the weight of attribute A_i to class C.

$$\mu_C(o) = \frac{\sum_{i=1}^{n} ID(dom(A_i), o(A_i)) \times w(A_i(C))}{\sum_{i=1}^{n} w(A_i(C))}$$

Consider the fuzzy class *Young students* and object *o2* above. Assume w (*Age* (*Young students*)) = 0.9 and w (*Height* (*Young students*)) = 0.2. Then $\mu_{\text{Young students}}(o2) = (0.9 \times 0.6 + 0.2 \times 1.0)/(0.9 + 0.2) = 0.67$.

In the above-given determination that an object belongs to a class fuzzily, it is assumed that the object and the class have the same attributes, namely, class C is with attributes {A_1, $A2$, ..., A_n} and object o is on {A_1, $A2$, ..., A_n} also. Such an object-class relationship is called *direct object-class relationship*. As we know, there exist subclass/superclass relationships in the *OODB*, where subclass inherits some attributes and methods of the superclass, overrides some attributes and methods of the superclass, and define some new attributes and methods. Any object belonging to the subclass must belong to the superclass since a subclass is the specialization of the superclass. So we have one kind of special object-class relationship: the relationship between superclass and the object of subclass. Such an object-class relationship is called *indirect object-class relationship*. Since the object and the class in indirect object-class relationship have different attributes, in the following, we present how to calculate the membership degree of an object to the class in an indirect object-class relationship.

Let C be a class with attributes {A_1, $A2$, ..., A_k, A_{k+1}, ..., A_m} and o be an object on attributes {A_1, $A2$, ..., A_k, A'_{k+1}, ..., A'_m, A_{m+1}, ..., A_n}. Here attributes A'_{k+1}, ..., and A'_m are overridden from A_{k+1}, ..., and A_m and attributes A_{m+1}, ..., and A_n are special. Then we have

$$\mu_C(o) = \frac{\sum_{i=1}^{k} ID(dom(A_i), o(A_i)) \times w(A_i(C)) + \sum_{j=k+1}^{m} ID(dom(A_j), o(A_j')) \times w(A_j(C))}{\sum_{i=1}^{m} w(A_i(C))}$$

Based on the direct object-class relationship and the indirect object-class relationship, now we focus on arbitrary object-class relationship. Let C be a class with attributes $\{A_1, A2, ..., A_k, A_{k+1}, ..., A_m, A_{m+1}, ..., A_n\}$ and o be an object on attributes $\{A_1, A2, ..., A_k, A'_{k+1}, ..., A'_m, B_{m+1}, ..., B_p\}$. Here attributes $A'_{k+1}, ...,$ and A'_m are overridden from $A_{k+1}, ...,$ and A_m, or $A_{k+1}, ...,$ and A_m are overridden from $A'_{k+1}, ...,$ and A'_m. Attributes $A_{m+1}, ...,$ and A_n and $B_{m+1}, ..., B_p$ are special in $\{A_1, A2, ..., A_k, A_{k+1}, ..., A_m, A_{m+1}, ..., A_n\}$ and $\{A_1, A2, ..., A_k, A'_{k+1}, ..., A'_m, B_{m+1}, ..., B_p\}$, respectively. Then we have

$$\mu_C(o) = \frac{\sum\limits_{i=1}^{k} ID(dom(A_i), o(A_i)) \times w(A_i(C)) + \sum\limits_{j=k+1}^{m} ID(dom(A_j), o(A_j')) \times w(A_j(C))}{\sum\limits_{i=1}^{n} w(A_i(C))}$$

Since an object may belong to a class with membership degree in [0, 1] in fuzzy object-class relationship, it is possible that an object that is in a direct object-class relationship and an indirect object-class relationship simultaneously belongs to the subclass and superclass with different membership degrees. This situation occurs in fuzzy inheritance hierarchies, which will be investigated in next section. Also for two classes that do not have subclass/superclass relationship, it is possible that an object may belong to these two classes with different membership degrees simultaneously. This situation only arises in fuzzy object-oriented databases. In the *OODB*, an object may or may not belong to a given class definitely. If it belongs to a given class, it can only belong to it uniquely (except for the case of subclass/superclass).

The situation where an object belongs to different classes with different membership degrees simultaneously in fuzzy object-class relationships is called *multiple membership of object* in this paper. Now let us focus on how to handle the multiple membership of object in fuzzy object-class relationships. Let $C1$ and $C2$ be (fuzzy) classes and α be a given threshold. Assume there exists an object o. If $\mu_{C1}(o) \geq \alpha$ and $\mu_{C2}(o) \geq \alpha$, the conflict of the multiple membership of object occurs, namely, o belongs to multiple classes simultaneously. At this moment, which one in $C1$ and $C2$ is the class of object o dependents on the following cases.

Case 1: There exists a direct object-class relationship between object o and one class in $C1$ and $C2$.

Then the class in the direct object-class relationship is the class of object o.

Case 2: There is no direct object-class relationship but only an indirect object-class relationship between object o and one class in $C1$ and $C2$, say $C1$. And there exists such subclass $C1'$ of $C1$ that object o and $C1'$ are in a direct object-class relationship.

Then class $C1'$ is the class of object o.

Case 3: There is neither direct object-class relationship nor indirect object-class relationship between object o and classes $C1$ and $C2$. Or there exists only an indirect object-class relationship between object o and one class in $C1$ and $C2$, say $C1$, but there is not such subclass $C1$' of $C1$ that object o and $C1$' are in a direct object-class relationship.

Then class $C1$ is considered as the class of object o if $\mu_{C1}(o) > \mu_{C2}(o)$, else class $C2$ is considered as the class of object o.

It can be seen that in Case 1 and Case 2, the class in direct object-class relationship is always the class of object o and the object and the class have the same attributes. In Case 3, however, object o and the class that is considered as the class of object o, say $C1$, have different attributes. It should be pointed out that class $C1$ and object o are definitely defined, respectively, viewed from their structures. For the situation in Case 3, the attributes of $C1$ do not affect the attributes of o and the attributes of o do not affect the attributes of $C1$ also. There should be a class C and C and o are in direct object-class relationship. But class C is not available so far. That $C1$ is considered as the class of object o, compared with $C2$, only means that $C1$ is more similar to C than $C2$. Class C is the class of object o once C is available.

Consider three fuzzy classes $C1$ with $\{A, B\}$, $C2$ with $\{A, B, D\}$, and $C3$ with $\{A, F\}$. There exists a fuzzy object o on $\{A, B', E\}$. Here, B' is overridden from B and $D \neq E \neq F$. According to the definitions above, we have

$$\mu_{C1}(o) = \frac{ID(dom(A), o(A)) \times w(A(C1)) + ID(dom(B), o(B')) \times w(B(C1))}{w(A(C1)) + w(B(C1))}$$

$$\mu_{C2}(o) = \frac{ID(dom(A), o(A)) \times w(A(C2)) + ID(dom(B), o(B')) \times w(B(C2))}{w(A(C2)) + w(B(C2)) + w(D(C2))}$$

and

$$\mu_{C3}(o) = \frac{ID(dom(A), o(A)) \times w(A(C3))}{w(A(C3)) + w(F(C3))}.$$

Assume

$w(A(C1)) = w(A(C2)) = w(A(C3))$,
$w(B(C1)) = w(B(C2))$,

and

$w(B(C2)) + w(D(C2)) = w(F(C3))$.

Also assume $\mu_{C1}(o) \geq \alpha$, $\mu_{C2}(o) \geq \alpha$, and $\mu_{C3}(o) \geq \alpha$, where α is a given threshold. Then object o belongs to classes $C1$, $C2$ and $C3$ simultaneously. The conflict of the multiple membership of object occurs. It can be seen that the relationship between o and $C1$ is an indirect object-class relationship. But the relationship between o and $C2$, which is the subclass of class $C1$, is not a direct object-class relationship. So class $C2$ is not the class of object o. It can also be seen that $\mu_{C1}(o) \geq \mu_{C2}(o) \geq \mu_{C3}(o)$. So $C1$ is considered as the class of object o. But in fact, there should be a new class C with $\{A, B', E\}$, which is the class in the direct object-class relationship of o and C. That $\mu_{C1}(o) \geq \mu_{C2}(o) \geq \mu_{C3}(o)$ only means that $C1$ with $\{A, B\}$ is more similar to C with $\{A, B', E\}$ than $C2$ with $\{A, B, E\}$ and $C3$ with $\{A, F\}$. When class C is not available right now, class $C1$ is considered as the class of object o.

9.3   Fuzzy Inheritance Hierarchies

In the *OODB*, a new class, called subclass, is produced from another class, called superclass by means of inheriting some attributes and methods of the superclass, overriding some attributes and methods of the superclass, and defining some new attributes and methods. Since a subclass is the specialization of the superclass, any one object belonging to the subclass must belong to the superclass. This characteristic can be used to determine if two classes have subclass/superclass relationship.

In the fuzzy *OODB*, however, classes may be fuzzy. A class produced from a fuzzy class must be fuzzy. If the former is still called subclass and the later superclass, the subclass/superclass relationship is fuzzy. In other words, a class is a subclass of another class with membership degree of [0, 1] at this moment. Correspondingly, the method used in the *OODB* for determination of subclass/superclass relationship is modified as

  (a) for any (fuzzy) object, if the member degree that it belongs to the subclass is less than or equal to the member degree that it belongs to the superclass, and

  (b) the member degree that it belongs to the subclass is great than or equal to the given threshold.

The subclass is then a subclass of the superclass with the membership degree, which is the minimum in the membership degrees to which these objects belong to the subclass.

Let $C1$ and $C2$ be (fuzzy) classes and β be a given threshold. We say $C2$ is a subclass of $C1$ if

$$(\forall o)\, (\beta \leq \mu_{C2}(o) \leq \mu_{C1}(o)).$$

The membership degree that $C2$ is a subclass of $C1$ should be $\min_{\mu_{C2}(o) \geq \beta} (\mu_{C2}(o))$.

It can be seen that by utilizing the inclusion degree of objects to the class, we can assess fuzzy subclass/superclass relationships in the fuzzy *OODB*. It is clear that such assessment is indirect. If there is no any object available, this method is not used. In fact, the idea used in evaluating the membership degree of an object to a class can be used to determine the relationships between fuzzy subclass and superclass. We can calculate the inclusion degree of a (fuzzy) subclass with respect to the (fuzzy) superclass according to the inclusion degree of the attribute domains of the subclass with respect to the attribute domains of the superclass as well as the weight of attributes. In the following, we give the method for evaluating the inclusion degree of fuzzy attribute domains.

Let $C1$ and $C2$ be (fuzzy) classes with attributes $\{A_1, A_2, ..., A_k, A_{k+1}, ..., A_m\}$ and $\{A_1, A_2, ..., A_k, A'_{k+1}, ..., A'_m, A_{m+1}, ..., A_n\}$, respectively. It can be seen that in $C2$, attributes $A_1, A_2, ...,$ and A_k are directly inherited from $A_1, A_2, ...,$ and A_k in $C1$, attributes $A'_{k+1}, ...,$ and A'_m are overridden from $A_{k+1}, ...,$ and A_m in $C1$, and attributes $A_{m+1}, ...,$ and A_n are special. For each attribute in $C1$ or $C2$, say A_i, there is a domain, denoted *dom* (A_i). As shown above, *dom* (A_i) should be *dom* $(A_i) = cdom$ $(A_i) \cup fdom$ (A_i), where *cdom* (A_i) and *fdom* (A_i) denote the sets of crisp values and fuzzy subsets, respectively. Let A_i and A_j be attributes of $C1$ and $C2$, respectively. The inclusion degree of *dom* (A_j) with respect to *dom* (A_i) is denoted by ID (*dom* (A_i), *dom* (A_j)). Then we identify the following cases and investigate the evaluation of ID (*dom* (A_i), *dom* (A_j)):

(a) when $i \neq j$ and $1 \leq i, j \leq k$, ID (*dom* (A_i), *dom* (A_j)) = 0,

(b) when $i = j$ and $1 \leq i, j \leq k$, ID (*dom* (A_i), *dom* (A_j)) = 1, and

(c) when $i = j$ and $k + 1 \leq i, j \leq m$, ID (*dom* (A_i), *dom* (A_j)) = ID (*dom* (A_i), *dom* (A'_i))) = max (ID (*dom* (A_i), *cdom* (A'_i)), ID (*dom* (A_i), *fdom* (A'_i))).

Now we respectively define ID (*dom* (A_i), *cdom* (A'_i))) and ID (*dom* (A_i), *fdom* (A'_i))). Let *fdom* $(A'_i) = \{f_1, f_2, ..., f_m\}$, where f_j $(1 \leq j \leq m)$ is a fuzzy value, and *cdom* $(A'_i) = \{c_1, c_2, ..., c_k\}$, where c_l $(1 \leq l \leq k)$ is a crisp value. We can consider $\{c_1, c_2, ..., c_k\}$ as a special fuzzy value $\{1.0/c_1, 1.0/c_2, ..., 1.0/c_k\}$. Then we have the following, which can be calculated by using the definition in Case 1 of Section 9.2.3.

$$ID \ (dom \ (A_i), cdom \ (A'_i)) = ID \ (dom \ (A_i), \{1.0/c_1, 1.0/c_2, ..., 1.0/c_k\})$$

$$ID \ (dom \ (A_i), fdom \ (A'_i)) = \max_j \ (ID \ (dom \ (A_i), f_j))$$

Based on the inclusion degree of attribute domains of the subclass with respect to the attribute domains of its superclass as well as the weight of attributes, we can define the formula to calculate the degree to which a fuzzy class is a subclass of another fuzzy class. Let $C1$ and $C2$ be (fuzzy) classes with attributes $\{A_1, A_2, ..., A_k, A_{k+1}, ..., A_m\}$ and $\{A_1, A_2, ..., A_k, A'_{k+1}, ..., A'_m, A_{m+1}, ..., A_n\}$, respectively, and w (A) denote the weight of attribute A.

Then the degree that $C2$ is the subclass of $C1$, written μ $(C1, C2)$, is defined as follows.

$$\mu (C1, C2) = \frac{\sum_{i=1}^{m} ID (dom (A_i (C1)), dom (A_i (C2))) \times w (A_i)}{\sum_{i=1}^{m} w (A_i)}$$

In subclass-superclass hierarchies, a critical issue is multiple inheritance of class. Ambiguity arises when more than one of the superclasses have common attributes and the subclass does not declare explicitly the class from which the attribute was inherited.

Let class C be a subclass of classes $C1$ and $C2$. Assume that the attribute A_i in $C1$, denoted by A_i $(C1)$, is common to the attribute A_i in $C2$, denoted by A_i $(C2)$. If dom $(A_i$ $(C1))$ and dom $(A_i$ $(C2))$ are identical, there does not exist a conflict in the multiple inheritance hierarchy and C inherits attribute A_i directly. If dom $(A_i$ $(C1))$ and dom $(A_i$ $(C2))$ are not identical, however, the conflict occurs. At this moment, which one in A_i $(C1))$ and A_i $(C2)$ is inherited by C dependents on the following rule:

If ID (dom (A_i (C1)), dom (A_i (C2))) $\times$ w (A_i (C1)) > ID (dom (A_i (C2)), dom (A_i (C1))) $\times$ w (A_i (C2)), then A_i (C1) is inherited by C, else A_i (C2) is inherited by C.

Note that in fuzzy multiple inheritance hierarchy, the subclass has different degrees with respect to different superclasses, not being the same as the situation in classical object-oriented database systems.

9.4 Flexible Constraints

Types and constraints are the basic building blocks of object-oriented database model. Here constraints are used for the definition of the semantics and integrity of the data and for the definition of query criteria (de Tre and de Caluwe, 2005). The classical view of constraints is the notion of imperative, all-or-nothing conditions. In this view, constraints serve as discriminators between alternatives that must be rejected and alternatives worthy of full consideration. In this view, a constraint cannot be violated and "cannot be compensated by the satisfaction of another constraint" (Dubois, Fargier and Prade, 1996). So over-constrained problem is inherent in classical constraint satisfaction problem (CSP). In order to overcome the shortage of classical constraints, more recently, flexible constraints are extensively studied and have become attractive in AI (Miguel and Shen, 2001).

Constraints have been one of the basic building blocks of object schemas. The identification and comparison of the semantic relationship of constraints are crucial in the object-oriented databases. As the result of the identification and comparison of the semantic relationship of constraints, the operations on constraints are needed. Although flexible constraints receive increasing interest, most work focuses on the joint satisfaction of constraints (Ruttkay, 1994). Little research has been done in comparison and operations of flexible constraints. Few operations were defined in (Dubois, Fargier and Prade, 1996). But they are incomplete. In particular, semantic relationships between flexible constraints are not considered when these operations are defined.

9.4.1   Constraints and Classification

A traditional (hard) constraint relates to a set of decision variables $\{X_1, X_2, ..., X_n\}$, which domains are $D_1, D_2, ...,$ and D_n, respectively. Then it is classically described by an associated relation R defined as follows.

$$R \subseteq D_1 \times D_2 \times ... \times D_n$$

Here, R is the crisp subset of Cartesian product of $D_1, D_2, ...,$ and D_n. The tuples with the form $d = (d_1, d_2, ..., d_n) \in R$ are compatible with the constraint. Formally, constraint $C_{X1X2...Xn}$ is represented by

$R_{X1X2...Xn}$ or R_C.

An alternative d satisfying constraint C is hereby expressed by $R_{X1X2...Xn}(d)$ or $R_C(d)$. The set $\{X_1, X_2, ..., X_n\}$ of variable related by R is denoted by $V(R)$.

Traditional constraints are qualified as "hard constraints" to distinguish them from their counterparts: flexible constraints.

Fuzzy Constraints

Dubois, Fargier and Prade (1996) use the notion of soft constraint. In their terminology, whereas hard constraints divide the solution space into feasible and non-feasible, soft constraints divide the space into three sub-spaces, non-feasible, somewhat feasible, and feasible. This subdivision is captured by a membership degree function μ_{RC} associated with constraint C. The function μ_{RC} takes the value 1 in the feasible space, 0 in the non-feasible space and a value between 0 and 1 in the somewhat-feasible space. Dubois, Fargier and Prade (1996) note that soft constraints are a combination of a hard constraint (defining the non-feasible space) and a preference criterion (ranking the somewhat-feasible and feasible solutions).

Prioritized Constraints

In an ideal situation, all constraints must be met. In practice, it is often the case that violating different constraints does not carry the same consequences. Not all constraints have the same level of criticality. Dubois, Fargier and Prade (1996) capture the level of criticality of constraints through a numeric priority level ρ_C associated with constraint C. The priority level expresses the degree of necessity of constraint C. A crisp (non-soft) constraint C with a degree of necessity ρ_C is represented by a fuzzy constraint C^* characterized as follows:

$$\mu_{R_{C^*}}(d) = 1 \text{ if } \mu_{R_C}(d) = 1$$

$$\mu_{R_{C^*}}(d) = 1 - \rho_C \text{ if } \mu_{R_C}(d) = 0$$

When C is a soft constraint with membership degree function μ_{RC} and priority level ρ_C, it is modeled by the fuzzy constraint C^* characterized by:

$$\mu_{R_{C^*}}(d) = \max(1 - \rho_C, \mu_{R_C}(d)).$$

Using the two concepts of fuzziness and prioritization, a variety of other concepts can be captured. Dubois, Fargier and Prade (1996), for example, use them to capture the concept of guards (constraints that must be satisfied up to some threshold level, no matter how low the priority), and the concept of hierarchical constraints (constraints that are only relevant if some other constraints are met/violated).

Fuzzy (soft) constraints and prioritized constraints are called flexible constraints in the paper. Since prioritized constraints are modeled by fuzzy constraints, the notion of flexible constraints here only refers to soft (fuzzy) constraints. Of course, classical (hard) constraints can be viewed as the special case of flexible constraints. In the following, we give the formal definition of flexible constraints.

Definition (flexible constraint): A flexible constraint C relates to a set of decision variables $\{X_1, X_2, ..., X_n\}$, which domains are $D_1, D_2, ...,$ and D_n, respectively, and is described by an associated fuzzy relation R_C that is the fuzzy subset of Cartesian product of $D_1, D_2, ...,$ and D_n. Formally, flexible constraint $FC_{X1X2...Xn}$ is represented by $R_{X1X2...Xn}$ or R_C. Each instantiation with the form $d = (d_1, d_2, ..., d_n) \in R$ is connected with a membership degree, denoted $\mu_R(d)$ ($0 \leq \mu_{RC}(d) \leq 1$).

9.4.2   Flexible Constraint Comparison

Since a flexible constraint is represented by a fuzzy relation, the semantic relationship between flexible constraints turns out to be the relationship between fuzzy relations. It should be pointed out that, however, the distributed knowledge may result in syntactic and semantic conflicts among flexible constraints, which affect the identification and determination of the relationships between flexible constraints. The issues about conflicts and solutions of flexible constraints will be discussed in other paper. Here we assume that all possible conflicts are identified and solved.

Let FC1 and FC2 be two flexible constraints represented by fuzzy relations R_{FC1} and R_{FC2}, respectively. Assume that $V(R_{FC1}) = V(R_{FC2}) = \{X_1, X_2, ..., X_n\}$, each ranging on its respective domain $D_1, D_2, ...,$ and D_n. Basically, equivalence relationship and inclusion relationship of flexible constraints have been identified (Dubois, Fargier and Prade, 1996).

Definition (equivalence relationship): Let R_{FC1} and R_{FC2} be the same as the above. We say R_{FC1} and R_{FC2} are equivalent to each other, denoted $R_{FC1} = R_{FC2}$, if

$$\forall (d_1, d_2, ..., d_n) \in D_1 \times D_2 \times ..., \times D_n., \; \mu_{R_{FC1}}(d_1, d_2, ..., d_n) = \mu_{R_{FC2}}(d_1, d_2, ..., d_n).$$

Definition (inclusion relationship): Let R_{FC1} and R_{FC2} be the same as the above. We say R_{FC1} includes R_{FC2}, denoted $R_{FC1} \supseteq R_{FC2}$, if

$$\forall (d_1, d_2, ..., d_n) \in D_1 \times D_2 \times ..., \times D_n., \; \mu_{R_{FC1}}(d_1, d_2, ..., d_n) \geq \mu_{R_{FC2}}(d_1, d_2, ..., d_n).$$

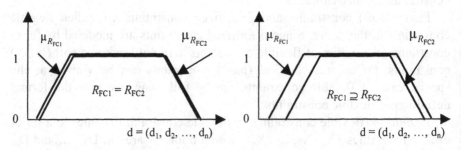

Figure 9-1. Equivalence and Inclusion Relationships of the Flexible Constraints

In (Mili, 2000), the situation $R_{FC1} \supseteq R_{FC2}$ is called as "R_{FC1} is more defined than R_{FC2}". It is clear that semantic equivalence is a particular case of semantic inclusion: if $R_{FC1} \supseteq R_{FC2}$ and $R_{FC1} \subseteq R_{FC2}$, then $R_{FC1} = R_{FC2}$. Figure 9-1 shows the semantic relationships above.

It should be pointed out that, however, $R_{FC1} = R_{FC2}$ or $R_{FC1} \supseteq R_{FC2}$ ($R_{FC1} \subseteq R_{FC2}$) is essentially the special case of semantic relationship. Generally speaking, the semantic relationship of flexible constraints should be fuzzy also since the constraints are flexible. In order to assess the semantic relationship of flexible constraints quantitatively, we introduce the notion of semantic inclusion degree.

Definition (semantic inclusion degree): Let R_{FC1} and R_{FC2} be the same as the above. The degree that R_{FC1} semantically includes R_{FC2}, denoted SID (R_{FC1}, R_{FC2}), is defined as follows.

$$SID\ (R_{FC1}, R_{FC2}) =$$
$$\sum \min (\mu_{R_{FC1}} (d1, d2, ..., dn), \mu_{R_{FC2}} (d1, d2, ..., dn)) / \sum \mu_{R_{FC2}} (d1, d2, ..., dn))$$

It can bee seen that the meaning of SID (R_{FC1}, R_{FC2}) is the percentage of the solutions of R_{FC2} that are wholly included in the solutions of R_{FC1}. Following this definition, the notion of semantic equivalence degree can be easily drawn as follows.

Definition (semantic equivalence degree): Let R_{FC1} and R_{FC2} be two flexible constraints and SID (R_{FC1}, R_{FC2}) be the degree that R_{FC1} semantically includes R_{FC2}. Let SED (R_{FC1}, R_{FC2}) denote the degree that R_{FC1} and R_{FC2} are equivalent to each other. Then,

$$SED\ (R_{FC1}, R_{FC2}) = \min (SID\ (R_{FC1}, R_{FC2}), SID\ (R_{FC2}, R_{FC1}))$$

Using the notions of semantic inclusion degree and semantic equivalence degree, the semantic relationship between flexible constraints can be assessed quantitatively. If a threshold is given, we can get approximate equivalence relationship and approximate inclusion relationship.

Definition: Let R_{FC1} and R_{FC2} be two flexible constraints and α be a given threshold. Then if SED (R_{FC1}, R_{FC2}) $\geq \alpha$, we say R_{FC1} and R_{FC2} are equivalent to each other, denoted $R_{FC1} \approx_\alpha R_{FC2}$. If SID ($R_{FC1}$, R_{FC2}) $\geq \alpha$, we say R_{FC1} includes R_{FC2}, denoted $R_{FC1} \supseteq_\alpha R_{FC2}$ or $R_{FC2} \subseteq_\alpha R_{FC1}$.

Example. Consider three flexible constraints represented by fuzzy relations R_{FC1}, R_{FC2}, and R_{FC3}, respectively, shown in Figure 9-2. Then,

SID (R_{FC1}, R_{FC2}) = (0.6 + 0.8 + 0.9 +0.7 + 0.5)/(0.6 + 0.8 + 0.9 +0.7 + 0.5) = 1.0

SID (R_{FC2}, R_{FC1}) = (0.6 + 0.8 + 0.9 +0.7 + 0.5)/(0.6 + 0.8 + 0.9 +0.7 + 0.5) = 1.0

and thus

$$\text{SED } (R_{FC1}, R_{FC2}) = \min (\text{SID } (R_{FC1}, R_{FC2}), \text{SID } (R_{FC2}, R_{FC1})) = 1.0$$

R_{FC1}			R_{FC2}			R_{FC3}		
X	Y	μ	X	Y	μ	X	Y	μ
2	3	0.6	2	3	0.6	4	5	0.7
4	5	0.8	4	5	0.8	6	7	0.9
6	7	0.9	6	7	0.9	8	9	0.6
8	9	0.7	8	9	0.7			
10	11	0.5	10	11	0.5			

Figure 9-2. Three Flexible Constraints Represented by Fuzzy Relations

Similarly,

SID $(R_{FC1}, R_{FC3}) = (0.7 + 0.9 +0.6)/(0.7 + 0.9 +0.6) = 1.0$

SID $(R_{FC3}, R_{FC1}) = (0.7 + 0.9 +0.6)/(0.6 + 0.8 + 0.9 +0.7 + 0.5) = 2.2/3.5$
$= 0.629$

and thus

SED $(R_{FC1}, R_{FC3}) = \min (\text{SID } (R_{FC1}, R_{FC3}), \text{SID } (R_{FC3}, R_{FC1})) = 0.57$

It is clear that R_{FC1} and R_{FC2} are equivalent to each other and R_{FC1} includes R_{FC3}.

Example. Consider two flexible constraints represented by fuzzy relations R_{FC4} and R_{FC5}, respectively, shown in Figure 9-3. Let $\alpha = 0.75$ be the given threshold.

R_{FC4}			R_{FC5}		
X	Y	μ	X	Y	μ
4	5	0.7	10	11	0.4
6	7	0.8	12	13	0.6
8	9	0.9	14	15	0.9
10	11	0.6	16	17	0.7
12	13	0.3			

Figure 9-3. Two Flexible Constraints Represented by Fuzzy Relations

Then,

SID $(R_{FC1}, R_{FC4}) = (0.7 + 0.8 + 0.7 +0.5)/(0.7 + 0.8 + 0.9 +0.6 + 0.3) =$
$2.7/3.3 = 0.82$

SID $(R_{FC4}, R_{FC1}) = (0.7 + 0.8 + 0.7 +0.5)/(0.6 + 0.8 + 0.9 +0.7 + 0.5) =$
$2.7/3.5 = 0.77$

and thus

SED $(R_{FC1}, R_{FC4}) = \min (\text{SID } (R_{FC1}, R_{FC4}), \text{SID } (R_{FC4}, R_{FC1})) = 0.77$

Similarly,

$$SID\ (R_{FC4}, R_{FC5}) = (0.3 + 0.4)/(0.4 + 0.6 + 0.9 + 0.7) = 0.7/2.6 = 0.269$$
$$SID\ (R_{FC5}, R_{FC4}) = (0.3 + 0.4)/(0.7 + 0.8 + 0.9 + 0.6 + 0.3) = 0.7/3.3 = 0.212$$

and thus

$$SED\ (R_{FC4}, R_{FC5}) = min\ (SID\ (R_{FC4}, R_{FC5}), SID\ (R_{FC5}, R_{FC4})) = 0.212$$

It is clear that R_{FC1} and R_{FC4} can be viewed as be equivalent to each other under the given threshold. That implies that R_{FC1} semantically includes R_{FC4} and R_{FC4} semantically includes R_{FC1} simultaneously. However, neither R_{FC4} semantically includes R_{FC5} nor R_{FC5} semantically includes R_{FC4} under the given threshold. Therefore, R_{FC4} and R_{FC5} are not equivalent to each other.

9.4.3　Operations on Flexible Constraints

Flexible constraints are represented by fuzzy relations. So the operations on flexible constraints turn out to be the operations on fuzzy relations. In the following, some operations on fuzzy relations are defined, which may be used in flexible constraint satisfaction problem (FCSP) or distributed knowledge integration.

Projection. Let R be a fuzzy relation and $V\ (R) = \{X_1, X_2, ..., X_n\}$. The projection of R on decision variable subset $\{X_i, ..., X_j\} \subseteq V\ (R)$ is a fuzzy relation on $\{X_i, ..., X_j\}$, denoted $R{\downarrow}\{X_i, ..., X_j\}$. It is clear that $V\ (R{\downarrow}\{X_i, ..., X_j\}) = \{X_i, ..., X_j\}$. The membership function of $R{\downarrow}\{X_i, ..., X_j\}$ is defined as follows.

$$\mu_{R{\downarrow}\{Xi, ..., Xj\}}\ (d_i, ..., d_j) = \max\nolimits_{\Pi_{\{xi,...,xj\}}(d1,d2,...,dn)=(di,...,dj)}\ (\mu_R\ (d_1, d_2, ..., d_n))$$

R					$R{\downarrow}\{X, Z\}$		
X	Y	Z	μ		X	Y	μ
4	5	2	0.7		4	2	0.8
4	7	2	0.8		6	4	0.9
6	5	4	0.9		8	6	0.3
6	7	4	0.6				
8	5	6	0.3				

Figure 9-4. Projection Operation on the Flexible Constraint

Here $\Pi_{\{Xi, ..., Xj\}}\ (d_1, d_2, ..., d_n)$ denotes the classical projection of $(d_1, d_2, ..., d_n)$ to $\{X_i, ..., X_j\}$.

Example. Consider a flexible constraint represented by fuzzy relation R shown in Figure 9-4. In light of the definition of projection of fuzzy relation above, we obtain the following fuzzy relation $R\downarrow\{X, Z\}$.

Cylindrical Extension. Let R be the same as the above. The cylindrical extension of R to decision variable set $\{X_i, ..., X_j\} \supseteq V(R)$ is a fuzzy relation on $\{X_i, ..., X_j\}$, denoted $R\uparrow\{X_i, ..., X_j\}$. It is clear that $V(R\uparrow\{X_i, ..., X_j\}) = \{X_i, ..., X_j\}$. The membership function of $R\uparrow\{X_i, ..., X_j\}$ is defined as follows.

$$\mu_{R\uparrow\{Xi, ..., Xj\}}(d_i, ..., d_j) = \mu_R(d_1, d_2, ..., d_n)_{\Pi_{V(R)}(di,...,dj)=(d1,d2,...,dn)}$$

Here $\Pi_{V(R)}(d_i, ..., d_j)$ denotes the classical projection of $(d_i, ..., d_j)$ to $V(R)$.

Selection. Let R be the same as the above. The selection of R is to choose some instances from the fuzzy relation. The chosen instances meet the given condition represented by a *predicate*. A predicate is formed through combining the basic clause $X\,\theta\,Y$ as operands with operators $\neg$, $\wedge$, and $\vee$. Here, $X \in V(R)$ is a decision variable, Y is either decision variable or a literal, and $\theta \in \{>, <, =, \neq, \geq, \leq$, between, not between, in, not in, like, not like$\}$. In order to implement flexibility to selection, first X is allowed to be the variable denoting the membership degree of instances. Such a selection may be "selecting the instances which membership degrees are greater than 0.95". Second, $X\,\theta\,Y$ is allowed to be imprecise. That means that Y may be a fuzzy term such as (*very*) *big* or θ may be a fuzzy relation such as (*very*) *close to*. When $X\,\theta\,Y$ is imprecise, a threshold must be given to evaluate the imprecise condition (Chen and Jong, 1997; Ma and Mili, 2002).

Let P_f be a predicate representing flexible selection condition. Then the selection on R for P_f is defined as follows.

$$\sigma_{Pf}(R) = \{t \mid t \in R \wedge Pf(t)\}$$

Combination. Let $R1$ and $R2$ be two fuzzy relations. The combination of $R1$ and $R2$ is to construct a fuzzy relation R. For this purpose, the following cases can be identified.

Case 1: $R1 \approx_\alpha R2$.

Here α is the given threshold. Since $R1$ and $R2$ are semantically equivalent to each other, $R = R1$ (or $R = R2$) such that $\mu_R(d) = \mu_{R1}(d)$ (or $\mu_R(d) = \mu_{R2}(d)$).

Case 2: $V(R1) = V(R2)$ and $R1 \not\approx_\alpha R2$.

Here α is the given threshold. We have three strategies for constructing R under this situation, which are *union operation*, *intersection operation*, and *different operation*, respectively.

The union of two fuzzy relations $R1$ and $R2$ is a fuzzy relation $R = R1 \cup R2$ over $V(R1)/V(R2) = \{X_1, X_2, \ldots, X_n\}$ such that

$$\mu_R(d_1, d_2, \ldots, d_n) = \mu_{R1 \cup R2}(d_1, d_2, \ldots, d_n) = \max(\mu_{R1}(d_1, d_2, \ldots, d_n), \mu_{R2}(d_1, d_2, \ldots, d_n)).$$

In particular, $R = R1$ and $\mu_{R1 \cup R2}(d_1, d_2, \ldots, d_n) = \mu_{R1}(d_1, d_2, \ldots, d_n)$ if $R1 \supseteq_\alpha R2$. If $R1 \subseteq_\alpha R2$, $R = R2$ and $\mu_{R1 \cup R2}(d_1, d_2, \ldots, d_n) = \mu_{R2}(d_1, d_2, \ldots, d_n)$.

The intersection of two fuzzy relations $R1$ and $R2$ is a fuzzy relation $R = R1 \cap R2$ over $V(R1)/V(R2) = \{X_1, X_2, \ldots, X_n\}$ such that

$$\mu_R(d_1, d_2, \ldots, d_n) = \mu_{R1 \cap R2}(d_1, d_2, \ldots, d_n) = \min(\mu_{R1}(d_1, d_2, \ldots, d_n), \mu_{R2}(d_1, d_2, \ldots, d_n)).$$

In particular, $R = R2$ and $\mu_{R1 \cap R2}(d_1, d_2, \ldots, d_n) = \mu_{R2}(d_1, d_2, \ldots, d_n)$ if $R1 \supseteq_\alpha R2$. If $R1 \subseteq_\alpha R2$, $R = R1$ and $\mu_{R1 \cap R2}(d_1, d_2, \ldots, d_n) = \mu_{R1}(d_1, d_2, \ldots, d_n)$.

The difference of two fuzzy relations $R1$ and $R2$ is a fuzzy relation $R = R1 - R2$ over $V(R1)/V(R2) = \{X_1, X_2, \ldots, X_n\}$ such that

$$\mu_R(d_1, d_2, \ldots, d_n) = \mu_{R1 - R2}(d_1, d_2, \ldots, d_n) = \min(\mu_{R1}(d_1, d_2, \ldots, d_n) - \mu_{R2}(d_1, d_2, \ldots, d_n), 0).$$

Example. Consider two flexible constraints represented by the fuzzy relations R_{FC4} and R_{FC5} shown in Figure 9-3. It has been shown that neither R_{FC4} semantically includes R_{FC5} nor R_{FC5} semantically includes R_{FC4} under the given threshold $\alpha = 0.75$. Then we have the fuzzy relations shown in Figure 9-5.

$R_{FC4} \cup R_{FC5}$				$R_{FC4} - R_{FC5}$		
X	Y	μ		X	Y	μ
4	5	0.7		4	5	0.7
6	7	0.8		6	7	0.8
8	9	0.9		8	9	0.9
10	11	0.6		10	11	0.2
12	13	0.6				
14	15	0.9				
16	17	0.7				

Figure 9-5. The Union and Difference Operations on the Flexible Constraints

Case 3: $V(R1) \neq V(R2)$ and $V(R1) \cap V(R2) \neq \Phi$.

We have two strategies for constructing R under this situation, which are join (conjunctive combination) operation and disjunctive combination operation, respectively. Then the join of two fuzzy relations $R1$ and $R2$ is a fuzzy relation $R = R1 \otimes R2$ over $V(R1) \cup V(R2) = \{X_i, ..., X_j\}$ such that

$$\mu_R (d_i, ..., d_j) = \mu_{R1 \otimes R2} (d_i, ..., d_j) = \min (\mu_{R1} (\Pi_{V(R1)} (d_i, ..., d_j)), \mu_{R2} (\Pi_{V(R2)} (d_i, ..., d_j)))$$

The disjunctive combination of two fuzzy relations $R1$ and $R2$ is a fuzzy relation $R = R1 \oplus R2$ over $V(R1) \cup V(R2) = \{X_i, ..., X_j\}$ such that

$$\mu_R (d_i, ..., d_j) = \mu_{R1 \oplus R2} (d_i, ..., d_j) = \max (\mu_{R1} (\Pi_{V(R1)} (d_i, ..., d_j)), \mu_{R2} (\Pi_{V(R2)} (d_i, ..., d_j))).$$

Case 4: $V(R1) \cap V(R2) = \Phi$.

To construct R under this situation, we use Cartesian product operation. The Cartesian product of two fuzzy relations $R1$ and $R2$ is a fuzzy relation $R = R1 \times R2$ over $V(R1) \cup V(R2) = \{X_i, ..., X_j\}$ such that

$$\mu_R (d_i, ..., d_j) = \mu_{R1 \times R2} (d_i, ..., d_j) = \mu_{R1} (\Pi_{V(R1)} (d_i, ..., d_j)) \times \mu_{R2} (\Pi_{V(R2)} (d_i, ..., d_j))$$

Example. Consider three flexible constraints represented by fuzzy relations R_1, R_2, and R_3, respectively, shown in Figure 9-6.

R_1				R_2				R_3		
A	X	μ		B	X	μ		C	Y	μ
2	3	0.6		12	5	0.6		24	5	0.7
4	5	0.8		14	7	0.8		26	7	0.9
6	7	0.9		16	9	0.9				

Figure 9-6. Three Flexible Constraints for Combination Operation

$R_1 \otimes R_2$					$R_1 \oplus R_2$			
A	B	X	μ		A	B	X	μ
4	12	5	0.6		4	12	5	0.8
6	14	7	0.8		6	14	7	0.9

Figure 9-7. Conjunctive and Disjunctive Combination Operations on the Flexible Constraints

It can be seen that $V(R1) \neq V(R2)$ and $V(R1) \cap V(R2) \neq \Phi$. Following the definition in Case 3, we have the fuzzy relations shown in Figure 9-7. But V

$(R1) \cap V (R3) = \Phi$ and $V (R2) \cap V (R3) = \Phi$. Following the definition in Case 4, we have the fuzzy relations shown in Figure 9-8.

$R_1 \times R_3$					$R_2 \times R_3$				
A	C	X	Y	μ	B	C	X	Y	μ
2	24	3	5	0.42	12	24	5	5	0.42
2	26	3	7	0.54	12	26	5	7	0.54
4	24	5	5	0.56	14	24	7	5	0.56
4	26	5	7	0.72	14	26	7	7	0.72
6	24	7	5	0.63	16	24	9	5	0.63
6	26	7	7	0.81	16	26	9	7	0.81

Figure 9-8. Cartesian Product Operation on the Flexible Constraints

9.5   The Fuzzy Object-Oriented Model

Based on the discussion above, we have known that the classes in the fuzzy *OODB* may be fuzzy. Accordingly, in the fuzzy *OODB*, an object belongs to a class with a membership degree of [0, 1] and a class is the subclass of another class with degree of [0, 1] also. In the *OODB*, the specification of a class includes the definition of *ISA* relationships, attributes, method implementations and constraints. In order to specify a fuzzy class, some additional definitions are needed. First, the weights of attributes to the class must be given. In addition to these common attributes, a new attribute should be added into the class to indicate the membership degree to which an object belongs to the class. If the class is a fuzzy subclass, its superclasses and the degree that the class is the subclass of the superclass should be illustrated in the specification of the class. Finally, in the definition of a fuzzy class, fuzzy attributes may explicitly be indicated.

Formally, the definition of a fuzzy class is shown as follows.

CLASS *class name* WITH DEGREE OF *degree*
   INHERITS *superclass_1 name* WITH DEGREE OF *degree_1*
   ...
   INHERITS *superclass_k name* WITH DEGREE OF *degree_k*
   ATTRIBUTES
     Attribute_1 name: [FUZZY] DOMAIN *dom_1*: TYPE OF *type_1* WITH
DEGREE OF *degree_1*
     ...
     Attribute_m name: [FUZZY] DOMAIN *dom_m*: TYPE OF *type_m* WITH
DEGREE OF *degree_m*
     Membership_Attribute name: *membership_degree*

```
    WEIGHT
      w (Attribute_1 name) = w_1
      ...
      w (Attribute_m name) = w_m
    METHODS
      ...
    CONSTRAINTS
      ...
    END
```

For non-fuzzy attributes, the data types include simple types such as integer, real, Boolean, string, and complex types such as set type and object type. For fuzzy attributes, however, the data types are fuzzy type based simple types or complex types, which allows the representation of descriptive form of imprecise information. Only fuzzy attributes have fuzzy type and fuzzy attributes are explicitly indicated in a class definition. Therefore, in the definition above, we declare only the base type (e.g., integer) of fuzzy attributes and the fuzzy domain. A fuzzy domain is a set of possibility distributions or fuzzy linguistic terms (each fuzzy term is associated with a membership function). For example, a fuzzy attribute *Age* is declared as follows.

Age: FUZZY DOMAIN {very young, young, old, very old}: TYPE OF integer

Then an object attribute defined fuzzy type will have either a crisp value or a fuzzy value given in the type definition. For example, *Age* = 21 or *Age* = *young*.

9.6   Query and Operations

The change in database model impacts the operations on the database model (Ma and Mili, 2002). In the following, we describe some operations based on the proposed fuzzy class model above. First, we briefly discuss several combination operations of the fuzzy classes. Finally, we investigate the issue of user request-queries based on the fuzzy classes. Depending on the relationships between the attribute sets of the combining classes, three kinds of combination operations can be identified: *fuzzy product* ($\tilde{\times}$), *fuzzy join* ($\bowtie$), and *fuzzy union* ($\tilde{\cup}$). Let $C1$ and $C2$ be (fuzzy) classes and let *Attr* ($C1$) and *Attr* ($C2$) be their attribute sets, respectively. Assume a new class C is created by combining $C1$ and $C2$. Then

$$C = C1 \; \tilde{\times} \; C2, \text{ if } Attr' \, (C1) \cap Attr' \, (C2) = \Phi,$$

$$C = C1 \bowtie C2, \text{ if } Attr'(C1) \cap Attr'(C2) \neq \Phi \text{ and } Attr'(C1) \neq Attr'(C2),$$

or

$$C = C1 \,\tilde{\cup}\, C2, \text{ if } Attr'(C1) = Attr'(C2).$$

Here, $Attr'(C1)$ and $Attr'(C2)$ are obtained from $Attr(C1)$ and $Attr(C2)$ through removing the membership degree attributes from $Attr(C1)$ and $Attr(C2)$, respectively. In the following, μ_C is used to represent the membership degree attribute of C. Assume we have an object o of C. Then $\mu_C(o)$ is used to represent the value of o on μ_C. For a common attribute in C, say Ai, $o(Ai)$ is used to represent the value of o on Ai. If we have a set of such common attributes, say $\{Ai, Aj, ..., Am\}$, $o(\{Ai, Aj, ..., Am\})$ is used to represent all values of o on the attributes in $\{Ai, Aj, ..., Am\}$. Furthermore, $o(C)$ is used to represent all values of o on the common attributes in C. In the following, we give the formal definitions of fuzzy product, fuzzy join, and fuzzy union operations.

9.6.1   Fuzzy Product

The fuzzy product of $C1$ and $C2$ is a new class C, which is composed with the common attributes of $C1$ and $C2$ as well as a membership degree attribute. The objects of C are created by the composition of objects from $C1$ and $C2$.

$$C = C1 \,\tilde{\times}\, C2 = \{o | (\forall o') (\forall o'') (o' \in C1 \wedge o'' \in C2 \wedge o(Attr'(C1)) = o'(C1) \wedge o(Attr'(C2)) = o''(C2) \wedge \mu_C(o) = op(\mu_{C1}(o'), \mu_{C2}(o'')))\}$$

Here, operation op is undefined. Generally, $op(\mu_{C1}(o'), \mu_{C2}(o''))$ may be $min(\mu_{C1}(o'), \mu_{C2}(o''))$ or $\mu_{C1}(o') \times \mu_{C2}(o'')$.

9.6.2   Fuzzy Join

The fuzzy join of $C1$ and $C2$ is a new class C, where $Attr'(C1) \cap Attr'(C2) \neq \Phi$ and $Attr'(C1) \neq Attr'(C2)$. Class C is composed with $Attr'(C1) \cup (Attr'(C2) - (Attr'(C1) \cap Attr'(C2)))$ as well as a membership degree attribute. The objects of C are created by the composition of objects from $C1$ and $C2$, which are semantically equivalent on $Attr'(C1) \cap Attr'(C2)$ under the given thresholds. It should be noted that, however, $Attr'(C1) \cap Attr'(C2) \neq \Phi$ implies $C1$ and $C2$ have the same weights of attributes for the attributes in $Attr'(C1) \cap Attr'(C2)$. This is an additional requirement to be met in the case of the fuzzy join operation. Let α be the given threshold. Then

$$C = C1 \bowtie C2 = \{o | (\exists o') (\exists o'') (o' \in C1 \land o'' \in C2 \land SE (o' (Attr' (C1) \cap Attr' (C2)), o'' (Attr' (C1) \cap Attr' (C2))) \geq \alpha \land o (Attr' (C1)) = o' (C1) \land o (Attr' (C2) - (Attr' (C1) \cap Attr' (C2))) = o'' (Attr' (C2) - (Attr' (C1) \cap Attr' (C2))) \land \mu_C (o) = op (\mu_{C1} (o'), \mu_{C2} (o'')))\}$$

Here, operation *op* is also undefined. Generally, $op (\mu_{C1} (o'), \mu_{C2} (o''))$ may be $min (\mu_{C1} (o'), \mu_{C2} (o''))$ or $\mu_{C1} (o') \times \mu_{C2} (o'')$.

9.6.3   Fuzzy Union

The fuzzy union of $C1$ and $C2$ requires $Attr' (C1) = Attr' (C2)$, which implies that all corresponding attributes in $C1$ and $C2$ have the same weights. Let a new class C be the fuzzy union of $C1$ and $C2$. Then the objects of C are composed of three kinds of objects. The first two kinds of objects are such objects that directly come from one component class (e.g., $C1$) and are not redundant with any object in another component class (e.g., $C2$) under the given thresholds. The last kind of objects is such objects that are the results of merging the redundant objects from two component classes under the given thresholds. Let α be the given threshold.

$$C = C1 \,\tilde{\cup}\, C2 = C = \{o | (\forall o'') (o'' \in C2 \land o \in C1 \land SE (o (C1), o'' (C2)) < \alpha) \lor (\forall o') (o' \in C1 \land o \in C2 \land SE (o (C2), o' (C1)) < \alpha) \lor ((\exists o') (\exists o'') (o' \in C1 \land o'' \in C2 \land SE (o' (C1), o'' (C2)) \geq \alpha \land o = merge (o', o''))\}$$

Here, *merge* is an operation for merging two redundant objects of the class to form a new object of the class. Let o' and o'' be two objects of class C and $o = merge (o', o'')$. Then $o (C) = o' (C)$ or $o (C) = o'' (C)$ and $\mu_C (o) = max (\mu_{C1} (o'), \mu_{C2} (o''))$.

9.6.4   Fuzzy Query

Query processing refers to such procedure that the objects satisfying a given condition are selected and then they are delivered to the user according to the required formats. These format requirements include which attributes appear in the result and if the result is grouped and ordered over the given attribute(s). So a query can be seen as comprising two components, namely, a boolean selection condition and some format requirements. For the sake of the simple illustration, some format requirements are ignored in the following discussion. An SQL (Structured Query Language) like query syntax is represented as

SELECT *<attribute list>* **FROM** *<class names>* **WHERE** *<query condition>*,

where *<attribute list>* is the list of attributes separated by commas: $Attribute_1$, $Attribute_2$, ..., $Attribute_n$. At least one attribute name must be specified in *<attribute list>*. Attributes that take place in *<attribute list>* are selected from the associated classes which are specified in the **FROM** statement. *<class names>* contains the class names separated by commas: $Class_1$, $Class_2$, ..., $Class_m$, from which the attributes are selected with the **SELECT** statement.

Classical databases suffer from a lack of flexibility to query. The given query condition and the contents of the database are all crisp. A query is flexible if the databases contain imprecise and uncertain information and the query condition is imprecise and uncertain. For the fuzzy object-oriented databases, it has been shown above that objects belong to a given class with membership degree [0, 1]. In addition, an object satisfies the given query condition also with membership degree [0, 1] because fuzzy information occur in the query condition and/or the object. Therefore, the query processing based the proposed fuzzy object-oriented database model refers to such procedure that the objects satisfying a given threshold and a given condition under given thresholds simultaneously are selected from the classes. It is clear that the queries for the fuzzy object-oriented databases are threshold-based ones, which are concerned with the number choices of threshold. Therefore, an SQL like query syntax based on the fuzzy object-oriented database model is represented as follows.

SELECT *<attribute list>* **FROM** *<Class₁* **WITH** *threshold₁*, ..., *Classₘ* **WITH** *thresholdₘ>* **WHERE** *<query condition* **WITH** *threshold>*

Here, *<query condition>* is a fuzzy condition and all thresholds are crisp numbers in [0, 1]. Utilizing such SQL, one can get such objects that belong to the classes under the given thresholds and also satisfy the query condition under the given thresholds at the same time. Note that the item **WITH** *threshold* can be omitted. The default of threshold is exactly 1 at this moment.

Assume we have a fuzzy class *Young Students* as follows.

CLASS *Young Students* WITH DEGREE OF *1.0*
  INHERITS *Students* WITH DEGREE OF *1.0*
    ATTRIBUTES
      ID: TYPE OF *string* WITH DEGREE OF *1.0*

    Name: TYPE OF *string* WITH DEGREE OF *1.0*

    Age: FUZZY DOMAIN {*very young, young, old, very old*}: TYPE OF *integer*
WITH DEGREE OF *1.0*

    Height: DOMAIN *[60, 210]*: TYPE OF *real* WITH DEGREE OF *1.0*

    Membership_Attribute name

   WEIGHT

     w *(ID)* = *0.1*

     w *(Name)* = *0.1*

     w *(Age)* = *0.9*

     w *(Height)* = *0.2*

   METHODS

    ...

   CONSTRAINTS

    ...

   END

A query based on the class may be

   SELECT Yong Students.Height *FROM* Yong Students *WITH* 0.5
   WHERE Yong Students.Age = *very young WITH* 0.8.

This query is to get the young students objects that have membership degree equal to or greater than 0.5 and have very young age with a membership degree equal to or greater than 0.8. The height values of the selected objects are provided to the users. Assume that we now have three objects of *Yong Students*: $o1$, $o2$, and $o3$ and they have membership degrees 0.4, 0.6, and 0.7, respectively. It is clear that $o1$ does not satisfy the query because its membership degree to *Young Students* is 0.4, which is less than the given threshold 0.5. Objects $o2$ and $o3$ may or may not satisfy the query, depending on if their ages are very young under the given threshold 0.8.

9.7   Summary

   Incorporation of imprecise and uncertain information in database model has been an important topic of database research because such information extensively exists in data and knowledge intensive application such as expert system, decision making, and CAD/CAM etc. Besides, that there are complex object structures is another characteristics of these systems. Classical relational database model and its extension of imprecision and uncertainty do not satisfy the need of handling complex objects with imprecision and uncertainty. Fuzzy object-oriented databases are hereby introduced. Furthermore, there have been several investigations into complex applications with uncertainty in the database models based on the fuzzy *OODB*. To handle complex data and knowledge with uncertainty, in (Koyuncu, Yazici and George, 1999), an intelligent fuzzy object-oriented database (*IFOOD*) architecture was proposed, in which fuzzy object-oriented databases (*FOODB*) were coupled with fuzzy knowledge bases (*FKB*) through a bridge that provides interoperability. Here, the *FOODB* is used to handle large scale of complex and fuzzy data and the *FKB* is used to handle imprecise knowledge of the application domain. The evaluation of imprecise queries in the *IFOOD* was presented in (Koyuncu, Yazici and George, 2000). It should be noted that the *FOODB* in the *IFOOD* (Koyuncu, Yazici and George, 1999; Koyuncu, Yazici and George, 2000) comes from the similarity-based object-oriented databases in (Yazici, George and Aksoy, 1998).

In this chapter, based on possibility distribution and the semantic measure method of fuzzy data, we presented a fuzzy object-oriented database model (*FOODBM*) to cope with imperfect as well as complex objects in the real world at a logical level. Some major notions such as objects, classes, objects-classes relationships, subclass/superclass, and multiple inheritances in fuzzy object-oriented databases have been extended under fuzzy information environment. Finally, a generic model for fuzzy object-oriented databases is proposed. The *FOODBM* framework proposed here differs from the *FOODB* framework proposed in (Koyuncu, Yazici and George, 1999; Koyuncu, Yazici and George, 2000; Yazici, George and Aksoy, 1998) in two aspects: first, the way that uncertainty is represented and second, the calculations of fuzzy object-class relationship and fuzzy subclass/superclass relationship.

References

Bordogna, G., Pasi, G. and Lucarella, D., 1999, A fuzzy object-oriented data model for managing vague and uncertain information, *International Journal of Intelligent Systems*, 14: 623-651.

Chen, S. M. and Jong, W. T., 1997, Fuzzy query translation for relational database systems, *IEEE Transactions on Systems, Man and Cybernetics–Part B: Cybernetics*, 27 (4): 714–721.

Cross, V., de Caluwe, R. and Vangyseghem, N., 1997, A Perspective from the fuzzy object data management group (FODMG), *Proceedings of the 1997 IEEE International Conference on Fuzzy Systems*, 2: 721-728.

Cross, V. and Firat, A., 2000, Fuzzy objects for geographical information systems, *Fuzzy Sets and Systems*, 113: 19-36.

de Tre, G. and de Caluwe, R., 2005, A constraint based fuzzy object oriented database model, *Advances in Fuzzy Object-Oriented Databases: Modeling and Applications*, Edited by Zongmin Ma, Idea Group Publishing.

Dubois, D., Fargier, H. and Prade, H., 1996, Possibility theory in constraint satisfaction problems: handling priority, preference and uncertainty, *Applied Intelligence*, 6 (4): 287-309.

Dubois, D., Prade, H. and Rossazza, J. P., 1991, Vagueness, typicality, and uncertainty in class hierarchies, *International Journal of Intelligent Systems*, 6: 167-183.

George, R., Srikanth, R., Petry, F. E. and Buckles, B. P., 1996, Uncertainty management issues in the object-oriented data model, *IEEE Transactions on Fuzzy Systems*, 4 (2): 179-192.

Gyseghem, N. V. and de Caluwe, R., 1998, Imprecision and uncertainty in UFO database model, *Journal of the American Society for Information Science*, 49 (3): 236-252.

Koyuncu, M., Yazici, A. and George, R., 1999, IFOOD: An intelligent object-oriented database architecture, *Proceedings of the 10th International Conference on Database and Expert Systems Applications*, Lecture Notes in Computer Science 1677 Springer 1999, 36-45.

Koyuncu, M., Yazici, A. and George, R., 2000, Flexible querying in an intelligent object-oriented database environment, *Proceedings of the 4th International Conference on Flexible Query Answering Systems*, 75-84.

Liu, W. Y. and Song, N., 2001, The fuzzy association degree in semantic data models, *Fuzzy Sets and Systems*, 117 (2): 203-208.

Ma, Z. M. and Mili, F., 2002, Handling fuzzy information in extended possibility-based fuzzy relational databases, *International Journal of Intelligent Systems*, 17 (10): 925-942.

Miguel, I. and Shen, Q., 2001, Solution techniques for constraint satisfaction problems: advanced approaches, *Artificial Intelligence Review*, 15 (4): 269-293.

Mili, F., 2000, Managing engineering knowledge federations, *Industrial Knowledge Management-A Micro Level Approach*, Edited by R. Roy, Springer Verlag, London, 513-524.

Ruttkay, Z., 1994, Fuzzy constraint satisfaction, *Proceedings of the 1994 International Conference on Fuzzy Systems*, 2: 1263 –1268.

Vila, M. A., Cubero, J. C., Medina, J. M. and Pons, O., 1996, A Conceptual approach for deal with imprecision and uncertainty in object-based data models, *International Journal of Intelligent Systems*, 11: 791-806.

Yazici, A., George, R. and Aksoy, D., 1998, Design and implementation issues in the fuzzy object-oriented data model, *Information Sciences*, 108 (1-4): 241-260.

Yazici, A., Soysal, A., Buckles, B. P. and Petry, F. E., 1999, Uncertainty in a nested relational database model, *Data & Knowledge Engineering*, 30 (3): 275-301.

Zicari, R. and Milano, P., 1990, Incomplete information in object-oriented databases, *ACM SIGMOD Record*, 19 (3): 5-16.

Chapter 10

CONCEPTUAL DESIGN OF FUZZY DATABASES

10.1   Introduction

Information modeling in databases can be carried out at two different levels: *conceptual data modeling* and *logical database modeling*. Therefore, we have conceptual data models and logical database models for database modeling, respectively. Conceptual data models are generally used for information modeling at a high level of abstraction. However, information systems are constructed based on logical database models. So at the level of data manipulation, i.e., a low level of abstraction, logical database models are used for information modeling. Here, logical database models are often created through mapping conceptual data models into logical database models. This conversion is called *conceptual design of databases*.

There have been several proposals for extending relational database model as well as nested relational database model in order to represent and query fuzzy data. Current efforts have been concentrated on fuzzy object-oriented databases and some related notions. Compared with the studies of the fuzzy database models, little work has been done in modeling imprecision and uncertainty in conceptual data model. It is particularly true in developing design methodologies for implementing fuzzy databases. To fill this gap, this chapter proposes the conceptual designs of the fuzzy nested relational databases using the fuzzy EER model and the fuzzy object-oriented databases using the fuzzy UML model. Also the mapping of the fuzzy XML model into the fuzzy relational database model is investigated in this chapter.

10.2   Transformation from the Fuzzy EER Model to the Fuzzy Nested Relational Databases

The transformations of the fuzzy ER data model to the fuzzy relational databases have been investigated in (Chaudhry, Moyne and Rundensteiner, 1999). The techniques for mapping the fuzzy EER model to the fuzzy relational databases were proposed and a sequence of steps to implement a fuzzy RDB from the extended fuzzy ER model was prescribed. It should be pointed out, however, being the extension of relational data model, NF^2 data model is able to handle complex-valued attributes and may be better suited to some complex applications such as office automation systems, information retrieval systems and expert database systems (Yazici, Soysal, Buckles and Petry, 1999). In (Yazici, Buckles and Petry, 1999), based on similarity relations (Buckles and Petry, 1982), the *IFO* model, which was proposed in (Abiteboul and Hull, 1987) as a formally defined conceptual database model that comprises a rich set of high-level primitives for database design, was extended to the *ExIFO* (Extended *IFO*) model to represent uncertainties at the levels of the attribute, the object, and class. Also a mapping process to transform the *ExIFO* model into the fuzzy extended NF^2 relations including uncertain properties that are represented in both models was also described in (Yazici, Buckles and Petry, 1999).

In Chapter 4 and Chapter 8, the EER and nested relational models have been extended, respectively, using the possibility-distribution theory. In order to transform the fuzzy EER model into the fuzzy nested relational database model, first of all, we should know how the fuzzy nested relational databases support the fuzzy EER model. As described in Chapter 4, three levels of fuzziness can be found in the fuzzy EER model, in which the first level of fuzziness occurs in metadata. The fuzzy nested relational databases do not support this level of fuzziness, which only model the fuzziness that occurs in type/instance and instance levels (i.e., attribute values). In addition, generally speaking, an entity in the EER model corresponds to a relation in the nested relational databases and each entity instance is mapped into a tuple of the relation. Correspondingly, the attributes of the entity correspond to the attributes of the relation. A relationship in the EER model can be mapped into the attributes of the relations that are created by the entities connected with the relationship.

Subtype/supertype entities in the EER model can be implemented in relational databases via the reference relationships between relations. It is clear that, based on such organization principles, the instances related to the structural relationships one another are represented in separate relational databases. In order to obtain some information, one may have to query multiple relational databases by using join operations. Besides, it is very hard to have a complete and clear picture about information model from the query answers. Relational databases obviously are not suitable to support the EER model. The reason is because of the restriction of first normal form (1NF) in traditional relational databases. Nested relational databases can solve this problem very well.

10.2.1 Transformation of Entities

Generally speaking, entities in the fuzzy EER model are transformed to relations in the fuzzy nested relational databases and the attributes of entities may be considered as that of the corresponding relation directly. Note that multivalued attributes the fuzzy EER model are mapped into set-valued attributes in the fuzzy nested relational databases. We can distinguish four kinds of entities in the fuzzy EER model as follows:

  (a) entities without any fuzziness at the three levels,
  (b) entities with the fuzziness only at the third level,
  (c) entities with the fuzziness at the second level, and
  (d) entities with the fuzziness at the first level.

For the first two kinds of entities, we can directly transform the entities into relations. For the third kind of entities, however, an additional attribute should be added to each relation transformed from the corresponding entity, which is used to denote the possibility that the tuples belong to the relation. It should be noted that for the entities with membership degree and the entities whose attributes have membership degree, the fuzzy nested relational model couldn't model the first level of fuzziness.

Notice that the entities mentioned above are not subclass entities, which mapping will be discussed below. In addition, a weak entity in the fuzzy EER model depends on its owner entity. A weak entity in FEER model can be mapped to a relation-valued attribute.

Figure 10-1 shows the transformation of entities.

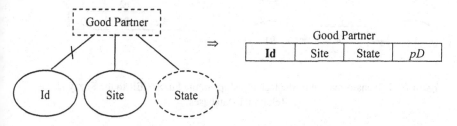

Figure 10-1. Transformation of the Entities in the Fuzzy EER to the Fuzzy Nested Relational Databases

10.2.2   Transformation of Relationships

A relationship in the EER model should be mapped into an association relation, which attributes serve as a group of pointer to combine an explicit reference from one tuple to another tuple. Considering the constraint of cardinality, such attributes in two associated tuples can be single-valued one or multivalued one.

Let entity $E1$ with attributes $\{K1, A1, ..., Am\}$ and entity $E2$ with attributes $\{K1, B1, ..., Bn\}$ be connected with relationship $R \{X1, ..., Xk\}$, where $K1$ and $K2$ are, respectively, key attributes of $E1$ and $E2$, and R may be one-to-one, one-to-many, or many-to-many relationship. In addition to the transformation processing given in the entity transformation discussion before, the relationship R is mapped into a relational schema with attribute set $\{K1, K2, X1, ..., Xk\}$, where $K1$ and $K2$ are key attributes. If the constraint of cardinality is a one-to-many relationship, i.e., R is a one-to-many relationship from $E1$ to $E2$, $K2$ is a set-valued attribute in $r1$ created by $E1$, and $K1$ is a single-valued attribute in $r2$ created by $E2$.

Considering the fuzziness in the fuzzy EER model, we can distinguish four kinds of relationships as follows:

    (a) relationships without any fuzziness at the three levels,

    (b) relationships with the fuzziness only at the third level (it means that the attributes of relationships may take fuzzy values),

    (c) relationships with the fuzziness at the second level, and

    (d) relationships with the fuzziness at the first level.

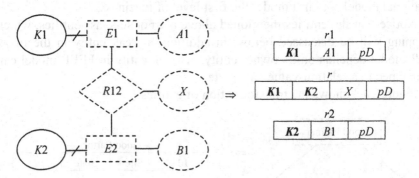

Figure 10-2. Transformation of the Relationships in the Fuzzy EER to the Fuzzy Nested Relational Databases

For the relationship R in case (a) or (b), the transformation of the relationships can be conducted according to the rules given above. For the relationship R in case (c), additional attributes denoting the possibility that the relationship instances belong to the relation should be added the relation r created by R. It should be noted that for the relationships with membership degree and the relationships whose attributes have membership degree, fuzzy nested relational model cannot model the first level of fuzziness and the transformation of such relationships is not complete.

Figure 10-2 shows the transformation of relationships.

10.2.3 Transformation of Generalizations

Let E_1 with attribute types named K_1, A_1, A_2, ..., and A_k and E_2 with attribute types named K_2, B_1, B_2, ..., and B_m be generated to supertype S. Assume $\{A_1, A_2, ..., A_k\} \cap \{B_1, B_2, ..., B_m\} = \{C_1, C_2, ..., C_n\}$. Generally speaking, E_1 and E_2 are mapped into schemas $\{K_1, A_1, A_2, ..., A_k\} - \{C_1, C_2, ..., C_n\}$ and $\{K_2, B_1, B_2, ..., B_m\} - \{C_1, C_2, ..., C_n\}$, respectively. As to the transformation of S, depending on K_1 and K_2, we distinguish the following two cases.

(a) K_1 and K_2 are identical. Then S is mapped into the schema $\{K, C_1, C_2, ..., C_n\}$, where K is $K1$ or $K2$.

(b) K_1 and K_2 are different. Then S is mapped into the relational schema $\{K, C_1, C_2, ..., C_n\}$, where K is the surrogate key created by K_1 and K_2 (Yazici, Buckles and Petry, 1999).

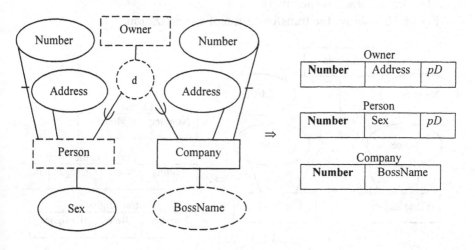

Figure 10-3. Transformation of the Generalizations in the Fuzzy EER to the Fuzzy Nested Relational Databases

Considering the fuzziness in the entities, the following cases for the transformation of generalization are distinguished.

(a) E_1 and E_2 are crisp. Then E_1 and E_2 are transformed to relations r_1 and r_2 with attributes $\{K_1, A_1, A_2, ..., A_k\} - \{C_1, C_2, ..., C_n\}$ and $\{K_2, B_1, B_2, ..., B_m\} - \{C_1, C_2, ..., C_n\}$, respectively. S is transformed to a relation r with attributes $\{K, C_1, C_2, ..., C_n\}$ just like the discussion above.

(b) When there is the fuzziness of type/instance level in E_1 and (or) E_2, being similar to case (a) also, relation r, as well as relations r_1 and r_2, are formed. Note that r, r_1 and (or) r_2) created by E_1 and (or) E_2 with the type/instance level of fuzziness should include the attribute pD.

(c) When there is the fuzziness of schema level in E_1 and (or) E_2, relation r, as well as relations r_1 and r_2, is formed. But the fuzziness at this level cannot be modeled in the created relations.

Figure 10-3 shows the transformations of generalization.

10.2.4   Transformation of Specializations

Let S be an entity type with n attributes named K, A_1, A_2, ..., and A_n, where K is its key. Let an entity type $S1$ with attributes named A_{11}, A_{12}, ..., and A_{1k} and an entity type $S2$ with attributes named A_{21}, A_{22}, ..., and A_{2m} be the subclasses of S. Since S_1 and S_2 are the subclasses of S, there are no keys in S_1 and S_2. At this point, S is mapped into the relational schema $\{K, A_1, A_2, ..., A_n\}$, and S_1 and S_2 are mapped into schemas $\{K, A_{11}, A_{12}, ..., A_{1k}\}$ and $\{K, A_{21}, A_{22}, ..., A_{2m}\}$, respectively.

Figure 10-4 shows the transformation of specialization.

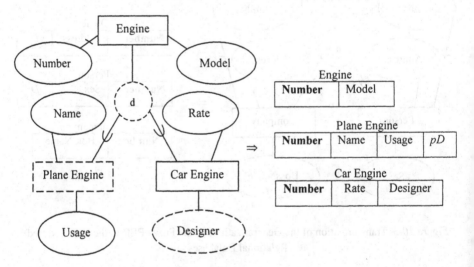

Figure 10-4. Transformation of the Specializations in the Fuzzy EER to the Fuzzy Nested Relational Databases

10.2.5 Transformation of Categorizations

Categorization is concerned with the issue of selective inheritance. Essentially, categorization shows the uncertainty that which entity in the categorization will take place in the schema is not known currently. The entities, fuzzy or not, in the categorization can respectively be mapped into relations following the methods given above. The categorization entity also follows the transformation. Some additional attributes, however, should be added into the corresponding relation. These attributes are a set of all attributes of the entities in the categorization.

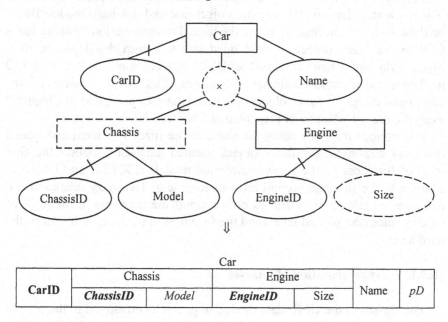

Figure 10-5. Transformation of the Aggregations in the Fuzzy EER to the Fuzzy Nested Relational Databases

10.2.6 Transformation Aggregations

Each aggregation in the fuzzy EER model can be mapped into a relation of the fuzzy nested relational schema with relation-valued attributes. Depending on the component entities, the aggregation entity may be crisp or fuzzy. As we know, there are four kinds of entities in the fuzzy EER model. Fuzziness of the component entities only on the attribute values does not influence the relation created by the aggregation entity. If there exists the fuzziness of the component entities at type/instance level, namely, one at the second level, however, an additional attribute must be appended to the relation created by the aggregation entity, indicating the aggregation degree of tuples. The fuzziness of the component entities at type level, i.e., one at the first level, however, cannot be modeled in the relation created by the aggregation entity.

Figure 10-5 shows the transformations of aggregation.

10.3   Transformation from the Fuzzy UML Model to the Fuzzy Object-Oriented Databases

In (Fong, 1995), some transformation rules have been presented to map object-oriented data model into the object-oriented database model. Based on these basic transformation rules, the formal transformation from the fuzzy EER to the fuzzy object-oriented databases has been developed in (Ma, Zhang, Ma and Chen, 2001). The UML reflects some of the best OO modeling experiences available. Therefore, this section discusses the conceptual design of fuzzy object-oriented databases presented in Chapter 9 using the fuzzy UML model presented in Chapter 5.

It is noticed that, not being the same as the fuzzy relational and nested relational databases, the fuzzy object-oriented databases support the first level of fuzziness of the fuzzy conceptual models (ER/EER and UML) in addition to the first and second level of fuzziness. The fuzzy relational and fuzzy nested relational databases only support the fuzziness at the level of type/instance (the second level) and the fuzziness at the level of instance (the third level).

10.3.1   Transformation of Classes

The classes in the UML data model, in general, correspond to the classes in the object-oriented databases and the attributes of the classes in the UML model correspond to the attributes of the classes in the object-oriented databases. If the classes in the UML data model are subclasses or superclasses, in the object-oriented databases, the inheritance hierarchies of the classes produced by these UML classes must be indicated explicitly.

For the purpose of the transformation from the fuzzy UML model into the fuzzy object-oriented databases, first we suppose that the classes in the UML model are neither subclasses nor superclasses. Then we can distinguish four kinds of classes in the fuzzy UML model as follows:

    (a) classes without any fuzziness at the three levels,

    (b) classes with the fuzziness only at the third level,

    (c) classes with the fuzziness at the second level, and

    (d) classes with the fuzziness at the first level.

While transforming the classes of the fuzzy UML model into the classes of the fuzzy object-oriented databases and the attributes of the former classes into the attributes of the later classes, the transformation of the classes with three levels of fuzziness are of particularly concern. For the classes in case (b), their attributes taking fuzzy values must be indicated in the transformed classes in the fuzzy object-oriented databases that these attributes have fuzzy value types, denoted by *FUZZY TYPE OF*. For the classes in case (c), an additional attribute, denoted by *pD*, should be added into each class transformed from the corresponding class in the fuzzy UML model, which is used to denote the possibility that the class instances belong to the class. For the classes in case (d), the classes or/and their attributes may be associated with membership degrees. Correspondingly, the transformed classes and attributes in the fuzzy object-oriented databases are associated with the membership degrees, if any. The membership degree is used to indicate the possibility that the created class belongs to the corresponding database model, or the attributes of the created class belong to the class.

Figure 10-6 shows the transformation of the classes in the fuzzy UML data models to the fuzzy object-oriented databases. For the sake of simplification, some components in the class definition of the fuzzy object-oriented databases such as *DOMAIN*, *WEIGHT*, *METHODS*, and *CONSTRAINTS* are not listed in the following definitions.

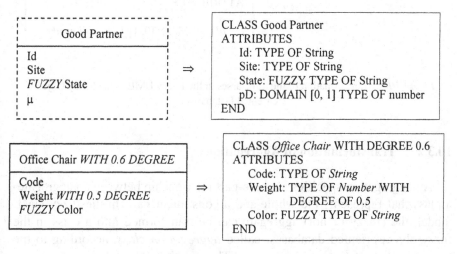

Figure 10-6. Transformation of the Classes in the Fuzzy UML to the Fuzzy Object-Oriented Databases

Now assume that the classes of the fuzzy UML model are superclasses, which may be any of the classes listed in cases (a)-(d) above. Then the transformation of such classes into the classes of the fuzzy object-oriented databases is the same as the transformation of the classes of the fuzzy UML model given above. As to the classes of the fuzzy UML model that are subclasses and may be any of the classes listed in cases (a)-(d) above, they can be transformed into the classes of the fuzzy object-oriented databases following the same principles of the class transformation given above. But, in the fuzzy object-oriented databases, the inheritance hierarchies of the produced classes (subclasses) must be indicated explicitly.

Figure 10-7 shows the transformation of the subclasses in the fuzzy UML data models to the fuzzy object-oriented databases.

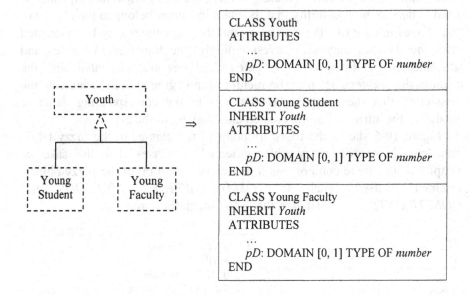

Figure 10-7. Transformation of the Subclasses in the Fuzzy UML to the Fuzzy Object-Oriented Databases

10.3.2   Transformation of Aggregations

An aggregation specifies a whole-part relationship between an aggregate- a class that represents the whole-and a constituent part. In the fuzzy UML model, the (fuzzy or not) aggregate can be transformed into a class in the fuzzy object-oriented databases, called *aggregation class*, according to the transformation of classes given above. The constituent part, being a (fuzzy or not) class, can also be transformed into a class in the fuzzy object-oriented databases, called *component class*. It should be noticed that, however, the attributes of the aggregation class consist of all attributes from the aggregate as well as its all component classes as complex class attributes.

Figure 10-8 shows the transformation of the aggregations in the fuzzy UML data models to the fuzzy object-oriented databases.

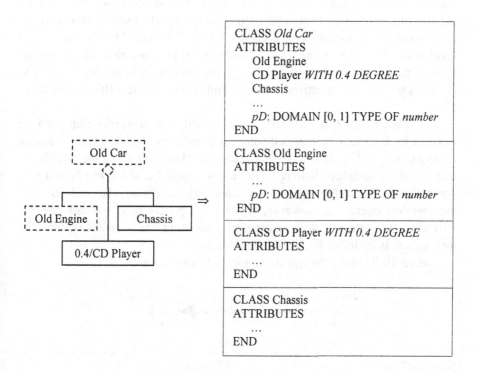

Figure 10-8. Transformation of the Aggregations in the Fuzzy UML to the Fuzzy Object-Oriented Databases

10.3.3 Transformation of Associations

An association in the UML model should be transformed into an association in the OO schema, which describes a group of pointer as an attribute in an object that combines an explicit reference to another object. Considering the constraint of cardinality, such attributes in two associated objects can be single-valued one or multivalued one. In the fuzzy UML model, three kinds of associations can be distinguished as follows:

(a) associations without any fuzziness at the three levels,

(b) associations with the fuzziness at the second level, and

(c) associations with the fuzziness at the first level.

Let class C_1 and class C_2 be connected with association relationship R, where R may be one-to-one, one-to-many, or many-to-many relationship. Also assume that C_1 and C_2 have such attributes, say $K1$ and $K2$, whose values serve as the object identification, respectively. Then, following the transformation process of the classes given above, C_1 and C_2 can be transformed into the classes in the fuzzy object-oriented databases. However, the influence of R and C_2 (or C_1) to C_1 (or C_2) must be considered when C_1 (or C_2) is transformed to a class of the fuzzy object-oriented databases. K_2 (or K_1) should be added into the class C'_1 (or C'_2) created by C_1 (or C_2) as a foreign key just like the relational databases. If the constraint of cardinality is a one-to-many relationship, i.e., R is a one-to-many relationship from C_1 to C_2, K_2 is a multivalued attribute in C'_1, and K_1 is a single-valued attribute in C'_2.

For relationship R in case (b), the possibility that a relationship instance belongs to R should be mapped into the possibility that an object instance belong to C'_1 or C'_2. Therefore, additional attributes denoting the possibility that the class instances belong to the class should be added to C'_1 and C'_2, respectively. For relationship R in case (c), i.e., the relationships with membership degree μ, however, K_2 in C'_1 and K_2 in C'_2 should be the attributes with membership degree μ, indicating the possibility that the foreign key is included for the created class.

Figure 10-9 shows the transformation of associations.

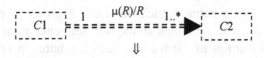

CLASS C'_1	CLASS C'_2
ATTRIBUTES	ATTRIBUTES
K_1:	K_2:
K_2: DOMAIN *set values*	K_1: DOMAIN *single values*
...	...
pD: DOMAIN [0, 1] TYPE OF *number*	pD: DOMAIN [0, 1] TYPE OF *number*
END	END

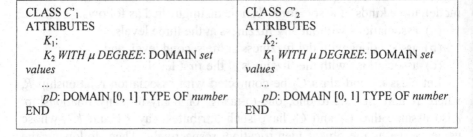

CLASS C'_1	CLASS C'_2
ATTRIBUTES	ATTRIBUTES
K_1:	K_2:
K_2 *WITH μ DEGREE*: DOMAIN *set values*	K_1 *WITH μ DEGREE*: DOMAIN *set values*
...	...
pD: DOMAIN [0, 1] TYPE OF *number*	pD: DOMAIN [0, 1] TYPE OF *number*
END	END

Figure 10-9. Transformation of the Associations in the Fuzzy UML to the Fuzzy Object-Oriented Databases

10.4 Mapping the Fuzzy XML Model into the Fuzzy Relational Database Model

XML is becoming the de facto standard for data description and exchange between various systems and databases over the Internet. To store, query and update XML documents, it is necessary to integrate XML and databases (Bertino and Catania, 2001). Concerning the kind of databases used for the integration, one can distinguish four different approaches (Kappel *et al.*, 2000).

- Special-purpose databases which are particularly tailored for processing XML documents (Goldman, McHugh and Widom, 1999; Kanne and Moerkotte, 2000);
- Object-oriented databases which are well-suited for storing XML documents (Chung *et al.*, 2001; Johansson and Heggbrenna, 2003);
- Object-relational databases which would be also appropriate for mapping to and from XML document (Surjanto, Ritter and Loeser, 2000; Runapongsa and Patel, 2002);
- Relational databases which might be the more promising alternative because of the widespread use and mature techniques (Lee and Chu, 2000; Kappel *et al.*, 2000; Du, Amer-Yahia and Freire, 2004).

To store XML documents within databases, the approach to mapping of XML to databases is extensively applied, where the structure of XML documents (XML DTD or XML Schema) is mapped into a corresponding database schema and XML documents are stored according to the mapping. In the following, we describe the mappings of the fuzzy XML DTD to the fuzzy relational database model.

10.4.1 DTD Tree and Mapping to the Relational Database Schema

The hierarchical XML and the flat relational data models are not fully compliant. So the transformation is not a straightforward task. Generally a DTD tree can be created from the hierarchical XML DTD. Its nodes are elements and attributes, in which each element appears exactly once in the graph, while attributes appear as many times as they appear in the DTD. The element nodes can be further classified into two kinds: leaf element nodes and nonleaf element nodes. So in the DTD tree, we totally have three kinds of nodes, which are *attribute nodes*, *leaf element nodes* and *nonleaf element nodes*. Note that there exists a special nonleaf element node in the DTD tree, i.e., *root node*. In addition, we also need to identify such attribute nodes that the corresponding attributes are associated with ID #REQUIRED or IDREF #REQUIRED in DTD. We call these attribute nodes *key attribute nodes*.

A DTD tree can be constructed when parsing the given DTD (Shanmugasundaram *et al.*, 1999). Figure 10-10 shows a simple DTD tree example.

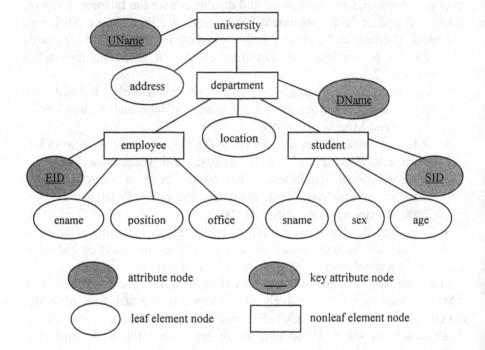

Figure 10-10. A Simple DTD Tree

The created DTD tree is then mapped into the relational schema following the processing as follows.

(a) Take the root node of the given DTD tree and create a relational table. Its attributes come from the attribute nodes and leaf element nodes connecting with the root node. Here the key attribute node(s) should become the primary key attribute(s) of the created table.

(b) For each nonleaf element node connecting with the root node, create a separate relational table. Its attributes come from the attribute nodes and leaf element nodes connecting with this nonleaf element node, and its primary key attribute(s) will come from the key attribute node(s).

(c) For other nonleaf element nodes in the DTD tree, apply the same processing given in (b) until all nonleaf element nodes are transformed.

Note that sometimes we need to link a created relational table to its parent relational table through the parent table's primary key.

The DTD tree in Figure 10-10 is mapped into the relational schemas shown in Figure 10-11.

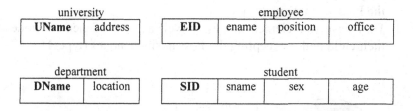

Figure 10-11. The Relational Schema Created by the DTD Tree in Figure 10-10

It should be pointed out that, however, the above-mentioned mapping of XML DTD to the relational schema using the DTD tree puts a focus on structural aspects of transformation.

10.4.2   Mapping the Fuzzy XML Model into the Fuzzy Relational Database Model

Generally speaking, the fuzzy XML DTD presented in Chapter 6 can be transformed into the fuzzy relational database schema using a similar processing given above under classical environment. That is, we first construct a DTD tree through parsing the given fuzzy DTD and then map the DTD tree into the fuzzy relational database schema. However, the DTD tree here, called the *fuzzy DTD tree*, is clearly different from the classical DTD tree above because the fuzzy DTD contains new attribute and element types, which are attribute Poss and elements Val and Dist. As a result, the transformation of the fuzzy DTD tree to the fuzzy relational database schema is also different from the transformation of the classical DTD tree to the classical relational database schema.

In the fuzzy DTD tree, in addition to (key) attribute nodes, leaf element nodes and nonleaf element nodes, there are three special nodes, which are *Poss attribute nodes*, *Val element nodes*, and *Dist element nodes*. Figure 10-12 shows a simple fuzzy DTD tree that basically comes from the fuzzy DTD in Figure 6-2. In this fuzzy DTD tree, the Dist element nodes created from Disk elements are used to indicate the type of a possibility distribution, being *disjunctive* or *conjunctive*. In addition, each Dist element node has a Val element node as its child node and a nonleaf element node as its parent node. From the figure, we can also identify four kinds of Val element nodes as follows.

(a) They do not have no any child node excepting the Poss attribute nodes (type-1).

(b) They only have leaf element nodes as their child nodes excepting the
   Poss attribute nodes (type-2).
(c) They only have nonleaf element nodes as their child nodes excepting
   the Poss attribute nodes (type-3).
(d) They have leaf element nodes as well as nonleaf element nodes as
   their child nodes excepting the Poss attribute nodes (type-4).

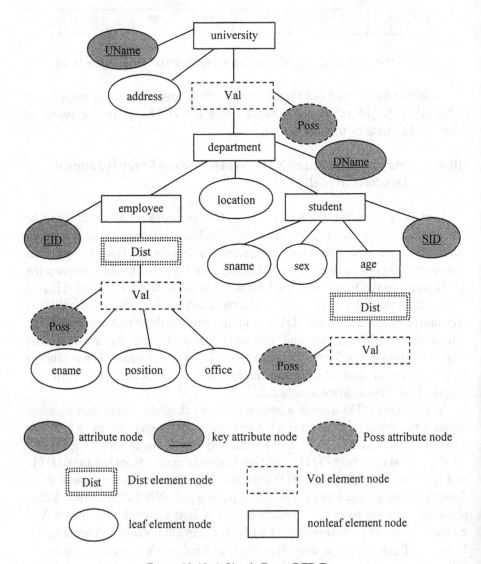

Figure 10-12. A Simple Fuzzy DTD Tree

In the following, we describe the transformation of the fuzzy DTD tree
into the fuzzy relational database schema. Being different from the

transformation of the classical DTD tree to the relational database schema, in the transformation of the fuzzy DTD tree to the fuzzy relational model, the Poss attribute nodes, Val element nodes, and Dist element nodes in the fuzzy DTD tree do not take part in composing the created relational schema and only determine the model of the created fuzzy relational databases. In details, we have the following the processing.

(a) Take the root node of the given fuzzy DTD tree and create a relational table. Its attributes first come from the attribute nodes and leaf element nodes connecting with the root node. Here the key attribute node(s) should become the primary key attribute(s) of the created table. Then determine if the root node has any Val element nodes or Dist element nodes as its child nodes. If yes, we need to further determine the type of each Val element node (we can ignore Dist element nodes because each Dist element node must has a Val element node as its child node only).

  (i) If it is the Val element node of type-2, all of the leaf element nodes connecting with the Val element node become the attributes of the created relational table. Also an additional attribute is added into the created relational table, representing the possibility degree of the tuples.

  (ii) If it is the Val element node of type-3, only an additional attribute is added into the created relational table, representing the possibility degree of the tuples.

  (iii) If it is the Val element node of type-4, we leave the nonleaf element nodes for further treatment in (b) and do the same thing as (i) for the leaf element nodes.

  It is impossible that the Val element nodes of type-1 arise in the root node.

(b) For each nonleaf element node connecting with the root node, create a separate relational table. Its attributes come from the attribute nodes and leaf element nodes connecting with this nonleaf element node, and its primary key attribute(s) will come from the key attribute node(s). Furthermore, determine if this nonleaf element node has any Val element nodes or Dist element nodes as its child nodes and identify the type of these nodes, if any. We still apply the processing given in (i)-(iii) of (a) to treat the Val element nodes of type-2, type-3, and type-4. For the Val element nodes of type-1, each of them should become an attribute of another relational table created from the parent node of the current nonleaf element. Note that this attribute is one that may take fuzzy values.

(c) For other nonleaf element nodes in the fuzzy DTD tree, apply the same processing given in (b) until all nonleaf element nodes are transformed.

The fuzzy DTD tree in Figure 10-12 is mapped into the fuzzy relational schemas shown in Figure 10-13, in which attribute "age" is one that may take fuzzy values.

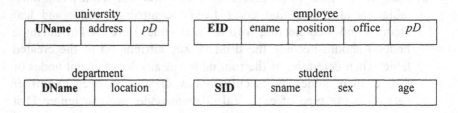

Figure 10-13. The Fuzzy Relational Schema Created by the Fuzzy DTD Tree in Figure 10-12

10.5   Summary

Conceptual data models are generally able to capture complex object and semantic relationships at a high level of abstraction. At the level of data manipulation, logical database models are used for data storage, processing, and retrieval activities related to data management. Database modeling often starts with conceptual data modeling and then the created conceptual data models are transformed into logical database models.

Focusing on conceptual design of the fuzzy databases, this chapter presents the transformation of the fuzzy EER and UML data models to the fuzzy nested relational and fuzzy object-oriented database models. In particular, with the fuzzy DTD tree, the transformation of the fuzzy XML model to the fuzzy relational database model is proposed in this chapter.

References

Abiteboul, S. and Hull, R., 1987, IFO: A formal semantic database model, *ACM Transactions on Database Systems*, 12 (4): 525-565.

Bertino, E. and Catania, B., 2001, Integrating XML and databases, *IEEE Internet Computing*, July-August, 84-88.

Buckles, B. P. and Petry, F. E., 1982, A Fuzzy Representation of Data for Relational Database. *Fuzzy Sets and Systems*, 7 (3): 213-226.

Chaudhry, N. A., Moyne, J. R. and Rundensteiner, E. A., 1999, An extended database design methodology for uncertain data management, *Information Sciences*, 121 (1-2): 83-112.

Chung, T. S., Park, S., Han, S. Y. and Kim, H. J., 2001, Extracting object-oriented database schemas from XML DTDs using inheritance, *Lecture Notes in Computer Science 2115*, 49-59.

Du, F., Amer-Yahia, S. and Freire, J., 2004, ShreX: Managing XML documents in relational databases, *Proceedings of the 2004 International Conference on Very Large Data Bases*, 1297-1300.

Fong, J., 1995, Mapping extended entity-relationship model to object modeling technique, *SIGMOD Record*, 24 (3): 18-22.

Goldman, R., McHugh, J. and Widom, J., 1999, From semistructured data to XML: migrating the Lore data model and query language, *Proceedings of the 1999 International Workshop on the Web and Databases*, 25-30.

Johansson, T. and Heggbrenna, R., 2003, *Importing XML Schema into an Object-Oriented Database Mediator System*, Master's Thesis in Computer Science, Uppsala University, Sweden.

Kanne, C.-C. and Moerkotte, G., 2000, Efficient storage of XML data, *Proceedings of the 2000 International Conference on Data Engineering*, 198-198.

Kappel, G., Kapsammer, E., Rausch-Schott, S. and Retschitzegger, W., 2000, X-Ray-towards integrating XML and relational database systems, *Lecture Notes in Computer Science 1920*, 339-353.

Lee, D. and Chu, W. W., 2000, Constraints-preserving transformation from XML document type definition to relational schema, *Lecture Notes in Computer Science 1920*, Springer, 323-338.

Ma, Z. M., Zhang, W. J., Ma, W. Y. and Chen, G. Q., 2001, Conceptual design of fuzzy object-oriented databases using extended entity-relationship model, *International Journal of Intelligent Systems*, 16: 697-711.

Naiburg, E. J. and Maksimchuk, R. A., 2001, *UML for Database Design*, Addison-Wesley Professional (1st edition).

Runapongsa, K. and Patel, J. M., 2002, Storing and querying XML data in object-relational DBMSs, *Lecture Notes in Computer Science 2490*, 266-285.

Shanmugasundaram, J., Tufte, K., He, G., Zhang, C., DeWitt, D. and Naughton, J., 1999, Relational databases for querying XML documents: limitations and opportunities, *Proceedings of the 1999 International Conference on Very Large Data Bases*, 302-314.

Surjanto, B., Ritter, N. and Loeser, H., 2000, XML content management based on object-relational database technology, *Proceedings of the First International Conference on Web Information Systems Engineering*, 1: 70-79.

Yazici, A., Buckles, B. P. and Petry, F. E., 1999, Handling complex and uncertain information in the ExIFO and NF2 data models, *IEEE Transactions on Fuzzy Systems*, 7 (6): 659.676.

Yazici, A., Soysal, A., Buckles, B. P. and Petry, F. E., 1999, Uncertainty in a nested relational database model, *Data & Knowledge Engineering*, 30 (3): 275-301.

Zvieli, A. and Chen, P. P., 1986, Entity-relationship modeling and fuzzy databases, *Proceedings of the 1986 IEEE International Conference on Data Engineering*, 320-327.

INDEX